Peace

崔희둡 ☺

Shattered by the Wars

But Sustained by Love

Hi-Dong Chai

InspiringVoices®
A Service of **Guideposts**

Inspiring Voices books may be ordered through booksellers or by contacting:

Inspiring Voices
1663 Liberty Drive
Bloomington, IN 47403
www.inspiringvoices.com
1 (866) 697-5313

ISBN: 978-1-4624-0796-5 (sc)
ISBN: 978-1-4624-0797-2 (e)

Library of Congress Control Number: 2013918880

Printed in the United States of America.

Inspiring Voices rev. date: 10/28/2013

This is a compelling story of a young boy coming of age during a very troubled time in Korea. It is the story of a family of faith, courage, and determination. The overriding theme is of a mother's love for her husband and children, and her unswerving faith in God's goodness. The events are told from the point of view of Hi-Dong, the youngest child in a family of ten. The struggles of keeping the family intact and facing the hazards and despair of a country at work with itself are faced with strength and a steadfast devotion to God. A good read and certain to be on the best-seller's list soon! —Betsy Shoup, Santa Clara, CA

Life experienced and seen through the eyes of a Korean boy under Japan during WWII and during the Korean War. A compelling story. Must *read* book for every American to appreciate how fortunate he is to live in America. —Pat Doran, Los Gatos, CA

Shattered by the Wars is certainly a moving and involving story. It is also an eye-opening picture of what it must have been like to be displaced by war and intolerance. I find that I am continually amazed and fortunate that I am now a friend with a person who survived all of that upheaval and mind-blowing trauma. What a story he has to tell … and surely there is much that we can learn from it. —John Hawes, San Jose, CA

An easy reading and fascinating true story of life in Korea during the Japanese occupation and the North Korean invasion. The author, a bright and curious young boy, is raised by his courageous mother, who endures heartache and sorrow, but scrimps and saves in order to send her son off to America, the land of opportunity. How the family copes with the difficulties encountered held my interest to the end.—Bill Slocum, San Jose, CA

Note from the author

I hate war. War kills. War maims. War widows. War orphans. According to Wikipedia, In WWII, 62 to 78 million lost their lives. Over 2.5 percent of the world population. In the Korean War, 2.5 million North and South Koreans were killed/wounded. In the Vietnam War, more than 4 million North and South Vietnamese, Cambodians, and Laotians lost their lives. And war leaves a deep scar not only on the land, that will take years to heal, but also in the hearts of those who are affected by the war. I am one of those who carry a deep emotional wound to this day, more than sixty years later.

During my earlier years in Korea, I lost three loved ones through WWII and the Korean War. During WWII under Japan, my father was imprisoned by the Japanese police because he was a Christian minister who refused to bow down to the picture of the Japanese emperor. My elder brother, my best friend, volunteered to join the Japanese military in the hope of having his father released from the prison. He left home as a vibrant 15 year-old boy, and returned home as a worn-out injured 18 year-old man when the war ended in 1945. He died from his injury a year later. In 1950, the Korean War broke out. North Korean communists occupied Seoul for 90 days, where we lived. One day two North Korean officers came to my house and took my father away. He never returned. Also, the day before the South Korean army returned to Seoul, my eldest brother, who had turned communist, disappeared. He also never returned.

Not only did I lose my father and two brothers, I also lost my beloved dog. One day during the Korean War, Mother said, "We don't have enough food, even for the family. We have to let Kwidong go." How could I say, "No", to Mother when there was not enough food even for the family? I had to let my best friend go. The picture of Kwidong turning her head toward me as if to say, "Good bye", as she was led down the street by a dog warden, still numbs my heart with pain and guilt.

*I wrote **Shattered by the Wars** with my heart that had yearned for peace and brotherhood through my growing years, in the hope that the readers would* *seek harmony at home and peace in the world. I picture a scene where people from diverse cultures hold hands across the vast continents and over the deep oceans, form a huge circle, look at each other with broad smiles, and sing a mighty song of brotherhood. Wouldn't it be wonderful if that day would come in our lifetime?*

Excerpt from *Shattered by the Wars*

Time: October, 1950
Place: Police station, Seoul, Korea

The captain said sitting down and lighting a cigarette. "You are all communists and liars. Your husband is a communist in a preacher's garb. He is not kidnapped, but escaped to the north. You know where your communist son is, and you don't tell us."

"OK, you brat," Captain said. "Where's your brother?"

"I don't know, Sir."

"I am getting sick of listening to your lies," he said. "Where is your worthless communist brother?"

"He really doesn't know, Captain," Mother spoke behind me.

"Shut up. I didn't ask you," Captain screamed. "That does it."

"Officer Kim." Captain made eye contact with Officer Kim.

I saw Officer Kim pulling out his revolver from the holster. I heard him cock the revolver. Then he placed the barrel against my temple. It felt cold and hard.

"Where's your brother?" Captain asked.

"I don't know, Sir." That's only answer I knew.

"Where's your brother?" Captain asked me again.

Is there something that I can say that will make the captain stop asking the same question? I asked myself.

"The night before the U.N. soldiers entered Seoul," I said, "Brother came home and took a few of his belongings and left us. He didn't tell us where he was going."

"I didn't ask you to explain," Captain yelled. "Now, the last time … Where's your brother?"

I closed my eyes ignoring his question. *What's the use of answering? He's not going to believe me anyway.*

"That does it." Captain sounded final. "Detective Kim ... Go ahead."

I heard the pulling of the trigger and the barrel of the revolver jerking on my temple. I imagined the bullet speeding through my head, making holes through my skull and flying out the other side, covered with blood and brain matter. But I felt nothing. I heard no blasting sound of the bullet. Instead, a dead silence.

Then I heard a voice, *Oh my God ...* Mother's voice. I heard someone falling. I turned. Mother was on the floor. Slouched. Staring at me with her sunken round eyes. The same eyes I saw when I had walked out of Father's office with Detective Lee a week ago. Her bent arms reaching out toward me. Trembling. I rushed to her, knelt down, and put my arm around her shoulder. She stared at me with round eyes as if she was seeing a ghost.

Shattered by the Wars

But Sustained by Love

This book is dedicated to my mother,
the greatest human being that I have known.

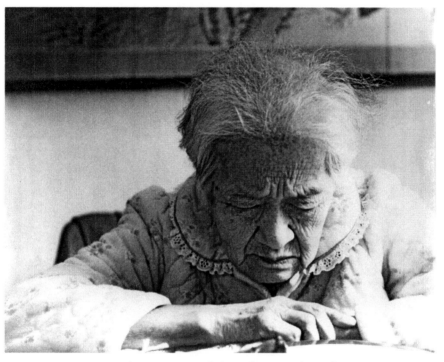

Mother in prayer (Photo by David Rim)

And to all mothers in the world whose love and sacrifice
have been permanently etched in the hearts of men and women
who were nurtured by them.

Table of Contents

1. My birth

I was born in Seoul, Korea, as the last member in a family of ten children, three of whom died before my birth. Mother was forty-two years old when she had me. In those days, because of the lack of proper nutrition and medical care, people aged early, and delivering a baby at the age of forty was a miracle, like a seventy-year-old woman of today having a baby. So when Mother delivered beautiful twin daughters at the age of thirty-seven, she thought that her baby-delivering mission was finally over. She felt relieved and grateful. She thought that Nature would free her from this painful task. The remaining years would be spent raising her children, watching them grow, marry and raise their own families. She would visit them and spend the afternoons playing with her grandchildren.

Then at the age of forty-two, she woke up one morning and felt something moving inside her.

Oh God, what's happening? Mother shuddered. *Another child at my age? Please God, don't let this be …*

Mother secretly visited an herbal doctor. The doctor put his three fingers on her wrist to check her pulse and other body signs; he put his hand on her stomach and closed his eyes to feel any movement inside her stomach. After a few minutes, the doctor opened his eyes with a broad smile. He pronounced to Mother that a new life was preparing to enter the world in seven months. Mother begged him for medicine that would cause miscarriage. But the doctor said, "I'm not an infant killer." Disheartened, she went to see her younger sister, Little Aunt, with her problem. Little Aunt was more understanding and suggested that Mother try several herbs. Eagerly Mother tried them, and none of them worked. Instead, they gave her a stomachache. She pounded her stomach with a wooden bat when nobody was around. It didn't work. She jumped up and down on a hard surface while pounding her stomach, but the little one in her stomach seemed to enjoy her antics. With each passing day her stomach grew bigger and rounder.

What will the people in the church think when they find out I am pregnant? she thought. *Women will gather in someone's house, giggle and make stories about their minister's wife being so sexually active past the age of forty. Men will make jokes about having a virile forty-seven-year-old minister who doesn't know when to stop.* She was dismayed and distressed, but there was nothing she could do but wait for the fateful moment.

On September 10, 1936, early in the morning, an infant boy rushed out of her womb with a mighty roar. His roaring shook the whole house waking up everyone from his sleep. The family members rushed to the room to see the baby. They marveled at his chubby arms and legs. They marveled—some worried—at his head, because it was the biggest head with a thin neck that they had ever seen. Father was grateful and relieved because his old wife survived the painful birth experience, especially delivering a baby with such a big head. He was also grateful because God gave him a son—not a daughter—who would carry on his family name. With the family members surrounding the mother and the baby, Father gave a prayer of thanksgiving and prayed that the baby would grow up happy, healthy and responsible, trusting in God's love.

The news spread fast. The neighbors and the women in the church visited Mother to see her newborn son. They all marveled at his big head, chubby arms and legs. His loud cry made them laugh. "He will be a singer when he grows up," one said. "Look at his legs and arms, another said. He is going to be a *jangsar*—Superman—who will look after his family and friends."

But Mother was depressed for days, having another human being to take care of. She was also worried. *His head is a little too big for his body. I wonder what he is going to turn out to be.* Without consulting Father, who believed that fortune-telling was a sin, Mother invited a fortune-teller, an old woman with wrinkles all over her face, to find out what kind of future lay ahead for her son. After gazing at him for a while from top to bottom and checking the lifelines on his hands, the old woman told Mother that her son would bring good fortune to the family and be a shining star in the east. So with the accolades from the visitors, encouraging remarks from the fortune-teller and the innocent little baby eagerly seeking his mother's milk, her worry and distress were gradually replaced by warmth and love toward him. She named him Hi-Dong, and he is the author of this story.

My father was a Christian minister and educator whose life was totally dedicated to serving God and his flock. With his born-again experience and the newfound zeal for Christ, he traveled all over the Land of the Morning Calm, the land of the Buddhists and Confucians, preaching the gospel to those who thought Christianity was a white man's religion. He traveled all over the countryside with American missionaries, preaching in village squares and building churches. He lived the life of St. Paul of old. He believed that his life's mission was to introduce Christ's message and lead as many Koreans to the bosom of Christ as he could. He wanted them to experience the deep inner peace and joy that he found when he had surrendered his life at the feet of Jesus, who died on the cross for people like him.

He was rarely home with his family. When he was in town, he was either at the seminary where he taught young, aspiring seminarians, or visiting parishioners of his church, which had hundreds of members scattered around the city of Seoul. For him, his precious time belonged to Christ. In order to maximize his time for preaching, he slept little. He washed and shaved hurriedly with his sharp old-fashioned shaving knife, worrying me no end that he might cut himself badly. He ate quickly. He took a spoonful of rice in his mouth, chewed six times, swallowed the rest, and went on to the next spoonful. As a child, I used to wonder, *How come Father doesn't get a stomachache eating so fast? Mother always tells me to chew every morsel in my mouth slowly until it becomes paste and then swallow. Otherwise, I will get a stomachache. But she never tells Father to slow down. Maybe she's scared to tell him.*

When he finished the meal, he always said to Mother, "*Yubo* (Honey in

Korean), your cooking is delicious as always. Now I have to run. There is so much to do today. Take good care of yourself."

Mother responded, "Please have a blessed day. Please be sure to take a few minutes rest here and there."

I never heard them say, "I love you," because they—like others—felt that spoken words were cheap. They believed that love was such an important word that it should be expressed through deeds, not words. Father used to say that a bowl of rice given to a hungry man would soothe his hunger pain, while a thousand times saying *I love you* would keep his stomach empty.

After saying good-bye to us, Father rushed out of the house. Then late in the evening, he came home for supper and also to rest and recuperate for the next day's activities. As a minister, he had no weekends off. Saturdays and Sundays were busier days for him because he had to prepare his sermons and lead the weekly worship services.

Even though Father spent all his time and effort for the church and seminary, his pay was miniscule. In that period there were no checks or credit cards, and the salary was paid in cash. So each month, he brought a pack of paper money to Mother, and she had to figure out how to stretch it as far as possible.

To supplement his small income, Mother sewed for people with her old treadle sewing machine. Ladies from the church and neighborhood brought dresses for altering and fabric for making new dresses.

When I was a child, a lady visiting Mother with a pink spring outfit in her hands said, "Myung-Hae was wearing this last spring. She looked very beautiful in it. But this year, it is too short for her because she has grown up so fast …"

"I know," Mother replied.

"These days young girls grow like weeds!" the lady said. "So, instead of throwing it away, I decided to let her younger sister, Myung-Ja, wear it this year."

"Let me look at it," Mother said, taking the outfit from her and holding it up in front of her. "This is a beautiful dress. It will be very good for your younger daughter. My memory tells me that Myung-Hae and Myung-Ja are about the same size except for the height. Myung-Hae is much taller."

"Yes, that is why I brought it to you."

"All I have to do is shorten the bottom somewhat."

"I think so."

"Can you tell me how much taller Myung-Hae is?"

"She is taller than her sister by my index finger," the lady answered, sticking her index finger up in the air.

"Let me see your finger."

The lady held her finger out toward Mother, and Mother compared it with her own and chuckled, "We have the same size fingers. I will have the dress ready for you by tomorrow."

"Thank you," the lady said. "How much will it be?"

"This is such an easy job," Mother replied. "You don't have to pay me at all."

"But—"

"Don't worry about it. Just come tomorrow with your daughter. It will be ready."

The next day the lady came with Myung-Ja, and Mother put the dress on her. Myung-Ja shyly stood in front of them.

"You like it?" Mother asked.

"Yes," Myung-Ja replied smiling.

"You are blessed with two beautiful daughters," Mother complimented.

"Thank you," Myung-Ja's mother said. "They are my pearls."

Myung-Ja's mother insisted on paying for the service, but Mother refused. After repeated *Please* and *Thank you and No*, they moved onto womanly talk on meandering topics while the daughter sat in one corner of the room, anxiously waiting to go home. After an hour or so, the lady asked for a glass of water. As soon as Mother stepped out of the room to get the water, the lady handed me an envelope, whispering to me to give it to Mother after they were gone.

That was how the payment was transacted; I ended up being the middleman between the ladies and Mother. It was a fun task. Also, I found out who was generous and who was very tight with money. When I told these details to my twin sisters, they would make sharp comments about those ladies who did not pay much, and they would cast evil eyes when they saw them coming, and walk away from them while whispering to each other, and speaking of them as being stingy.

Rarely a day passed without having visitors. In those days no one had a telephone, and visitors came unannounced. They came in the morning. They came in the afternoon. They came just before mealtime and at night to stay over. Mother welcomed them all. For those who came just before a mealtime, she would make a quick adjustment to the food so that they could also be fed, though it meant that the children got less. Some visitors came and spent the night. The people from the countryside often came with live chickens, fish, potatoes, fruit, or whatever they could bring, and stayed with us for days. Mother, whose love for people was in-born, treated all with such empathy that our house was like a village square. First-comers, usually men, came to see Father for advice or to discuss church-related matters. But when they found out what Mother was like, they sent their wives and children to see her with their personal problems.

As a child, I found life to be exciting with all the visitors and the commotion that accompanied them. I did not, however, like those who came just before the mealtime because it meant that my portion of food would be less. Above all, the people loved me. They played with me. They brought sweets, and I enjoyed receiving them. I remember Mother saying with a smile to those who brought gifts, "Your coming is itself an honor. Why do you have to bring a gift also?"

The visitors, in turn replied, "Please do not mention it. This is nothing at all."

I said to myself, *Don't listen to Mother. You can bring as much as you wish. Especially sweet things.*

In those days, the gifts were mostly food items, and I snuck out to the kitchen with great anticipation to sample the foods that people brought. Most foods were homemade; as a result, each had a unique flavor, and I used to savor them.

Mother was like the warm, pleasant sunshine. She had a way of helping people open themselves and share their innermost thoughts. Many came with a look of despair, and after being with Mother, they left with a smile on their faces. She made them feel good. Sometimes they poured out their problems with a voice of anguish and tears dripping down their cheeks. Mother listened with empathy and patience. By asking the right questions she helped them to solve their own problems.

Thus with a wonderful mother and father, a lot of friends to play with, and an unending stream of visitors, who were sometimes a pain but who also brought gifts, excitement and love, my childhood was a very happy one. I looked forward to every tomorrow.

2. My mother and father—their early years

Mother told me that she was married early in her teens. In the early 1900s, Korea still carried on the feudal tradition of the Lee dynasty—the last dynasty before Japan annexed Korea in 1910—the dynasty that was heavily influenced by Confucius. Father was the king of the family and children his subjects. Father ruled, and the children obeyed. Boys and girls had no voice in the selection of their mates. If a father said, "Min-Ja, you marry Myung-Shin," that was the end of her daydreaming about what kind of man that she would want to marry. Myung-Shin could be a foot shorter and fifteen pounds lighter than Min-Ja. Myung-Shin could have a high soprano voice that she didn't like in a man. Myung-Shin could be a habitual snorer. Min-Ja had no choice. Either obey or get kicked out of the house. Fortunately, most fathers loved their children, and they wanted the best for their sons and daughters.

It was the same for Mother. Her father decided that, based on the family background, personalities and astrological signs, Suk-Mo was the best choice for her. Both of them were from aristocratic backgrounds and from the same province. He was dynamic, aggressive and headstrong. She was gentle, wise and understanding. He was born in the year of the tiger, and she in the year of the lamb. He would rule, and she would obey. It was a combination that could not be beaten.

One afternoon her father called from the living room, "Kyung-In."

"Yes, Father," Mother replied. She was mopping the floor outside the living room.

"I have good news for you," Father said. "Come."

"Yes."

What's the good news? Mother wondered. *I have been begging Mother for months to send me to school where I can learn to write and read. Did she talk to Father about it, and did Father decide to go against the tradition and send me to school?*

Mother left the mop on the floor. Controlling her excitement, she quietly walked into the living room. Her father looked at her with a broad smile with her mother sitting next to him. She was smiling also. Mother sat in front of them with her head bowed as a sign of respect.

"You are fifteen years old," her father said. "And you are turning into a beautiful woman."

What does a beautiful woman have to do with my going school? Mother was getting suspicious but couldn't ask her father about it. She remained silent waiting for his next pronouncement.

"Your mother and I have found a man who will make the perfect husband for you," Father said. "His name is Suk-Mo. We went to visit his parents a few weeks ago and met Suk-Mo. A fine young man. His parents and we agreed that you two would make a wonderful couple."

"But ..." Mother wanted to resist.

"Kyung-In," her mother chimed in. "I know and your father knows that you want to go to school to learn to read and write. But you know it's against the tradition. Also Mr. and Mrs. Choi saw you a month ago when they visited us. They fell in love with you when you greeted them with a nice smile. Since then we have been corresponding with each other. Suk-Mo is the perfect choice for you."

"But ..."

"The wedding will take place in the spring. Three months from now," Father said.

That was all there was to it. Her parents made a decision, and the decision was final.

Even though I had heard Mother's story many times, I had difficulty believing that she would marry a man without ever seeing him. In that time there were no pictures to exchange, and her parents did not bother to describe what her future husband looked like except to say that Suk-Mo was the perfect choice. What was more surprising was that Mother didn't bother to ask about him. Tall or small. Fat or skinny. Aggressive or passive. No such questions. She forsook her desire to learn to read and write, and accepted her parents' decision and waited for the day when she would start living with the man, a total stranger.

During my growing years, Mother often said that my perception of a girl's physical beauty was determined by my feeling toward her. Mother said that if I did not like her, she would not look beautiful even if she were a beauty queen. But if I liked her, she would look pleasing even if she were a one-eyed hunchback.

"Didn't you really know what Father looked like?" I asked her one day when she was sewing my torn pants.

"No," Mother said.

"Didn't your parents show his picture to you?"

"We didn't have cameras to take pictures then," Mother said. "Even if we did, it was not the custom to see the bridegroom's face."

"So only after the wedding, you found out what Father looked like," I said.

"Not even after the wedding," Mother chuckled.

"Are you telling the truth?"

"I promise."

"Then you saw his face on the wedding night," I said.

"You shouldn't ask such a question."

"All I'm asking is whether you saw his face."

She stopped sewing and looked at me with a smile.

"I closed my eyes tight like this," she said closing her eyes like a vise.

"Why did you have to close your eyes?"

"It was the custom."

How could I argue about the custom? After the wedding, Mother cooked for him. She took a tray of food to him. She served him tea during the day. At night she slept next to him. But for days, she did not know what her husband looked like because in his presence she bowed her head low, never looking straight at him. All because it was the custom of the day.

"Weren't you curious to find out what Father looked like?" I asked.

"Very much," she said. "He sounded so firm and yet gentle, and I wanted so much to find out what he looked like."

"Why didn't you?"

"My mother told me not to look at him for a month," Mother said.

"If you did, then what?"

"It would bring misfortune."

"What kind of misfortune?"

"Like a baby born with one leg or a fire burning down your house," Mother said. "In that time the people believed in evil spirits who brought misfortune to those who disobeyed the custom."

Mother said that she counted the days when she could see her husband. Then, on the thirtieth day after her wedding, she looked out the window and saw someone walking toward her house. She figured that he was her husband. She was excited. She closed the curtain in order not to be caught by him, and peeped through the opening.

"Did he look OK to you?" I asked.

Mother said, with a chuckle, that she was very disappointed. She sighed, *Oh God, is he the man I have been living and sleeping with for a month? How come my parents got such an ugly-looking man?* He was short and wore thick-rimmed glasses. His small, narrow face was dark and angled. He was not like her father: tall, fair-skinned and handsome with a broad smile. But something must have worked though. In my teens Mother was married to him close to forty years and bore ten children, and she created a warm loving environment for her children. Mother honored Father. Father loved Mother, and he loved us. We were a very happy family.

As a child, watching Mother and Father relating to each other, I felt that there was a genuine bond between them. When Father looked at her, a smile was on his face, and warmth in his voice. Even after coming home feeling exhausted, his tired face came alive when he saw her waiting at the door. He was grateful for her care of the children and making ends meet with his meager income.

Mother respected his total dedication to his mission of serving God. She treated him like a king. When he came home from his office, she greeted him at the door, ushered him to his seat, and brought a wet towel to wipe his hands and face, asking him how his day was. Then she rushed out to the kitchen to bring his favorite tea with some sweets or fruit to him.

She never argued with Father, regardless of how much she disagreed with him. She just listened and asked him questions. Only after putting him in a receptive mood, she gently expressed her position. By then he would listen to her, nodding his head, and often he would end up siding with her.

In my growing years, Mother often said, "Man has a head that thinks and a heart that feels. If you want to have your way, you need to win his heart first."

She said that the first few years of her married life were ones of hardship and poverty. Father then was a young man, a newly born-again Christian, filled with the missionary zeal and ready to engulf the Land of the Morning Calm with the good news of Jesus Christ. He wanted to lead as many Koreans as possible to the bosom of Christ and to experience peace and freedom in their hearts. He did not worry about the well-being of his family because he believed that God would take care of them. His waking hours were spent going from village to village with American missionaries, preaching the Gospel. His pay was meager, and Mother's job was to stretch it as far as possible. Even for a small item such as a freshly caught mackerel she checked at many stores and haggled with the clerks for the best bargain. Good-quality rice was too expensive to afford. So she bought a cheaper grain, like barley, and mixed it with rice to cook.

There was not enough money to buy clothing for her children. So she bought a used treadle sewing machine to make dresses and to alter the old dresses for her younger kids. The oldest sister and brother got new clothes because there were no old ones to alter. But the younger ones got the altered clothes to fit their frames. As the youngest in the family, mine were altered the most. But with her sewing skill, they all appeared nice and new, and I did not mind wearing them. Sometimes, though, I wished that I could have brand-new clothes like my friends.

The hardest season for Mother was winter. There was not enough wood to heat the *ondul*—a cement floor covered with wear-resistant oiled paper. Underneath the floor was a series of ducts through which the heated air and smoke from the wood fire circulated, thus heating the floor before leaving through the chimney. The heated floor kept the room warm. On some cold nights she almost froze in bed because there was not enough wood to heat the floor. In that period there was no electricity, no electric heaters, plumbing, and a piped water system. In the cold dark morning, when the rooster crowed, she got out of bed shivering, walked to the freezing kitchen, started a fire, made soup and rice and side dishes, and served her husband a hot breakfast. During the day, she took laundry to a well to wash, even in freezing weather. When she brought the laundry home, it was frozen stiff like a bundle of sticks. Her hands ached and were numb from the cold.

I detected a note of sadness and pain in her voice when she spoke of her early years. She did not say, but I was sure that sometimes she was resentful of Father, who was so busy serving God that he was not sensitive to her hardship. Even as a child, I often thought, *Life is weird. Doctors are busy healing the sick, but often cannot heal themselves. Those who are so involved in helping others, like Father, often neglect to help those closest to them. It just does not seem right. But that seems to be the way it is in life. A lamp lights up a room, but it casts its own shadow around its base.*

I was glad to know that Mother's life turned easier as Father became more established. By the time I was born, our life was comfortable. In fact, she created the environment such that I felt that we were rich and secure.

3. My childhood

My early childhood was filled with happy memories. I can picture the peaceful seminary and church compound where we lived, where Father taught and preached, where I played with my two close friends: Yung-Suk, a boy who was a year older, and my beloved dog. Yung-Suk's father was also a minister like mine whose family lived in the compound at a house, a stone's throw from mine. He, like my father, was busy preaching the gospel as he traveled throughout the Land of the Morning Calm. Yung-Suk was tall, about three inches taller than I. He had the eyes of a boxer, ready to land a knockout punch to any boy whom he didn't like. He spoke his mind without caring what others might think or say. The only person he was afraid of was his mother because she was a no-nonsense lady who did not hesitate to whip her son with her bare hand, a wooden rod or a thick bamboo stick on his calves, his head, his shoulders as her spirit moved, while shouting in her tiger-like voice. He was also careful not to show his aggressiveness in front of Yung-Ja, his older sister by three years, because she would report him to her mother, and he would get punished. Yung-Ja used to call me Bow-Legs, because my legs had grown like a bow. But for whatever the reason, Yung-Suk's mother loved me. Whenever I went to her house, she greeted me with a broad smile saying, "How's my adopted son?" Then I would respond, "Good morning, Yung-Suk *urmony*—mother—can I play with Yung-Suk?" "Of course," she always said in a warm tone of voice, "you are a good example that my son should learn from."

Yung-Suk and I played and grew up together from the time I was about five years old. Even though Yung-Suk was not friendly to other kids in our neighborhood, he was protective of me like my brother, Hi-Seung. One day we were walking along on a neighborhood street. A couple of boys playing ball saw us. One called out, "Hey, watermelon head with bow legs. Don't fall down and get your head all splattered." Yung-Suk rushed toward them, knocking one down with his fist to the boy's chin and kicking the other boy with his foot to the boy's shin. They cried and ran away. After that, no boys bothered me. So I felt secure when I was with Yung-Suk.

Also I had a dog, named Kwidong—Precious One. When I wasn't with Yung-Suk, I walked into the wooded area in the compound to look for crawling things like frogs, snakes, or whatever I could find to catch while Kwidong followed me, sniffing along the way. When Kwidong saw a cat, she dashed toward it barking. The cat climbed up a nearby tree and teasingly look down at Kwidong, who barked looking up at her nemesis, her front feet on the tree trying to climb. I picked up a stick and threw it at the cat, who then moved up to a higher branch to avoid getting hit.

Kwidong loved my rubber ball that Brother Hi-Seung bought for me to learn how to throw and catch. I used to throw the ball against the brick wall of my house, and I tried to catch the ball bouncing off the wall while Kwidong watching me intensely. When I missed the ball and it passed me by, Kwidong dashed to get it, and brought it back in her mouth while wagging her tail, wanting me to do it again and again. With Kwidong around, I didn't have to run to get the ball. As soon as she saw that I was ready to throw the ball, she was prepared to run with her eyes focused on the ball. Sometimes I threw the ball gently to her saying, "Catch it before it lands on the ground." Sometimes I threw the ball straight up in the air telling her to catch it, but she just waited for the ball to bounce off the ground. Apparently, she knew that she could get her teeth broken catching the ball coming down at a high speed. But she loved me throwing the ball far away so that she could run and bring it back.

So with Yung-Suk and Kwidong to play with, and a lot of crawling and flying things that I could catch in the woods, I looked forward to every day to go out to the beautiful seminary compound to spend the day. When I got thirsty and hungry, I went to Mother for a drink and snack. And Mother was always there to welcome me with a smile, giving me something to eat, and listening to tales of my exploration.

In the springtime, the area was covered with cherry blossoms and golden buds of forsythia. Mother brightened our rooms with the bell-shaped, yellow forsythia flowers. She said looking at the tiny yellow flowers, "Isn't God a wonderful artist?" And I nodded in agreement. Another time she said, arranging the cherry blossom branches in a vase in the living room, "Hi-Dong, take one blossom and examine it carefully. Feel how soft those petals are. Look at the blending of colors. Follow the contour of each petal. Look at the center. How many stems with anthers are there? Can you count them? Do you see that hairy looking stigma at the center? That is where bees bring pollen and sit on it. The pollen gently goes down the tube and makes seeds."

As she spoke gently and quietly, I sensed that she was really enraptured by the delicate beauty of God's creation. I was fascinated by the detailed work that God had done on such a tiny blossom. I examined one blossom after another. I compared the size, and counted to see whether all had the same number of petals. I wondered why one blossom was smaller than the others, and why some petals had more cherry tones than the others. Because of that experience, I still carry that fascination when I see flowers.

In the summertime, I went out with Yung-Suk and Kwidong, and explored the wooded areas in the seminary compound. Sometimes I crawled into Kwidong's kennel and lay down next to her while she licked my nose and lips with her tongue, and I patted her fur. Other times I came home with a pocketful of dragon-flies, beetles, butterflies, and snails. I proudly displayed my catch of the day on the kitchen table, and Mother, smiling, listened to the details of my exploration. She never showed a sign of repulsion at the sight of a pocketful of dead insects on the table. Sometimes they were all squashed together for some reason, and they looked gruesome even to me. But somehow she made me feel good about what I was doing. She did not squelch my inborn curiosity about nature, but rather helped me to continue the exploration of the world around me.

Oh, yes, I remember one evening I brought home an old frog. It was an ugly-looking one, with small dark bumps all over its skin like a leper, and with one eye partially closed. I had found it in our front yard, and I jumped around to catch this frog hopping away from me. After minutes of hopping, the frog seemed tired and I reached out and grabbed it with my hand. I was excited to catch a live frog with my bare hand all by myself. I rushed into the house to show it to Mother.

"Mother, Mother," I yelled. "Where are you?"

"I am in the kitchen." I heard Mother's voice.

"Guess what I caught."

"What?"

"A live frog," I yelled. "I caught it all by myself with my hand."

I rushed into the kitchen. Mother looked at me while slicing potatoes with a sharp knife on the chopping board.

"Look," I said while setting the frog on the kitchen table.

Before Mother had the time to figure out what it was, this ugly little thing jumped right at Mother. Her eyes turned round. Then she shrieked and ran away with the knife in her hand, yelling at me to take it outside. It was such a funny sight that I laughed until tears ran down my cheeks while I jumped all over the kitchen trying to catch the slippery frog. It hopped into the tofu soup that she was preparing. I saw the soft flames fluttering beneath the pot from red hot charcoals. I was nervous. *That frog's going to be cooked*, I thought. *Hope the soup is not boiling.* I put my finger in the soup to feel the temperature, and to my relief it was not hot. The frog was on the edge trying to get out. I quickly grabbed the wiggly frog, ran out of the house and tossed the frog far in the air, as if I was throwing a baseball in a large arc.

Apparently she did not realize that the frog jumped into the soup because Mother served it for dinner. I looked around, and everybody seemed to enjoy the tofu soup that the frog had bathed in.

"Your tofu soup is always the best," Father said while taking a spoonful in his mouth.

But my stomach felt queasy thinking of the ugly frog with dark bumps all over his skin sloshing around the pot an hour ago. But if I did not eat, Mother would ask me why. And I would have to answer. And I could not tell a lie because if I did, I would end up in hell, where I would be walking on a track covered with red, hot charcoal, not only for a day but for eternity. My choice was clear. Eat the soup. And I did. With great effort.

That night at bedtime, Mother told me a frog story. "Once upon a time in a wooded pond near a small village lived Papa Frog and Mama Frog with little baby frogs. They were very happy in that pond because there was plenty of food to eat, and plenty of leaves falling on the pond where they played hide-and-seek. Every day Papa Frog went into the water to catch minnows for the baby frogs, and Mama Frog went into a grassy area near the pond to catch flies and mosquitoes for food.

Then one day as Papa Frog dived into the water to gather the daily meal, there was a huge fish waiting for him. The fish, in one gulp, swallowed Papa Frog and swam merrily away. Now Mama Frog was left all alone and was sad. But she did not want to see her little babies go hungry. She was not good at catching minnows like Papa Frog. So every day she went to the grassy area to collect insects. She had to work twice as hard now since Papa Frog was not there to help.

One day she could not gather enough food in the grassy area. And she had to move further out toward a dirt road leading to the village. It was getting dark. Right then a little boy with a fishing rod was passing by. As soon as the boy saw the Mama Frog, he laid the fishing rod on the road and jumped after her. She hopped desperately all over the road to avoid the boy's hand, but to no avail. The boy put Mama Frog on the hook and happily walked toward home. Swinging her with his rod.

Meanwhile, those twelve cute baby frogs were waiting for Mama to bring their food. They waited many, many hours for her. But she did not come. It was getting dark and started to rain. The babies started to cry, hoping that Mama Frog might hear them. They were getting hungry and missing her. But she didn't come back. Never again. And to this day, we hear frogs cry loudly, especially at an eventide."

That night, I couldn't sleep. For some reason, I associated that ugly-looking frog that I caught with Mama Frog in the story. I pictured the frightened Mama Frog crying as she was thrown high in the air, "Oh, I am going to be smashed on the ground. Who is going to take care of my twelve babies? They are going to be left all alone without me and Papa, and starve to death." I felt very guilty and couldn't sleep. I hoped that the frog had landed safely on the soft turf without getting hurt.

As soon as I woke up the next morning, I rushed outside toward the area where I threw the frog, fearing that she might have been smashed to death. I walked around all over, without finding a trace of her. I came back home, somewhat relieved at not finding the dead frog. Since that time, I have never caught frogs again.

Fall was an exciting season. Persimmon trees, which abounded in the compound, were filled with golden fruit. While my brothers climbed the trees to pick the ripe ones, I watched them with Kwidong standing next to me from the ground, marveling at their agility and balance, and wished I were up there too. I walked around with a basket and picked up those on the ground, and looked for ripe and mellow ones to eat.

For weeks we feasted on persimmons. Some were placed by sunny windows so that they would ripen quickly. Some were placed in the rice chest for later use. Some were taken down to the cool, dark basement and put in chaffs for delayed ripening. Now and then, Mother picked a couple ripe persimmons, scooped the insides out into a cup, and gave it to me to enjoy while she told me fruit stories as I ate.

Fall was also a time of brilliant golden foliage where we lived. I enjoyed looking out the window to behold the leaves in colorful red and orange hues surrounding the house. One day Mother was looking out through the living room window.

She said in a reflective mood, "Human life is like the seasons: Spring is like childhood. It is the time to grow, develop roots, experience the warmth of the sun, and taste the soothing and thirst-quenching rain.

Summer is like the period of being a youth. A person will grow stronger. His roots will sink deeper into the ground. There may be heavy winds and torrential rain, but he will stand firm if he has strong and deep roots.

Fall resembles middle age, with fruit and brilliant foliage. As some trees bear an abundance of fruit while others do not, a person who was nurtured well in childhood and developed strength and deep roots during his youth expects to be rewarded for his accomplishments, and to be admired and respected by people around him.

In late fall leaves start to fall, like a man losing his hair. Branches will lose their suppleness like a man's muscles and joints turning stiff. Winter is like old age, without leaves to protect the tree from the cold and without suppleness to bend with the wind. A person waits for God to call his name to come Home.

Seasons come and go in cycles, year after year. But the human seasons have only one cycle. A person is born once and dies once."

Then Mother looked at me, somewhat embarrassed at being so philosophical in front of a small child.

She said, "Some people are born to be apple trees and some to be willow trees, Mother said with a smile. And Hi-Dong, you are going to be a big, big oak tree, bigger than the tree you see out there. People will come, and sit by you, feel your strength and enjoy the shade that you provide."

I did not know what she was talking about, but it sounded good. So I held her hand and returned a smug smile as if I understood.

A few weeks before the frost set in, it was time for preparing winter *kimchee*. Mother went to the vegetable market to order Chinese cabbage, radish, pounds of hot, ground red pepper, garlic, a sack of salt, green onions, and smelly fish sauce. A hundred heads of cabbage and dozens of radishes needed to be cleaned, salted, grated, stuffed, and put into big clay urns.

This was the season for ladies. Some neighborhood ladies, as well as relatives, volunteered to help out in the big *kimchee*-making event. The house bustled with activities, with women scurrying around in their white skirts almost touching the ground, in and out of the house, some washing cabbage in a big tank outside with a water hose, some grating radish that would be used as *kimchee* stuffing, and some chopping green onions on a board with the sound of a woodpecker pecking on a tree. Each person had a job to do. Everyone's hands were busy with her chores, and at the same time all the lips were busy with womanly talk. I noticed that their lips moved much faster than their hands. It was a busy time for the ladies, but also a happy get-together for chatting and gossiping.

I loved the pungent odor of freshly chopped garlic permeating through the house. I marveled at the ladies who could talk for hours uninterrupted while busily doing their chores. As a kid, who was not good at speaking, I could not imagine myself talking and doing something at the same time.

It was an exciting time for me. I walked around with my hands behind me as if I were an inspector, and checked on what the women were doing, sampling a salted piece of cabbage here and grated radish stuffing there, and sometimes was scolded by my sisters who did not want to be bothered. When I went to Mother, she described what she was doing and gave me something to taste.

When the winter *kimchee* was all prepared, and the huge crocks were set in place, some in the ground for winter use, and some in the basement for near-term use, there was a feast, celebrating the successful completion of the yearly event. For the feast, the fresh crop of rice was cooked. The smell of finely cut beef, marinated in soy sauce, broiled on a hot charcoal grill whetted my appetite.

After the dinner with dishes of the broiled beef, cabbage and radish, the evening was spent in the living room with ladies in an unending round of talk, going over the events of the past few days. I sat beside Mother with my hands on her lap, listening until it was time for the women to leave. She was always generous to the ladies with food and kind words. As the relatives and neighbors left, she loaded them down with a bagful of cabbage, some radishes or a jar of *kimchee* to take home. She showered them with words of appreciation. They went home feeling good about themselves for helping, and were happy to have something to share with their families.

One of the joys of winter was tasting and eating *kimchee*. The hot radish stuffing put between the cabbage leaves tasted so good that I could eat it without ever getting tired of it. As long as I had the winter *kimchee* with rice and soup, I was satisfied. The *kimchee* tasted best a few weeks into the winter, when it was fully ripened. As the winter drew to a close, the *kimchee* started to turn sour. Then Mother made soup out of it with small pieces of pork. The pork needed some fat to enhance the flavor of the broth. When the *kimchee* soup was cooking, the house was filled with the pungent odor of garlic, scallions, and a sourness that I could not describe. The odor was strong, but the soup was very delicious.

The happiest part of the winter was the family getting together in the living room around the wood-burning stove. The stove was placed in the middle of the room keeping the room warm and comfortable. Father, wearing his glasses set close to the edge of his nose, read newspapers or the Bible on one side. My sisters, attending an elementary school, did their homework either on a meal table or on the floor. Sometimes they complained that they had too much homework, or that it was difficult. Father would look at them, making encouraging remarks. Mother spent most of her time sewing—torn pants or whatever else needed to be sewed. I sat beside her watching how she put the thread into the tiny eye of a needle. She let me try it now and then. I felt very good when I would thread the needle with my inexperienced fingers. I watched with curiosity how Mother patched torn holes. I also went over to Father and sat beside him as he read the Bible. He put his arm around me, sometimes reading a passage aloud so that I could hear. Often my sisters did not like me watching them work; they felt bothered. So they said, "Get away. Don't bother us."

When they told me to go away, I played tough and did not budge. A hassle would start. Either Mother or Father intervened to stop the squabble, usually saying, "Hi-Dong wants to learn. As long as he is just watching your work, leave him alone." I felt triumphant, and my sisters kept quiet, but they stared at me with evil eyes, which I fondly remember to this day.

I cherish the memory of those evenings, because peace and warmth permeated that room. I felt very secure and comfortable, seeing our family members there together, each doing his or her work and feeling good about being him- or herself, and I could explore the world around me to satisfy my curiosity.

4. My two brothers

When I was born, my eldest brother, Hi-Bum, was fifteen years old. My elder brother, Hi-Seung, was eight years old. As I was growing up, I heard from Mother's friends and our neighbors that Hi-Bum was the brightest and most well-mannered son in the family and Hi-Seung the dumbest and most rude. From elementary school on, Hi-Bum brought home straight A's while Hi-Seung brought home mostly C's and on rare occasions some B's. When Hi-Bum came home from school, he went straight to his room and did his homework before doing other activities. Unlike Hi-Bum, when Hi-Seung came home from school, he went straight to his room, threw his school-bag on his bed, and rushed outside to mingle with the neighborhood bullies. He made catcalls at the girls walking by. He tried to mount a he-dog on the back of a she-dog to see them mate—often getting bitten by one of the dogs. He got into fights with neighborhood bullies and came home with a bloody nose.

Hi-Bum, on the other hand, was not only bright but also articulate. When he gave his understanding of a Bible passage in the church, Father sat in his chair on the podium with a smile on his face while listening to his son talk, and others listened spellbound. At high school, Hi-Bum won many debates on various topics and impressed his Japanese teachers. After graduation, Japanese teachers sent Hi-Bum to a university in Manchuria founded by Japan to teach bright young students from its conquered countries so that they would return to their homelands and be the puppets of their Japanese masters.

This was not the case with Hi-Seung. He was crude in his language. He did not express his thoughts well to others and was often ridiculed by

Hi-Bum. At school Hi-Seung didn't pay attention to his Japanese teachers. He didn't do his homework. He spoke Korean, which was forbidden in his school. He talked back to his teachers and got slapped and kicked. He got into fights with his classmates. Thus Father was often called to school for consultation.

At home Hi-Bum was well-mannered. He greeted visitors at the door with smile, saying, "Welcome Mr. Kim. Have you been in peace? Please come in. I will go upstairs and tell Father that you are here." Or he said, "Welcome Mrs. Park, how have you been? Mother's in the living room, waiting for you. Please go in." On the other hand, when Mr. Kim knocked at the door, Hi-Seung opened the door and stared at him with the *don't bother me* look. When Mr. Kim asked, "Is your father home?", Hi-Seung's reply was, "Upstairs," and left the guest at the door. As a result, visitors poured accolades on Hi-Bum, but there was no such praise for Hi-Seung. On the contrary, the visitors conveyed their concern for Hi-Seung to Father. And our neighbors and friends considered him to be the black sheep of the family and a disgrace to his minister father. Thus Hi-Bum was the pride and joy to Father, whereas Hi-Seung was an embarrassment to him. As a result he got the most whipping from Father. I often heard Father yelling while Hi-Seung begged for mercy behind the closed door of Father's office. Scared, I used to run to Mother for protection.

Strangely though, from the time when I could walk and talk I was drawn to Hi-Seung. I often wondered why. *Why not model myself after Hi-Bum, the brightest and the jewel of the family instead after Hi-Seung, the dumbest and the embarrassment to the family?* One day I asked Mother why, and she told me the story. Mother said that Hi-Seung was all smiles when he saw his infant brother, me, in her arms. Hi-Seung watched with fascination how eagerly I sucked Mother's nipple. He said to Mother with a chuckle, "The way he drinks your milk, he's going to be a strong boy." When Mother asked him to look after me if she was away for an evening, Hi-Seung willingly obliged to feed me and babysit for me. When I was sick with fever, he came and sat by me with a worried look on his face, touching my wrist to check my pulse and putting his hand on my forehead to see whether I had a temperature. So from my birth, a love relationship developed between Hi-Seung and me.

As a child, I was a tender, innocent boy—afraid of loud noises, afraid of the dark, afraid of water, and afraid of bullies. When I heard a loud thunder with lightning, I ran to Mother screaming, "Mother, I'm scared," and hid under her skirt for protection. While walking next to Mother on a street, if I saw a scary-looking old man walking toward me, instinctively I moved close to Mother holding her hand tightly like a vise—fearfully watching the old man passing me by. Then Mother said with a smile, "Please excuse my son. He's afraid of my brother who looks like you."

We had a basement, and its door was outside the house. We walked a dozen concrete steps down to open the double door to get into the dark basement illuminated only by the light coming through the dusty glass windows of the door. It was the coolest place in the house, and Mother kept fresh vegetables, *kimchee*, and fish there. Mother often asked me to go down to the basement to get something for her, but I refused.

One day, Mother said, "Hi-Dong, I am going to make you a delicious charcoal-broiled mackerel for dinner."

"Oh, really?" I said with my taste buds rising with anticipation.

"Why don't you go down to the basement and get the mackerel that I bought this morning?"

"No way, Mother."

"Why not?"

"Because I'm scared."

"Scared of what?"

"A ghost."

Mother smiled looking at me with her tender eyes.

"There's no ghost, Hi-Dong."

I heard what Mother said, but I wasn't sure. For whatever the reason, I thought a bony lady ghost with sharp fingernails in a dark gown and scarf lived in the dark basement. Waiting for me. I pictured her grabbing me by the neck and flying with me far, far away into space saying, "You will have fun playing with my ghost children. I will tell them not to scratch you too much with their sharp fingers because when they play, they like to scratch each other."

"I'm still scared." I said to Mother.

"OK," Mother said, standing. "Let's walk down together."

I followed Mother to the basement holding her hand tightly, with my body rubbing against Mother's leg. I didn't want to be snatched away by the lady ghost.

"Ghost, where are you?" Mother called in her alto voice. "Come and meet my son, Hi-Dong."

"Don't, Mother," I whispered. Shaking.

We waited for a few seconds, which seemed like forever. But no ghost showed up.

"Hurry up, Ghost," Mother yelled again. "I'm in a hurry."

But no ghost. We waited a few more seconds. Still no ghost.

"Do you believe me now?" Mother smiled. "There's no ghost."

"I'm still scared," I said holding on to her.

The next day as I was watching Mother getting ready for dinner, Hi-Seung walked in.

"What's for dinner?" Hi-Seung asked.

"I bought a fresh rock cod this morning," Mother said. "Hi-Dong, why don't you go down to the basement and get the fish?"

My immediate response was to say, "No, Mother." But I didn't want to say it in front Hi-Seung because I knew that he would make fun of me. I hesitated, rubbing my hands.

"Hi-Dong is afraid of going down to the basement alone," Mother said.

Hi-Seung looked at me with a teasing smile. "Little Brother, I see you are still afraid of the dark."

"He thinks there is a lady ghost living in our basement." Mother smiled. "He is afraid of her."

"Let's go to the basement together," Hi-Seung said winking at Mother.

"Why don't you go by yourself?" I said.

"I will show you how to use my slingshot to shoot at the ghost," he said.

"Slingshot?" I said. I was still scared, but I thought it would be so much fun to shoot at the lady ghost with Brother standing next to me.

"Yes, I will show you how/"

"OK," I answered back.

"You wait by the door," Hi-Seung said. "I'll go to my room and get the slingshot."

I rushed to the front door and waited while he walked to his room. Within minutes he came out with the slingshot, and we walked outside, picked up a few pebbles and walked down the steps to the basement. I wasn't too afraid this time with Hi-Seung next to me because I knew he could surely knock the lady ghost down with his bare hands.

"OK, Hi-Dong," Hi-Seung said handing me the sling and a pebble. "You stand at the wall and aim it at the place where you think that the lady ghost may come out."

"OK," I said with excitement building but still feeling scared.

I aimed the slingshot at a tall cabinet set in one corner, thinking that the lady ghost would come out from the back of the cabinet.

"You stay there," he said picking up the rock cod, "I will take this to Mother and be right back."

"Hurry," I said aiming the sling at the cabinet with the rubber band stretched.

I wasn't too afraid because Brother would come right back, and also I had the slingshot aiming at the cabinet. If the lady ghost came out, I was sure that I could hit her with the pebble and hurt her. While she cried with pain, Brother would be back and kick her away. But as Hi-Seung walked out, I heard the double-door slam shut. I heard the click, sounding like the door latch snapped in place. The basement became dark. I ran to the door. I tried to open the door. But it was locked!

"Brother," I shouted pounding the wooden door. "Open the door."

"I will be back in an hour," Hi-Seung said. "Be sure to get the slingshot ready to shoot at the lady ghost. If you don't and she shows up, you will be in trouble."

I heard his footsteps fading away. I banged on the door with my foot, calling Brother to help me. But there was no response. The place became silent. Totally silent. I froze with fear expecting at any moment that the lady ghost might appear and grab my neck with her sharp fingers saying, "Now I got you. I'm going to take you to my boys far, far away so they can play with a human boy." Then I felt the slingshot in my hands. I remembered Brother telling me to have the slingshot ready to shoot the lady ghost if she ever showed up. That was the only thing I could do to keep myself from being taken away by the ghost. Also I should aim at her eye so that I could blind her, and that way she could not know where I was. Then I could hide until Brother came back.

Mustering enough courage, I turned around. With light coming through the dusty window, I saw the *kimchee* jar in one corner. Green onions and several Chinese cabbages on a wooden table in another corner. I saw a spider weaving its web in one corner of the ceiling. And then I saw the cabinet. I pictured the lady ghost hiding behind the cabinet ready to appear at any moment. I aimed the slingshot at the cabinet. I pulled the rubber band with a pebble in the strap ready to release it toward the lady ghost as soon as she appeared. I waited with the rubber band stretched. Minutes passed. The ghost did not appear. My hand was getting tired from keeping the band stretched. I looked at the spider. It kept moving around ever so slowly—weaving. It didn't seem to be afraid. It just kept weaving a strand at a time. More minutes passed. No lady ghost showed up. I said to myself, *I think Mother is right. There is no ghost. I'm just imagining it.* I let go of the band, and I felt my hands, arms and shoulders relax. I walked to the spider to watch how it was weaving its web. I saw how the spider took a fine thread with its legs, bringing it to another thread and connected it in a given pattern. The thread seemed to come out of its body, but I did not know where it was coming from. But it was so interesting. Then I realized that I wasn't too afraid. The fear disappeared somehow. I looked around the basement, and it was still dark. But the darkness didn't seem to be so scary.

After the basement lockup, Hi-Seung took me to wooded area in the compound and left me there for hours at night on occasions. He called it a darkness training. The training to help me to get rid of the fear of darkness. On the first night, the howling sounds of animals and cuckooing sounds of night birds made me so scared that I froze in total darkness. I came home with my pants all wet from the fear of being bitten by animals in the woods. But after several trips into the woods, I found that the darkness did not bother me at all. The howling sounds still bothered me, but also I knew that in that woods there were no big animals to hurt me badly. In fact, I enjoyed looking at the millions of twinkling stars gracing the sky.

Next came the 'I love water' training. My family used to go to the Han River on sunny summer days. We took a boat and rowed across the river to have a picnic on the sandy beach. While others swam, I sat next to Mother watching the people swim because I was afraid to go into the water. I was afraid that the father of the koi fish in the living room aquarium, the one I killed to find out what made it swim, might recognize me in the water and tell his friends, "Look, guys, who I have here. See a little guy trying to swim like a frog? That little guy killed my boy. Let's get him." I pictured a swarm of big fish speeding up toward me, grabbing my arms and legs with their huge mouths, and pulling me down to the bottom of the river. I tried to fight them off, but they were too strong. I gasped for air. Instead, I swallowed water. I saw myself drowning at the bottom of the river while the fish circled around me with their unblinking eyes in celebration.

Often Hi-Seung came over and pulled me to the river to a place knee-deep while I resisted.

"OK, Hi-Dong, this is how far I am going to go," Hi-Seung said one day. "Let's see who can stay in the water longer without breathing. You count while I stick my head in the water."

It sounded like fun.

"OK," I said.

"As soon as I stick my head into the water," Hi-Seung said, "start counting like the grandfather clock ticking in the hallway. One ... two ... three ... like that."

"OK," I said.

Brother took a deep breath and put his head into the water, and I counted.

"One ... two ... three ... four ... five ..."

His head was still in the water.

"Six ... seven ... eight ... nine ... ten."

Still in the water. I was impressed.

"Eleven ... twelve ... thirteen."

His head came out of the water

"How many counts?" Hi-Seung asked without even gasping.

"Thirteen," I said.

"Good, I counted fifteen," he said. "Now it's your turn."

I took a deep breath like Hi-Seung and put my head in the water. The water was cold. Much colder than the tap water at home. I opened my eyes to see any big fish around while counting in my head. The first five counts were a breeze. As I got close to eight, I felt like I needed to breathe. But I did not want to be too far behind my brother. I counted to ten. I could not continue any longer. I felt like dying. I lifted my head gasping.

"Good job," Hi-Seung patting my back. "I counted eleven."

"It's hard work," I said taking a deep breath.

"You didn't seem to be afraid in the water," Hi-Seung said.

I realized that standing knee-deep in the water was not scary at all. In fact it was fun playing the breathing game with Brother.

"OK," Hi-Seung said. "I will teach you how to swim and breathe so that you can swim a long distance."

For the next several weeks, Hi-Seung took me to a community swimming pool nearby and taught me the breaststroke. I couldn't keep my head out of the water all the time, but I could stick my neck out to breathe after several strokes.

"For your good work," Hi-Seung said, "I am going to take you to the Han River for a boat ride this weekend."

"A boat ride?" I was excited. "Will you teach me how to row?"

"The oars are too heavy for you now," he said. "But when you get older, I will show you."

The weekend came, and we took a trolley to the Han River. We walked to the dock, rented a small row boat, and Hi-Seung started to row across the river toward the sandy beach where I saw children swimming naked. It was a beautiful day with a clear blue sky and the river without a ripple. As we got close to the beach about sixty feet away from the children, he said, "Take off your clothes."

"Why?" I asked in surprise.

"I saw how well you swam in the pool," he said. "Now swim toward the children."

Fear crept into me. I wasn't afraid of the pool because even at the deepest place, I could stick my head out of the water and because there was no fish. But here, it was much deeper, and there were a lot of fish. I was sure Hi-Seung would not be able to stick his head out of the water.

"I don't want to," I protested.

"You have a choice," he said. "Either you swim toward the children, or I'll tip the boat over so that you swim toward the shore in your clothes and shoes."

I knew Brother Hi-Seung meant what he said. Just like Father, to Hi-Seung 'No' was 'No', and 'Yes' was 'Yes'.

"OK," I said. "But let me have my underpants on."

"You see the other children swimming naked." He pointed to the children splashing the water and having a good time. "You can do the same."

I had never been naked in public, and I did not want to expose myself in full view of others. I hesitated.

"OK," Hi-Seung said. "Let's go over there where no one is around."

He turned the boat and rowed further away from the children.

"Take off your clothes while I row next to you," he said.

Reluctantly I took my clothes off to get ready to jump off the boat.

"Be sure to relax," he said. "And think you are swimming in the pool."

Hi-Seung counted, "One … two … three … Get set … Go." I followed his count and as soon as he said, "Go", I jumped into the water making a splash. Unlike the pool water, the river water felt cold. I opened my eyes and found that I could see the bottom way down. It was covered with white sand—not gray concrete. I saw a group of tiny fish swimming and wiggling their tiny fins. It was a beautiful sight to behold. Now I needed to breathe and swim toward the shore.

As Hi-Seung suggested, I relaxed. Swimming several strokes with my head in the water, and lifting my head for breath for the next stroke. I found I liked it.

"Seems like you are having fun," Hi-Seung said following next to me in the boat.

"Sort of," I said.

"You are doing fine," he said. "Just relax and enjoy."

With each stroke the shore was getting closer, and I felt that it wasn't bad at all. In fact it was fun. Then suddenly I thought of the fish down below. Especially the father of the koi fish that I killed. I pictured him telling his friends swimming next to him, "See that little fellow up there swimming like a frog without the pants? He killed my son. Let's swim up and bite off that tiny thing between his legs. Let's show him we can hurt him too." I hurried my pace.

"Hey, Hi-Dong," Hi-Seung said, "what's going on? If you rush like that, you are not going to make to the shore. Relax."

I slowed down the pace taking frequent breaths, still worrying that Father Fish might come any time and bite off my private part. When I hurried thinking of Father Fish under me, Hi-Seung said, "Slow down and relax." I slowed down. Then the thought of Father Fish made me hurry. Again, Hi-Seung reminded me to slow down. I kept swimming, hurrying, thinking of Father Fish and slowing down by Hi-Seung's reminders. To my good fortune, Father Fish didn't come, and by the time I reached the shore, I was half-dead. But I felt so proud of myself.

"Boy, I'm impressed for a five year old boy," Hi-Seung said getting off the boat. "Even a ten-year-old boy wouldn't be able to swim like you did."

"Thanks," I said returning a smug smile.

As we were coming home, he kept patting my back for the good job that I did.

"Now there's one more thing that I want to teach you," Brother said.

"What?"

"I will show you how to knock down those bullies who bother you," he said, "and be Tarzan of the human jungle."

As a child, I was not just afraid of the dark and the water, but I was also afraid of tough kids. When I saw boys fighting in the street, I ran away to Mother for protection. When I was with a boy talking tough to me, I ran away to Mother, shaking. I did not like myself acting like a mushy bean curd. I wanted to be like Tarzan whose stories I had read in comic books. So my ears took notice when I heard the word, Tarzan, who was not afraid of tigers and giant snakes in the African jungle. On the contrary, the tigers and snakes stayed away from Tarzan because they did not want him to twirl them around, throw them hundreds of feet high in the air, fall down to the ground, and be smashed into pieces. I wanted to be like Tarzan who was not afraid of anything—not even bullies.

For five days a week, after Hi-Seung came home from school, he took me to the neighborhood exercise ground that had chin-up bars, parallel bars, a basketball net, and a running track. He showed me how to do push-ups. How to pull myself up on the chin-up bar. He ran around the track with me. After two months of training, I could do twenty push-ups without breaking a sweat. I could do ten chin-ups with some sweat. I could run a quarter mile without stopping, even though I was way behind him.

Hi-Seung also taught me how to defend myself and counter-attack and knock a bully down using both my arms and feet. "OK, Hi-Dong, I am the bully," he said. "I'm going to attack you. You defend yourself and counter-attack." In the beginning, I had a rough time because his hands and feet were so fast. I had a hard time avoiding his fist touching my chin and his foot touching my shin. If it were a real fight, I would have ended up with a broken jaw and a bleeding shin. In time I was able to block his fist coming toward my chin and his foot coming toward my shin. It was fun, and I looked forward to the next day.

During the training, he told me to recite, like his gym teacher had told his class to do, "I am not afraid of anything. I can do anything that I set my mind to." He told me to say it ten times every morning before I got out of my bed.

After a few months of training, he said, "Now I can call you Tarzan."

"Did you call me Tarzan?" I looked at him in disbelief.

"Yes, Hi-Dong," Hi-Seung shouted, grinning at me. "You are Tarzan of the human jungle."

It was the happiest moment of my life. I was Tarzan—not a mushy bean curd. And I looked forward to every tomorrow to see Brother Hi-Seung coming home from school and to teach me new skills.

Unfortunately, the war came. Not only one war but two wars: World War II and the Korean War. In December, 1941, Japan bombed Pearl Harbor in the hope of destroying the U.S. naval power in the Pacific so that it could conquer all the countries in Asia without the U.S. intervention.

Japan dreamed of whole Asia under the rule of its *divine* emperor, Emperor Hirohito. In June, 1950, nine years later, North Korean broke though the 38th parallel line and rammed southward. North Korea's esteemed leader, Kim Il-Sung, wanted to take over South Korea and rule the unified Korea under his command. Thereafter, the garden of happiness, which had been my home, was mercilessly trampled by the ruthless Japanese military and the onslaught of the North Korean army.

5. Pearl Harbor—Japan tightens its vise

Soon after the bombing of Pearl Harbor on December 7, 1941, Japan's control over Korea was tightened. Like a vise. Japan announced, "No Korean alphabet will be taught in elementary schools. No Korean will be spoken in schools and in public places. No Korean flag will be displayed anywhere—even inside homes. The cherry blossom—not the rose of Sharon—will be Korea's national flower. Every Korean will have a Japanese name. Christian churches will be closed … Anyone who breaks any of the rules will be punished or imprisoned."

With WWII the Japanese carried out the rules they set up for Koreans with the utmost diligence. When I was in first grade at Mee Dong Elementary School, all my classmates were called by Japanese names. Mine was Yamamoto Yoshimitsu—not Chai Hi-Dong, my Korean name. Anyone who got caught speaking Korean in the class was ordered by the teacher to come to the front and put their arms out straight and hold them there for minutes. Some teachers hit students with bamboo sticks or slapped them with their calloused hands for speaking Korean. Every morning before the class started, we, thirty Korean children, stood straight in front of our desks, raised our arms high in the air, and shouted, "Tenno Heika, Bansai"—long live the emperor. We sang the Japanese national anthem. Regularly, the whole school marched in formation to the Shinto temple high above Mount Nam San and respectfully bowed down to the picture of the Japanese emperor. Japan expected every Korean, both young and old, to carry out this honored ritual.

Many Christians went to Mount Nam San to pay respect to the Japanese emperor. They said, "It's just a ritual anyway. As long as my heart is in Christ, I am a Christian. And God will understand." One day Mother's younger sister, Little Aunt, visited us. Her house was an hour walk from my house, and she came to see her sister every three weeks. Even though Little Aunt was not a Christian, I liked her because she always called me 'little young man'—not *mangnei*, the last son—in her husky voice with a broad smile. I called her *Jargun Eemo*, Little Aunt. She was always bubbly and laughed a lot. When she laughed, it sounded like a *Jangsah*—a big muscular man—laughing. It shook the house, and I liked it. But today she looked somber. She smiled at me but did not laugh. *Did she have a fight with her husband and lose? Did her house get robbed?* I wondered.

"What's the matter, Kyung-Ja?" Mother asked.

"These Japanese …" she shouted.

"Shhh …" Mother whispered looking around fearing that someone might be listening.

"I hear that the Japanese are rounding up the Christian ministers and taking them to prison."

"Ministers?" Mother said putting her hands on her chest.

I felt fear creeping up inside me. *Are they going to take Father to prison also?*

"Yes, ministers," she said. "Unless …"

"Unless what?"

"Unless they visit the *Shinto* shrine."

"Bow down to their emperor?"

"Yes," Little Aunt said. "Bow down to the Japanese emperor."

"Do you think Hi-Dong's father will do that?" Mother looked at Little Aunt.

"You and I both know the answer." She sighed. "Somehow, you have to persuade him."

"You used to tell me he was a mule-head." Mother smiled. "I don't think he will ever take even a first step up to the shrine."

"But he has to think of his family," Little Aunt said. "It's just a ritual anyway. All he has to do is go up to the temple and bow down to the dumb-looking old man so that he can keep you and your children secure."

"I don't know what's right and what's wrong these days," Mother sighed.

"A meaningless ritual to save his family or standing up for his God and put his family in danger."

Well, Father sided with his God—not with my Little Aunt. I remember him reciting the Bible the night after Little Aunt's visit,

"Who shall separate us from the love of Christ? Shall tribulation, or distress, or persecution, or famine, or nakedness, or peril, or sword? ... For I am convinced that neither death, nor life, nor angels, nor principalities, nor things present, nor things to come, nor powers, nor height, nor depth, nor any other created thing, shall be able to separate us from the love of God, which is in Christ Jesus our Lord." Romans 8:35-39

Little Aunt's premonition was right. A week later two policemen came, knocked at our door, and took Father to prison.

6. World War II—Hi-Seung volunteers

"Hey, Buddy, how come you look so glum?" Hi-Seung said, walking up toward the porch where I sat on a step. I was thinking of Father, wondering what the police were doing to him. "Did you get beaten up by that bully at school?"

"No," I replied with my head down. I didn't want to look at him because I might start crying.

"Well, then what's the matter? I have never seen Tarzan looking so scared."

He stood next to me looking down at my eyes, and then sat beside me with his arm around my shoulder.

"What happened?" His usual rough voice softened.

"Father's not home," I said.

"Oh, God," he muttered.

Then he pushed me with his usual roughness, and I almost tipped over on my side. But I regained my balance. He laughed his loud laugh and shouted. "I don't know what to do with my little brother," he said. "I thought I toughened him up to be Tarzan. Now he's afraid that Father's not home."

I got upset.

"That's not it," I said loudly, mustering enough courage. I looked straight at him as he had taught me a year ago. "Two policemen took Father away this morning."

"The Japanese?" he shouted jumping up.

"Yes, the Japanese police," I said, lowering my voice since Mother told me to speak quietly when talking about the Japanese.

"Did the Japanese take Father away?" He shouted loud enough for all the neighbors to hear. He shook his arms in the air shouting, "Those Japanese. Those Japanese." I got nervous. I stood and looked around to see whether there were Japanese policemen around. Then I heard the front door open. I looked. Mother was running out wiping her hands. Her eyes looked scared like mine.

"Quiet, Hi-Seung," Mother said with an unusual sharp tone.

She looked around with her round eyes like I had done seconds ago. Then she looked straight at Hi-Seung.

"I have told you many times not to say, 'Japanese'," Mother said. "It's not right to speak of other people in a demeaning way. And also you can bring more trouble to your family."

"I'm sorry, Mother." Hi-Seung said, calming down. "Did the Japanese police really take Father away?"

"Yes, this morning," Mother said.

"Did they say why?"

"They didn't."

"Did they say where they were taking him?"

"No."

"Did they just take him away?" Hi-Seung raised his voice. "Without telling you why? Without telling you where?"

"Yes. They didn't say why. They didn't say where," Mother said. "They just took him away."

"Those Japanese …" Hi-Seung gritted his teeth and walked up to his room.

After Father was taken away, Mother spent much of her waking hours in prayer while the rest of the family lived in moody silence. I saw her praying when I got out of the bed in the morning. I saw her praying when I came home from school. I saw her praying in the kitchen while waiting for the rice to cook. She prayed with me before my bedtime. A long prayer. Praying that Father would be OK. Praying that Father would not be beaten too badly. Praying that Father would come home soon.

Brother Hi-Seung didn't pray like Mother, but he changed after the Japanese took Father away. I used to enjoy his shouting, banging something in his room, chasing neighborhood dogs with a stick, making—what Mother called—lewd remarks to girls walking down the street, and getting into fights with neighborhood bullies. I wished that I was like my brother, who didn't mind being himself. Not afraid of anybody. Not afraid of anything. I loved him, and in some ways I wished that I was like him.

But with Father gone, he didn't do those bad things that I looked forward to every day. Instead, he turned quiet. He talked to Mother nicely. He still smiled at me but without much action. Like patting my back. Boxing as if he was going to hit me on my chin with his right fist. Asking me to attack with both my arms and feet. *What has happened to Brother Hi-Seung?* I wondered. *Is he worried that the Japanese may whip Father so badly that he may die?*

Months passed. By then it was obvious why Father was taken away. With the war intensifying, Japan did not want to see any problem on the home-front. It wanted all its focus in winning the war, not controlling riots and demonstrations. One way to keep the masses at bay was to eliminate leaders in religion, education and politics, who could incite discontent among the masses, thus creating social disorder. The Japanese police had figured that Father could be one of those leaders.

One afternoon, Hi-Seung, fifteen years old, returned home from school and came to the living room where Mother was sewing my torn pants. He looked pensive and nervous.

"Are you all right?" Mother asked.

"I guess so," Hi-Seung said.

"You look bothered."

No response.

"What happened?" Mother asked with a hint of grin. "Did you beat a boy up at school and get punished by your teacher?"

"No, Mother," he said. "Not this time."

"Then?"

"I ... I ..." Hi-Seung stuttered.

What is happening to Brother? Is he sick? I started to worry. Mother stopped sewing and looked at Hi-Seung.

"Can I get you a glass of *ggul mool*—water mixed with honey?" she asked.

This had been one way Mother used to find out what bothered Hi-Seung. When he was in a good mood, his response was, "Sure, Mother, I will be like baby Hi-Dong." But when he was in a foul mood, he shouted, "Don't insult me, Mother. I'm not Hi-Dong."

Today he just said, "No, thank you, Mother."

Mother looked at him. She was trying to figure out what was going on in his mind. I wondered also why he was not acting like his usual self. No one talked for a while.

Then Hi-Seung said, avoiding Mother's gaze, "I will be leaving for Japan."

His eyes twitched, and his hands were balled into fists.

"What?" Mother gasped.

"I will be leaving for Japan," he said again.

"Did you say Japan?"

"Yes, Mother. I will be joining the Japanese Youth Military Corps," he said. "In a week."

Mother's face turned white and motionless, and her eyes gazed at him with a blank stare. Her right hand was in the air with the thread dangling down from the needle in her fingers. There was a long silence, as if all the movement in the universe had ceased.

After gaining her composure, Mother asked, "Why?"

Another long silence. Hi-Seung's lips twitched, but there was no sound. He struggled to stay calm. I heard him breathe deeply. Then he spoke with tears welling up in his eyes.

Since Father was taken away to prison by the Japanese police, he could not sleep in peace. He imagined Father in prison garb, being tortured, starved, and mistreated by heartless prison guards. He pictured Father being kicked by heavy leather boots and his face repeatedly punched and slapped in a torture chamber because he refused to worship the Japanese emperor and because he had worked closely with American missionaries. He saw Father in a corner of a cement cell, curled up like a baby in a womb. He saw Father bruised and swollen. He had to get Father out some way. But how?

One day he went to the prison. His desire to see Father was not granted. However, he did get to talk to one of the jail officers—a Korean officer.

"The only way your father will be released," the officer said, "is if he will write a statement denying his Christian faith and submit to *Shinto.*" *Shinto* was the Japanese national religion that considered their emperor as divine.

"Knowing my father," Hi-Seung said, "He would rather die than deny his faith in Christ."

"Then he is in the right place," the officer scoffed.

"Can I be in prison in place of him?" Hi-Seung asked.

"Don't be ridiculous," the officer said. "This is not a circus."

"I'm sorry for saying it, Officer," He-Seung said. "But I just want to get my father released some way."

Apparently, the Korean officer was touched by the young boy's sincerity. "How old are you?"

"Fifteen years old, Sir."

"You are too young for any military service," he said. "My son is also your age."

The officer said turning his gaze toward the southern sky far away. Then he turned to Hi-Seung and looked at him. "I wonder whether my son would give his life for me like you are doing."

"I may be young," Hi-Seung said, "but I can do anything that older boys can."

There was a moment of silence. "Let's go and see the Japanese officer in the prison," the officer said. "I'll talk to him about you."

Hi-Seung was all excited now.

"Do you think he will take me?" Hi-Seung asked.

"I'll find out soon," the officer said. "He is here today to conscript able prisoners for the military service."

They went to the office where the officers in military uniforms sat in front of a long table while prisoners lined up for questioning. The Korean officer talked to one of the officers while Hi-Seung waited by the wall. Within a minute, Hi-Seung was asked to come to the table. The request was granted. The necessary papers were filled and signed. And my brother was ready to go to Japan to join the Japanese Youth Corps. In a week.

While he detailed the story, our eyes were filled with tears. My tears spoke of having to live without my best friend. Mother's tears were tears of sadness for the imminent departure of her son. They were the tears of loneliness and yearning that would ensue during his absence. They were also the tears of gratitude for having such a son who was willing to give his life for his father. She was moved by the act of his courage and sacrifice. After all, he was only a young boy of a carefree age who should have been playing and having fun with friends.

When he finished his story, Mother reached out and held his hand and started to sob. Hi-Seung bowed his head and cried. I felt tears welling up in my eyes as I watched them cry.

A question bubbled up from deep inside me: *Why do the Japanese hurt us so? They took Father to prison even though he didn't do any harm to them. He didn't beat them up. He didn't yell at them. All he did was to refuse to bow down to the picture of their emperor. He just said that his God was the God of Jesus Christ. Not the Japanese emperor. Now Brother Hi-Seung, my best friend, is leaving for Japan. "To have Father come home from the prison," he said. I have been wondering why he has not acted like his usual self after Father was taken away: yelling and acting angry, but quiet and thinking. Now I know. He was trying to figure out how to have Father home. Now he has found out that to have Father home, he has to go to Japan.*

He will leave us in a week. Making us worry every day wondering whether he will be sent to fight the Americans and get killed, or whether he will get into a fight with Japanese soldiers and get beaten up. I hope that God will cool his temper so that he doesn't get beaten up. I hope that God will keep him safe until he comes home.

I am sad to see my brother leave. But I am also very sad for Mother. With Father in prison and Brother in Japan, she has to work extra hard to feed us. What am I going to do if Mother gets sick and dies? Please God, don't let Mother get sick. Don't let Mother die.

Another question that troubled me was, *My Sunday school teacher says that God will reward those who worship Him and punish those who worship other gods. Then how come does God let Father be taken to prison by the Japanese? Father worships the God of Jesus while the Japanese worship their emperor. Mother prays every day—probably more than anybody in the whole world. The Japanese do not pray. Instead, the Japanese give Korean Christians a hard time. But God doesn't come to help them. And the Japanese seem to have more fun pushing us around. I don't understand.*

Hi-Seung's action was all the more touching because he was not an easy son to raise. He had an ongoing allergic rash from childhood. The itching and pain gave him such discomfort that his personality seemed to be affected by it. He complained a lot. He yelled often. He did not listen to Mother. There was no cure for his problem, and Mother did her best by trying to provide a proper diet for him.

Also Hi-Seung was the black sheep of the family, embarrassing his parents, while the rest of the children were admired by people and brought joy and pride. Yet, this black sheep, who had received the most whipping from Father, put his life on the line for Father. Then I was too young to appreciate Hi-Seung's action, but now I understand why Mother was so moved.

For me, his going to Japan was like losing a mother. Next to Mother, I felt closest to him in my family. When I was a little child, he acted like Mother toward me, always helpful and encouraging in his own way. When I broke his pencil lead by pushing it too hard on the paper to write, he did not ridicule or scold me like he would to other kids. Instead, he put his fingers around mine and helped me to put the proper pressure on the paper. When I could write without breaking the lead, he patted my back with a nice smile. When I greeted him coming home from school at the door, he put his hand in my pocket and pinched my flesh with a grin while I protested; later I found candy in my pocket. When Mother was away for an evening, he went into the kitchen and fixed food for me to eat. When I was sick in bed, he came and held my hand looking worried but saying that I would get better.

Also Hi-Seung was the one who toughened me, a tender child, who was afraid of the dark, who was afraid of water and who was afraid of bullies. He freed me from the fear of darkness by locking me in our dark basement for hours and also by taking me out in the woods in the dark of the night to show me that there was nothing to be afraid. To help me overcome the fear of water, he taught me how to swim and took me to the Han River and dumped me in the river for me to swim ashore. He also taught me how to defend myself from bullies and knock them down with my bare hands and feet. Above all, he helped me to feel that there was nothing I should be afraid of.

Soon my dear brother, my best friend, would leave me for Japan, to save his father from prison.

Dear God, please take good care of my brother while he is in Japan. Please let the war come to a quick end so that he can come home soon. So that I can play with him like the old times.

7. World War II—my house taken away

We didn't have much time to mourn the departure of Hi-Seung to Japan. We didn't even have time to go to his room and clean up the mess that he had left behind. It was a sunny afternoon, and I was in the kitchen watching Mother washing rice for supper. We heard a loud bang at the front door. Bang! Bang! Bang!

"Who's banging on the door like that?" Mother looked up. "Hi-Dong, go and see who's there."

"It may be Byung-Jin," I said. Hi-Seung's close friend. "He may be here to make us feel less sad."

"He wouldn't bang on the door like that," Mother said.

I went and opened the door. The man who knocked at the door wasn't Byung-Jin. Instead, there stood a tall policeman with a long sword at his side. Behind him were two laborers standing, holding a cot between them, where a man lay under a blanket. My shoulders stiffened.

"Where's your mother," the policeman said in a brusque manner.

"In the kitchen," I said haltingly. "She's washing rice."

"Tell her to come," he said. "Tell her that I brought the traitor home."

What's a traitor? I wondered while running to the kitchen.

"Mom, come," I said. "A policeman wants you at the door."

Mother quickly wiped her hands and went to the door, I following behind. As soon as she saw a figure lying under the blanket, she jumped toward him with her arms stretched toward the cot, but the policeman stepped in front of her, blocking her move. Mother shook, her gaze glued to the figure under the blanket.

"The traitor had a stroke in prison," he said. "We brought him here under house arrest."

"Oh *Yubo*—Dear," Mother cried, her arm reaching out toward Father.

"Where is his room?" the policeman said ignoring Mother's cry.

"Up ... upstairs," Mother said. "Please follow me."

The policeman ordered the laborers to follow Mother. They carefully held the handles and followed Mother upstairs while the policeman and I followed behind them. I worried that Father might slip down the cot and fall on the stairway, but the laborer in the back lifted his end high so that Father could lie flat. In his room the laborers put the cot on Father's bed, asked me to pull the cot out while they lifted Father on both ends. I carefully pulled the cot out, and they laid Father down on his bed.

Mother and I looked down at Father. Father lay on his bed with his eyes closed, seemingly unaware of what was going on around him. Mother's eyes glistened with tears. The policeman looked down at Father in contempt for a second, and turned to Mother.

"We will come any time of the day or the night to check on him," he said. "Don't ever think of taking him in hiding. Do you understand?"

Mother nodded her head without saying a word. Then the policeman stomped out of the house with the laborers following behind him.

Almost every day, sometimes in the dark of the night, a policeman pounded on the door. He could just knock. Instead, he pounded with his fist. Some nights he banged on the door with his leather boot, frightening everyone in the house. He marched straight into Father's room making loud footsteps in his leather boots with a pistol in his hand. He banged open the door to see whether Father was in bed. Then he stomped out of the house without bothering to close the door.

It was especially scary when we heard a bang in the dark of the night when everything was dead quiet or when we were sound asleep. Suddenly we were awakened by a loud bang. Bang! Bang! "Open the door!" Bang! Bang! "Open the door!" The sound echoed through the hallway. Pulling the blanket over my head, I shook with fear in my bed. Mother turned the light on. Put on her robe and rushed out to open the door while I was under the blanket shaking and listening. I heard loud footsteps. Someone was walking up the stairs, each step sounding like him walking into Father's room to shoot my father dead. The sound of the footsteps on the second floor echoed down to the bedroom. I heard the banging of the door. Then silence. *What is he going to do now?* I worried. *Is he going to shoot Father?* Seconds later I heard the footsteps again. This time, coming down the stairs and out the door into the night. Mother returned. Her face ashen. Her body shaking. I got out from my cover and watched her shake, wondering how I could help her. All I could do was to crawl to her, hold her shaking hand, praying that God would come to her aid. Praying that the policeman would be more thoughtful the next time.

When Father recovered from the stroke and was able to walk, the police permitted us to have Father go to a remote village bounded by high mountains on three sides with an ocean inlet. Mother wanted him to go there where he could recover in an unhurried environment. I guess the Japanese figured that he was too weak and too old to be a threat in that remote location.

Several weeks after Father had left for the village, we received a letter. The envelope looked like a formal letter with the address written in Chinese characters that the Japanese used. Mother opened it and found that the letter was written in Japanese mixed with Chinese characters. I could read the Japanese letters but not the Chinese characters, and the letter was full of characters that I did not know. We went to Mother's friend, Mrs. Chung, in our neighborhood who knew thousands of Chinese characters and who read Japanese.

As Mrs. Chung was reading the letter in Japanese, I watched her. After a couple lines, she stopped reading aloud, and her face turned sad. Tears filled her eyes.

"What is it?" Mother asked.

She didn't answer. Instead she sobbed.

"What does it say?" Mother asked again.

"I don't know why the good Lord does not come to your aid," she said. "Instead ..."

Mother's face turned white, just like the nights when we had the police visits.

"Is it the letter about Hi-Seung?" Mother's voice shook. "Is he dead?"

"No. No," Mrs. Chung said loudly.

"Oh, thank God," Mother said letting out a deep breath.

"But ..."

"But what? Mrs. Chung?"

"The letter says ..."

"What?"

"The Japanese police want your house."

"What? Want my house?"

"Yes. They want you to vacate your house in three weeks."

Mother's eyes turned blank. Her lips twitched, but no words came out. Then she closed her eyes with her hands on her chest. My heart sank. *What are we going to do? Are we going to end up on the streets? Begging for food and sleeping on street corners at night? Like beggars? And what about in the wintertime? Are we going to freeze to death like the frozen man I saw on the street last winter? What will they do with all our belongings? Grandfather clock in the hallway. Koi fish in the aquarium. My bed. My desk. My comic books. Hi-Seung's books. His slingshot. Father's desk. His chair. His Bible. His whip. Mother's sewing machine. Her cooking pans. Dishes ... So many things. Will the police let us take them? Or will they throw them out in our backyard and burn them to ashes? ... I'm so scared.*

We lived in a two-story brick house built by a missionary family from America who had worked closely with Father. It was situated inside the seminary compound where my father and the other minister both taught. When the missionary family left Korea, they offered their house to us. The upstairs had three large bedrooms and a balcony that faced Mount Nam San, where my class went to worship the Japanese emperor at the Shinto temple and where Father had refused to go, thereby ending up in prison. The room by the balcony was Father's office. Next to Father's was Hi-Bum's room, and the last room was Hi-Seung's, where I went almost every day to play with him or read comic books while Brother complained aloud about his homework. The downstairs had a dining room right under Father's office, a living room that could hold twenty people for worship, and a kitchen. Father added two Korean-style bedrooms by the living room where Mother and I slept. The floor of a Korean bedroom was covered with the oiled rice paper that was glued to a cement or clay slab. Under the slab was a series of ducts connected between a fireplace in the kitchen and the chimney. Above the fireplace was a big iron pot that was used to heat water since we did not have an automatic water heater that we enjoy today. When the pot was heated with a wood fire, the heat and the smoke went through the ducts and out to the chimney, thus heating the floor warm. Then there was a huge dark basement where I was afraid to go down until my brother taught me to be brave.

After frequenting the house to check on Father, the police must have decided that it would make a nice police office, where they could even make hot tea and *udon* in the kitchen. They could walk out to the balcony in the morning before their work, face Mount Nam San, bow down to the portrait of their emperor far away, and raise their arms high in the air shouting, "Tenno Heika, Bansai"— Long live, Emperor. They could do their morning exercise and practice drills with their swords and guns in the spacious yard facing the living room surrounded by persimmon trees. Also they could use our dark basement to keep thieves as a prison.

Now I will have to leave my house. The house where I was born and raised. The house where I cut open the koi fish to find out what made it swim. The house where I tore apart Father's favorite grandfather clock to find out what made it tick-tock. Without being whipped by Father who loved those fish and the clock. The house where I had so much fun with Brother Hi-Seung. In three weeks I will have to say, "Goodbye," to my house. "In three weeks," the police said. That was all there was to it. "Just move out." "Where to?" "That's your problem." "Can you give us more time?" "Are you kidding? Just move out."

When Father was in prison, Mother had prayed a lot. For his safety and for his release. Since Hi-Seung left for Japan, Mother prayed a lot that he would not get killed. But when the Japanese wrote us to move out, Mother didn't pray much. Instead, she became frantic. "What am I going to do? What am I going to do?" She said the same thing over and over rushing around from room to room throughout the day. A thousand times a day, it seemed like. She didn't even sit down to sew.

"Can't we go and stay with Father in the village?" I asked.

"That would be nice," Mother said. "But they don't have a school for you."

"I don't have to go to school."

"Hi-Dong, time moves only in one direction," Mother said looking at me. "You cannot go back to your past and do things over."

"So?"

"If we go to the village for a year, you will be a year behind in your schoolwork," Mother said. "And you will be studying with Dae-Wook and Jong-Ju."

Dae-Wook and Jong-Ju were six-year-old kids in our neighborhood. I was a seven-year-old boy. The thought of studying with those kids who were inches shorter than I didn't sound good. So I changed the subject.

"Where are we going to live then?"

"Our loving God will help us find a place," Mother snapped.

If Mother really believes that our loving God will find a place for us, why is she so jumpy? And if God is so loving, how come does God let the Japanese take Father to prison? Got him sick, and brought him home under house arrest? If God is so loving, how come does God let the Japanese take our home in the first place? It didn't make sense to me, a seven-year-old boy. But I didn't ask Mother because I was afraid that God might listen and put me in hell.

The news spread fast. Mother's brothers and sisters—especially Little Aunt—offered their places even though they didn't have extra rooms to spare. Also their homes were far away from my school. The distance was too far for me to walk to school since we didn't have a car, just like the other families around us. Church members came and prayed for us. They prayed that God would touch someone's heart and offer us a place to live, but they didn't offer their own.

Mother visited real estate agents around my school. She seemed to be in a hurry. She walked very fast, not her usual pace so that I could walk leisurely next to her. I tagged behind her, marching fast like the Japanese soldiers I had seen on the streets, pointing the toe of my shoe straight toward the sky with each step I took. Sometimes I ran so that I would not be too far behind. We found there were houses for sale, but those that we liked were beyond our means and those that we could afford were shanties that no church members would visit in class-conscious Korea. Mother returned home downtrodden. I returned home dead tired with my legs feeling like a pair of iron bars. Also I returned home worrying that Mother might get sick and die from all her worries. The worry about her weak husband in the village. The worry about her son in Japan. The worry about where to live. I prayed, "Please God. Help Mother find a place for us as quickly as possible."

A week into our search for a place, Mrs. Lee, wife of Dr. Lee who lived in our neighborhood, visited us. Unlike other visitors who came with sad faces, she came with a smile. Others greeted me saying, "Poor Hi-Dong," but Mrs. Lee greeted me with a broad smile, "How's our curious child?" I thought she had no manner calling me child instead of boy and smiling when there was nothing to smile about. Without responding to her question, I gave her a quick forced smile and walked away. Mother greeted her with her usual welcome, but Mother's smile was like mine also. Forced.

While Mother and Mrs. Lee talked, I sat by the window in the living room looking out watching the leaves of the persimmon trees fluttering by the breeze under the clear blue sky.

"I came home from Yong-ju yesterday," Mrs. Lee said, "and heard your terrible news from my next-door neighbor."

Mother sighed looking blankly at the wall.

"You must have been really shocked," she said. "To say the least."

"I don't know why the good Lord has been testing us so," Mother said, turning to Mrs. Lee.

"We said the same thing last night," Mrs. Lee said. "God should have blessed you more than anyone else in the world. But instead … this curse."

"I guess God works in mysterious ways. All I can do is to pray and wait."

"Also the neighbor told me that you have been looking for a place to stay," she said. "Have you found one yet?"

Mother let out a deep and long sigh, but no response. I turned to see her face. Sad and helpless face. Poor mother. I wished I could help her some way. Tears filled my eyes. I turned to the window because I did not want Mrs. Lee see me in tears. "Only babies cry," I remembered Hi-Seung saying when I came home crying, beaten by a bully one day. "I will teach you to be tough like me." Thinking of my brother far, far away in Japan filled my eyes with more tears. I wiped the tears with my fingers and bravely looked straight out the window tightening my lips. *Brother,* I said to myself. *I'm tough now like you trained me. Can you see me now? Strong and brave. Like you?*

"I went to Yong-ju because my father-in-law was very ill," Mrs. Lee said.

"Oh really?" Mother's eyes turned wide like the times when she was concerned for others.

"Only a year ago, he walked, talked and laughed like my fifty-year-old husband," she said. "But after the stroke he is a changed man. He cannot walk by himself without someone assisting him. He didn't even smile at me when I bowed down to him. I can barely hear his voice and understand his words. All I could hear him say was 'Uh … Uh …'"

"How sad," Mother said. "Dr. Lee must be concerned."

"Yes," she said. "Also, as the eldest son, he feels guilty healing others when his father needs his help."

"As a loyal son," Mother said, "he must feel that way."

"Last night he decided to go to be with his father until he passes away."

"Leave his family alone?"

"Since it may be weeks or months, I will go with him."

"What about his office?"

"His assistant and his nurses will keep it open."

"What about your two daughters?"

"They will stay with my sister who lives close to their schools."

"What about …" Mother stopped short of finishing her words.

"There is one more thing that we have to take care of before we leave," Mrs. Lee said, "That's why I am here to ask your help."

Not believing my ears, I turned to look at Mrs. Lee. *She must have turned crazy after seeing her sick father-in-law,* I thought. *She knows we are going to be kicked out from our house in two weeks, and she knows Mother has been looking for a place to live. Now she wants Mother to help her? How crazy. Should I yell at her? I am sure Brother Hi-Seung would yell and tell her to get out of the house.*

I looked at Mother to hear what she was going say. Her face turned strange. She didn't look sad. She didn't look happy. Mother just stared at Mrs. Lee looking as if she had wakened from a dream. There was no response from Mother. For seconds.

"Can you come," Mrs. Lee continued, her voice soft, "and stay at our house?"

I looked at Mother's face. Her lips twitched. Her shoulder stooped. Her eyes welled up with tears. She bowed her head without a response holding her hands over her chest. Mrs. Lee reached over and held Mother's hand. Then Mother let out a deep sigh. The sigh turned into a loud sob, filling up the room. My eyes filled up with tears too. I wanted to cry aloud like Mother. Instead, I bit my lip strong and hard because Hi-Seung had toughened me to be a strong and tough boy, who would not be afraid of anything. Not a cry-baby, who was afraid of the dark, afraid of the water, afraid of the bullies … But I could not push down the feeling welling up from my heart to my throat. This feeling pushed open my tightened lips and rushed out of me. I ran to Mother and sat behind her with my arms over her shoulders, and joined in her cry while wondering, *Maybe this is what Mother meant when she said, "God works in mysterious ways. All I can do is pray and wait." Thank you, Mrs. Lee.*

A week after Mrs. Lee's visit, we moved to her house. Our neighbors, ladies and young men, helped us to move what we wanted to keep and what we needed: Father's desk and chair, his books, Mother's sewing machine, the grandfather clock, blankets and pillows, clothes and shoes. We didn't have to bring cooking utensils because Mrs. Lee left hers for us to use. We took the items that we didn't need to our basement and piled them in corner and covered them with bedspreads, hoping that the police would leave them untouched and also hoping that we would be able to return to our house someday.

I was very sad walking out of the house. My house. This was the house that filled me with happy memories. This was the house that was filled with laughter, singing and cozy winter evenings when all the family sat around in the living room. Father reading, Mother sewing, brothers and sisters doing their homework with their bodies crouched on the floor, and I sitting next to Mother watching her sewing. I remembered the stove right in the middle of the living room, keeping us warm and comfortable. I could hear the crackling sound of the wood in the stove. I could see the steam from the tea kettle on the stove gently floating upward in the air. I felt so at peace there. I felt so secure and comfortable there. Now I would no longer experience those evenings, except through the flight into my memory world.

A few days after we moved to Dr. Lee's house, I saw two police cars and two trucks parked by the street leading to my house. The trucks were loaded with desks and chairs and bookshelves. Half a dozen laborers unloaded them and carried them toward my house led by a policeman. Other policemen carried boxes of papers to my house. When I saw the policemen walking up to my house, for the first time in my life I felt hate welling up inside me. I was seven years old then. I pictured myself being Superman. I imagined that I grabbed those policemen, one in each hand, lifted them, twirled them around for a while, and released them high in the air. I pictured them flying like ceramic figurines, and falling on a hard bed of rocks and breaking into pieces. I imagined repeating this until every policeman in and around the house was broken into pieces. I imagined myself taking all those desks, chairs and other pieces of furniture outside, smashing them on the ground into small broken pieces, and piling them up high, starting a fire, and watching them go up in flames. I felt a tinge of hate in my eyes and chest as they passed by me, carrying the furniture into my house. My house. Not theirs.

Mother had to work twice as hard. At home she had to take care of us. Also she had to look after Father in the village. To go to see Father she took a twenty-mile train ride, and walked the rest of the five miles over a mountain. Mother went there almost every other week. I remembered going to see Father with Mother one day. The train ride was fun, but the five-mile walk over the mountain was torture. The dirt road through the mountain meandered up and down and was wide enough for one person. Some parts were wet from the streams. Some parts were blocked by huge rocks, and we walked around them. I wasn't tough enough to walk the five miles without stopping. But I tried to maintain a tough outside and didn't ask Mother to stop. But she somehow knew that I needed rest. Every mile or so, Mother said, "I need a break. Can we stop for a while? And I replied, Sure, Mother."

I remember one evening that she came home all haggard and limping. I noticed the flesh around her right shin bone, all bruised and black and blue. I asked her what had happened. She replied in tears. A young Japanese policeman had stopped her at the train station. He wanted to search her bag, but she refused. He slapped her. She was angry and yelled at him. Then the policeman threw her on the ground and kicked her repeatedly with his heavy leather boot. While passers-by watched her helplessly, she yelled at him in Korean, which he did not understand. He did not like her defiant look, and kicked her some more. She was hurt. She was in pain. Above all, she felt humiliated. Mother had never been beaten in her life, not even by her father. But this young Japanese policeman, in full public view, humiliated her. For the first time in my life, I sensed great anger in her voice as she shared her ordeal. Her eyes through tears shone with bitterness.

As I saw her bruised and discolored shin, I wanted to run out, find that policeman, and cut him into pieces. I felt great hatred spreading like a brushfire, affecting every cell of my body. What kind of a savage would do such a gross deed to an innocent and caring person like my mother? I was angry, but also I knew that I was too small and powerless. All I could do was to carry out the revenge in the safe haven of my imagination.

I also sensed in me the hatred surfacing, not only to that particular Japanese policeman who hurt her, but to all Japanese. When I saw a Japanese person on the street, wearing his *kimono* and walking in his *gheta*, wooden Japanese footwear, my usual friendly face turned to anger and disdain.

In my later years, thinking of what the Japanese police had done to my mother, I realized: *This must be how people learn to hate a group of people, nation or a race. This must be how a nation gets to hate another nation, and one race gets to hate another race. A small incident gives a spark to a dormant seed of hatred in a person. This hatred, if left unchecked, grows like weeds and spreads to other people and to an entire nation.*

Mother taught me to love. She said love was like the spring sunshine. It helped people to get out of their cocoons and mingle with others as brothers and sisters. It helped them to take off the heavy jackets of winter from their shoulders, and experience the gentle warmth of the sun. It brought people to a garden of flowers to smell the fragrance of spring, and feast their eyes on the display of heavenly colors.

How do I stop hating and love instead? I did not try to hate. I did not tell myself that I was going to hate. It happened without my trying. When I saw Mother bruised, hurt and humiliated, I saw in me the ugly face of hate cajoling, and the dark hand of hate with the red banner of death, coaxing me to revenge. Can I shove this hate in a chamber of will power and keep it enclosed permanently? Will it not explode with a mighty fury sometime? Or should I pray to God, and tell Him that I find hate in me, and ask Him to diffuse it?

8. The war is over

World War II seemed to drag on forever. Every day, I waited for my dear brother, Hi-Seung, to come home, but as long as the war continued, I was not likely to see him soon. He had been away more than two years, and we did not hear from him often. Letters that he sent were very brief, just telling us that he was OK. He was probably too busy being pushed around by his Japanese masters and too tired to write long letters. For us, short letters were good enough, because seeing his handwritten letters meant that he was alive.

For two years, Hi-Seung's safety was constantly on Mother's mind. Everyday she prayed for his safety. Whenever she heard of the U.S. bombing military installations in Japan, she went into her prayer closet. She stayed there for more than an hour, praying. She came out of the closet with red eyes and a red nose from crying. Everyday she said, "Wonder what Hi-Seung is doing now?" When the mailman brought letters, she searched for Hi-Seung's letter with fear in her eyes. When she found Hi-Seung's name on an envelope, her eyes brightened. She hurriedly opened and read the letter. If she found that he was OK, she let out a big sigh of relief. She rushed into the prayer closet. She came out of the closet with red eyes and a red nose, but this time it was from the tears of thanksgiving and relief.

Waiting for my best friend for a year had been tough for me. But now almost two years had passed, and I was nine years old. I was almost as good as Hi-Seung in slingshots. I could hit five cans out of ten—not the one or two cans when Hi-Seung was teaching me. I could run like he told me, moving my right foot forward while my right hand moved backward—not moving my right foot and my right hand forward at the same time. More than anything else, I wanted to challenge him in putting our heads in the water in the bathtub to see who could stay there longer without breathing. I was pretty sure I could beat him because I had practiced it a lot using a bucket filled with water. But listening to old people, I realized that the war would not come to an end in a year—or even two years. Because the Japanese were fierce warriors, and they would never surrender to any country, even a huge one like America. They would never surrender even if every one of its young people was killed. They would fight until the last man in Japan gave his life. There was nothing I could do, but wait and pray that the Japanese would not be that fierce as the old people described them to be.

August 15, 1945. Father was in his office—back from the countryside a few months before—recovered from the stroke. He could walk, talk, and think as before, but with less energy in his stride, less strength in his voice, and forgetful. I found it strange and worrisome when he asked, "Hi-Dong, do you see my glasses somewhere? I cannot find them," because I saw his glasses on his forehead. Mother and I were in the living room. Mother sewing as usual and I reading a comic book about hungry monkeys jumping from one tree to another to find food. I heard a loud knock at the door. Not just once, but many times. Bang! Bang! Bang! I ran to the door expecting to see Byung-Jin, Hi-Seung's high school friend who often visited us. Instead, there stood my favorite aunt, Mother's younger sister. Little Aunt was huffing and puffing as if she had run away from a bandit.

"Are you OK, Aunt?" I asked. She ignored my question.

"Are your father and mother home?" She asked in her husky voice while taking her shoes off.

"Yes," I said. "Father's upstairs, and Mother's in the living room."

"Tell Father to come to the living room," she said rushing into the living room. "Right away."

Why is she in such a rush? I wondered while walking upstairs to get Father. *Why does she want Father in the living room? She always comes to see Mother. Never to see Father.* I could not figure it out.

When Father and I entered the living room, we saw Aunt and Mother sitting in front of the radio. Aunt quickly stood and bowed to Father.

"There's going to be an important announcement on the radio," Aunt said to Father.

"What announcement?" Father asked.

"Please sit," Aunt said. "It will come at any moment."

Puzzled, Father and I walked behind them and sat, not knowing what to expect.

There was no sound from the radio. No man's voice. No Japanese songs. Only the hissing noise. We waited. And waited. After about a minute, a voice came through the radio. It was the sound of an old man. The old man said,

"To our good and loyal subjects: After pondering deeply the general trends of the world and the actual conditions obtaining to Our Empire today, we have decided to effect a settlement of the present situation by resorting to an extraordinary measure."

I looked at Father. His narrow eyes became round, like circles. His face solemn.

Mother whispered to Aunt, "Who's that man talking?"

"Japanese emperor," Aunt whispered.

"Japanese emperor?" Mother looked at Little Aunt, surprised. Then Mother glanced at Father.

"Yes, Japanese emperor." Aunt snapped.

"What is he saying?" Mother asked.

"Sh ...," Aunt tapped Mother's hand. "I'll tell you later."

"We have ordered Our Government to communicate to the Governments of the United States, Great Britain, China and the Soviet Union that Our Empire accepts the provisions of their Joint Declaration."

"To strive for the common prosperity and happiness of all nations as well as the security and well-being of Our Subjects is the solemn obligation which has been handed down by Our Imperial Ancestors, and which we lay close to heart. Indeed, We declared war on America and Britain out of Our sincere desire to ensure Japan's self-preservation

and the stabilization of East Asia, it being far from Our thought either to infringe upon the sovereignty of other nations or to embark upon territorial aggrandizement. But now the war has lasted for nearly four years. Despite the best that has been done by everyone--the gallant fighting of the military and naval forces, the diligence and assiduity of Our servants of the State and the devoted service of Our one hundred million people, the war situation has developed not necessarily to Japan's advantage, while the general trends of the world have all turned against her interest. Moreover, the enemy has begun to employ a new and most cruel bomb, the power of which to damage is indeed incalculable, taking the toll of many innocent lives. Should We continue to fight, it would not only result in an ultimate collapse and obliteration of the Japanese nation, but also it would lead to the total extinction of human civilization. Such being the case, how are We to save the millions of Our subjects; or to atone Ourselves before the hallowed spirits of Our Imperial Ancestors? This is the reason why We have ordered the Acceptance of the provisions of the Joint Declaration of the Powers."

"We cannot but express the deepest sense of regret to our Allied nations of East Asia, who have consistently co-operated with the Empire towards the emancipation of East Asia. The thought of those officers and men as well as others who have fallen in the fields of battle, those who died at their posts of duty, or those who met with untimely death and all their bereaved families, pains Our heart day and night. The welfare of the wounded and the war sufferers, and of those who have lost their homes and livelihood, are the objects of Our profound solicitude. The hardships and sufferings to which Our nation is to be subjected hereafter will certainly be great. We are keenly aware of the inmost feelings of all ye, Our subjects. However, it is according to the dictate of time and fate that We have resolved to pave the way for a grand peace for all the generations to come by enduring the unendurable and suffering what is insufferable."

I peeked at Father. He laid his glasses on the coffee table next to him. He had his clasped hands on his chest. Tears fell from his eyes.

61

"Having been able to safeguard and maintain the structure of the Imperial State, We are always with ye, Our good and loyal subjects, relying upon your sincerity and integrity. Beware most strictly of any outbursts of emotion which may engender needless complications, or any fraternal contention and strife which may create confusion, lead ye astray and cause ye to lose the confidence of the world. Let the entire nation continue as one family from generation to generation, ever firm in its faith of the imperishableness of its divine land, and mindful of its heavy responsibilities, and the long road before it. Unite your total strength to be devoted to the construction for the future. Cultivate the ways of rectitude; foster nobility of spirit; and work with resolution so as ye may enhance the innate glory of the Imperial State and keep pace with the progress of the world."

Source: http://en.wikipedia.org/wiki/Gyokuon-h%C5%8Ds%C5%8D

I looked at Aunt. Aunt sobbed, holding Mother's hand. Her face was bathed in tears. Mother looked at Aunt with wondering eyes. Then I heard Father shouting in his tenor voice.

"*Daehan-mingook, Marnsei!*" Long live, Korea.

He shouted again with his arms raised to the heavens.

"*Daehan-mingook, Mansei!*"

And again. His face turned toward the ceiling.

"*Daehan-mingook, Mansei!*"

Then Father plopped down on the floor and cried aloud. Like a child. Mother rushed over and held his hand.

"Thank You, God," Father sobbed taking a deep breath. "The war is over. After thirty-five years, our country is free again."

I looked at Mother. Her eyes also were welling up with tears. I joined them crying because I knew Brother Hi-Seung would be coming home soon. To play with me.

I thought Father would cry forever with Mother next to him. But I saw Father and Mother praying facing each other, holding hands. Their heads bowed low. He prayed for minutes, not his usual short prayer. I couldn't hear him too well because his words were jumbled, not his usual sharp and clear voice. But I heard the words, 'Thank you', many times. 'Hi-Seung', several times.

As soon as I heard him say, "Amen", Father sat straight and looked at me.

"Hi-Dong," Father said with a broad smile. "Don't you have a Japanese flag that you take to school on occasion?"

"Yes," I replied wondering what he was up to.

"Bring it to me," Father said. "Also bring the brush and the black ink that you used to learn to write *Kanji*, Chinese characters used by the Japanese. Hurry."

I rushed to my room to get the flag, brush and ink. When I returned to the living room, Father sat in front of the dining table waiting for me. Father spread the Japanese flag on the table. He dipped the brush into the inkwell and pulled it out. He made three black dots on the red circle of the Japanese flag: two on the opposite edge of the circle and the one at its center. He drew a semicircle upward from the dot on one edge to the center and another semicircle—this time downward—from its center to the other dot. He brushed the top half of the circle with the black ink. He brushed on three parallel bars on the four corners of the flag: one corner with three bars; the opposite corner, two broken bars at their centers; the other corner, two broken bars with a bar at their center; and two bars with a broken bar at the center.

He looked down at the flag for a few seconds. Then he lifted his head and closed his eyes as in prayer. I heard his breathing. A very deep breathing. He looked sad. *What is Father thinking?* I turned to Mother, wondering. Mother put her finger in front of her lips—her signal to tell me, "Keep silent." I looked at Little Aunt. Her eyes were closed. Her face was wet with tears. I turned to Father. His eyes were still closed. I sat next to Father listening to the quiet sound of the grandfather clock tick-tocking in the hallway, waiting to see what Father would do next.

After a long silence, I heard Father's voice.

"Thank You. Thank You. Thank You," Father whispered. "We are free … After thirty six years, we are finally free."

Father opened his eyes and turned to me.

63

"Hi-Dong," he said looking down at the flag. "This is our flag. Our own Korean flag. Let us take this flag outside and join the crowd in celebration."

Celebration? What kind of celebration? I wondered. Will he dance with the crowd waving the flag in the air, moving his feet floating up and down, like the dancing ladies on stage? I have never seen Father dance in my life, and it will be fun to watch him. But I don't think he will. He's too formal.

I walked to the front door and waited for Father. Mother and Little Aunt walked behind me to see us go.

"Hi-Dong," Mother said. "Stay close to Father all the time. I don't want you get lost in the crowd."

"Mother, don't worry," I said. "I'm a nine-year-old boy now."

I waited for Father, who had gone upstairs to change. I was anxious to see what Father was going to do when we joined the crowd. Within a minute I heard his footsteps coming down the stairs—not his usual footsteps which were solid and solemn but more like mine: light and hasty. He was dressed, not in his usual suite with a necktie, but in an outfit for a picnic. He came down with the flag in his hand with a broad smile on his face.

"Let's hurry," he said rushing out of the door.

As I was hurrying out, I heard Mother saying again, "Be close to your father always." I said to myself, *I am a nine year old boy. A big boy now. And I don't like Mother still treating me like a kid. But she means well. Leave her alone. She wants me to be safe.*

Father hurried toward the crowd waving the flag high in the air just like when I ran to greet our victorious soccer team. I ran to catch up with him. As we hurried toward the main street, I saw Korean flags hung outside the houses. People yelled, *Mansei*, standing in front of their houses with their arms high in the air.

Streets were filled with people, young and old, men and women, with makeshift Korean flags—just like Father's—walking jubilantly from street to street. Smiling. Old people smiled, but their smiles were mixed with tears. I wondered why.

"*Daehan-mingook, Mansei,*" Father shouted in his tenor voice waving the flag high in the air.

"Hi-Dong," Father said looking at me. "Join us in celebration."

"*Daehan-mingook, Mansei,*" I imitated Father, but it didn't sound real. I was too shy.

"Let's do it together," Father said. "You watch me."

Father raised his arms high in the air, I following his motion. As soon as he said, "*Daehan,*" I joined him.

"*Daehan-mingook, Mansei,*" we shouted, I shouting as loudly as I could.

Then I heard a little girl's voice, "*Daehan-mingook, Mansei.*"

I looked. A little girl holding her mother's hand looked at us with a smile.

Father knelt down, his arms reaching out toward her in a warm embrace. I saw tears streaming down on Father's face. The tears that he had kept inside him for thirty-six long years.

Father walked the streets, not bothering to look at his watch. Not being in a hurry as he usually did. He walked shouting, *Daehan-mingook, Mansei,* over and over. He walked waving his flag high in the air like others in the crowd. Nobody seemed to be in a hurry. Nobody seemed to be conscious of others' presence. They walked shouting, *Daehan-mingook, Mansei.* They felt free. They were free.

Finally, the tight grip that the Japanese had on Korea was broken. The curtain of repression was lifted. Koreans could speak in Korean—not Japanese—without being punished. We could use our own alphabet, *Hangul*—not the Japanese *Hiragana* or *Karagana*—to write letters to friends and to study in schools. We could lift our flags high in the air without them being taken down and torn apart. Our church doors would be open, and we would be free to worship our God instead of being forced to walk up to the *Shinto* temple to bow down to the picture of their emperor. Our young men, who were forcefully sent to Japan and to battlefields would come home soon if they were lucky enough to be alive. Our young sisters, who were forcefully taken away to their factories to manufacture guns and swords to kill Americans would come back to their homes.

Thank you, God. Finally we are free.

9. Hi-Seung comes home and dies

For my family it was a time of joy and gratitude. We moved back to our house to start our lives anew. We did not have to worry about the Japanese police because they were no longer with us. No longer could they take Father to prison. No longer could they take our house away, leaving us homeless. No longer could they bang at our door in the dark of the night, frightening us from our sleep and causing Mother to shake—uncontrollably. No longer could a young Japanese policeman kick my dear mother in full view of strangers.

For my family, it was also a time of our anxiously waiting for Hi-Seung's return from Japan. We didn't know where he was because there was a total blackout of communication between Hi-Seung and us near the end of the war. He could have been sent to the front line. He could have become one of the casualties in the unending U.S. bombings. He could have been shot by the Japanese during the closing hours of the war. There was nothing we could do but pray and wait.

In the coming weeks, every day Mother and I went to the Seoul train station, a mile away, hoping to see He-Seung walking down the steps of the train. Every now and then, a train-load of young people, some in Japanese uniforms, some in plain clothes wearing the Japanese military hats, some with Japanese flags painted over to turn them into Korean flags, arrived from Busan. The station was filled with families, waiting to greet their long-lost sons and husbands. There were clusters of joyful reunions among those families who were reunited with their loved ones. There were loud cries of joy. There was hysterical laughter. There was an unending round of *Daehan-mingook, Mansei* echoing in the hall of the station. After those happily united families were gone, there was silence for the families who were waiting for the next train. They looked discouraged. They looked pensive. And we were a part of them.

Everyday I went to the station with Mother to see Hi-Seung coming off the train so that I could run to him with my outstretched arms shouting, "Welcome home, Brother," and expecting to be greeted by Brother's warm embrace saying, "So glad to see you, Tarzan." But it didn't happen. I returned home feeling sad with an empty heart. As we walked home, Mother held my hand and did not say a word. Like me she was sad and worried. After many trips to the station, her motion lost its strength and grace. She moved as if she was sleepwalking. Her face turned dark.

After two months, Mother said, "What's the use of going. Let's just stay home, pray and wait."

I still wanted to go to the station and see my brother coming off the train, but Mother did not let me.

"Mother, I know where the train station is," I protested. "I have been there thirty three times already with you."

"I know," Mother said.

"Then why can't I go?"

Mother was quiet. She did not look at me.

"Why not?"

Mother looked at me with her pleading eyes.

"You are my only son I have with me," she said quietly. "I am terribly afraid that I may lose you also."

How can I argue further with Mother, whose suffering I have witnessed since my birth? I remember her face when Father was taken to the prison. I remember her face at the front door when she rushed to the cot, held by two workers, where Father lay motionless while the Japanese police ordered the workers to take him to his room. I remember her face when Brother Hi-Seung came to her and told her that he would be leaving for Japan. How can I forget those faces? Sad faces. Helpless faces. How can I protest when she is worried about losing her baby son?

Every day I sat on a rock by the front of my house, hoping to see a glimpse of Brother Hi-Seung among the crowd down the street. I sat on the rock and waited for him to walk toward me. I waited and waited for him, but Brother did not appear. After weeks of waiting I decided to be like Mother. *Just pray and wait.* I didn't know how to pray like Mother, whose prayer was eloquent even though it was very long. All I could pray was, *Dear God, please don't let my brother die. I want to see him walking toward me and calling me Tarzan. Soon. Very soon.*

Then in the third month, I heard a knock on the door. I went and opened it. There in front of me stood a soldier wearing a worn light-green outfit and a backpack on his back. He looked more like a beggar than a soldier. He looked like Brother Hi-Seung, but I wasn't sure. I wondered, *Am I seeing my brother's ghost?* I froze and was scared. I just stood at the door staring at him—dazed and speechless. The soldier smiled at me and said, "You have grown so much since I left home." His voice sounded like my brother. My heart pounded. My eyes were glued to him. When he took a step toward me, I was going to step back because I wasn't sure whether he was real Hi-Seung. But a voice inside me said, *Don't.* I stood motionless and scared. When he bent down and put his arms on my shoulders, my shoulders stiffened. Only when he put his arms around me in a warm embrace, saying, "So nice to see you, Tarzan," did I know he was really my brother. *He's really my brother, Hi-Seung,* I convinced myself. *My brother is home. Finally.* Big tears streamed down my cheeks, and I couldn't stop. I wanted to shout aloud, *Welcome home, Brother,* but I couldn't. I stood there motionless in his embrace, not bothering to stop the tears, not rushing to Mother to tell her the joyful news.

Brother Hi-Seung must really have missed home. He said over and over while he knelt down to untie his shoes, "It's so nice to come home. So nice to come home."

I looked up to see his face with my tear-filled eyes. He was all smiles, but I noticed that he was not well. He looked very pale. His eyes were deeply sunken. His face was skin and bones. His arms around me had no strength. As I watched him taking his shoes off, my eyes welled up again. This time with tears of sadness, feeling the suffering that he had endured in Japan. Wiping the tears with one hand, holding his hand with the other, I led him to the living room where Mother was sewing my torn shirt.

"Who was it?" Mother asked without looking up.

"Look, Mother," I said.

She stopped sewing and looked at us. For an instant, I saw fear in Mother's face. Her hand jerked. She stared at Hi-Seung without words. Even when Hi-Seung walked over to her and bowed, she just stared at him. When He-Seung said, "Mother, I am home," her lips twitched. She tried to utter a word, but she couldn't. Only when he said again, "Mother, I am home," did she finally break down and said, "M-m-m-y son, ... Hi-Seung ... You are home!" She let her needle drop on the floor, reached out and held Hi-Seung's hand. Tears fell on the floor like rain washing away the years of longing and anguish. Standing by their side, I joined in their tearful reunion. *Thank you, God, for bringing my brother home.*

After minutes of sobbing, holding Hi-Seung's hand, Mother wiped her tears with her skirt.

"I was so busy crying that I forgot all about your father," Mother said looking at me. "Hi-Dong, run upstairs and tell Father the good news."

"Mother," Hi-Seung said, "I'll go upstairs and greet him."

"That's a better idea," Mother said. "He has been waiting and praying for your safe return since you left home."

"I'll go with you," I said. "You follow behind me. I will go to his office and tell him that you are here."

"OK," Hi-Seung smiled.

We turned toward the stairway to go to Father. Mother followed behind us. When I walked up the stairs, his door was closed. I knocked.

"Who's there?" Father said.

"It's me," I said loudly. "Hi-Dong."

"Oh, my *mangnei*. Come in," he said. "You sound excited."

When I opened the door, I saw Father writing something, his head glued to the desk.

"Brother is here," I said.

"Who?" Father said, without looking at us.

"Brother Hi-Seung," I shouted.

"Hi-Seung?" Father jerked his head toward us with his hand in the air.

Hi-Seung stepped forward and bowed to Father without a word. Father stared at Hi-Seung like Mother did minutes ago. The same stare, as if he was seeing a ghost. The room turned silent. The pen slid out of Father's fingers and fell on the wooden floor, making a sharp knocking sound. Then I saw Father's eyes fill with tears. The tear drops slid down his cheeks.

Father stood with his hand trembling and walked over to Hi-Seung. Father held Hi-Seung's hands and made him stand straight. Then Father stepped back and bowed low to Hi-Seung as if he was greeting an emperor.

"Thank you, my son," Father said in a teary voice, "for your sacrifice … to save me."

Then Father reached over for Hi-Seung's hands. He held them between his two hands and sobbed with his head bowed. Saying the words, 'Thank you', over and over. Without trying to control his tears.

Hi-Seung had a difficult time as an enlisted Korean in the Japanese military. He was the lowest on the totem pole. Because he was a Korean, he was mistreated by his Japanese counterparts. He was given hard physical labor whereas his Japanese counterparts received military training. A few months before the end of the war, he and other Koreans were ordered to do demolition work—tearing down buildings beyond repair from the U.S. bombings.

One day while working on the roof of a damaged building, he slipped and fell face down on the ground. He fell on a blunt object in the abdominal area. The pain was excruciating, and he couldn't stand up. By the time he was rushed to a military hospital, his abdomen was swollen like a balloon. A doctor, busy caring for the Japanese soldiers, decided to do quick exploratory surgery. In the rush, he mistakenly cut the urinary tract from his bladder. The doctor bypassed it with a red rubber tube through an opening in his lower abdominal area so that he could urinate. Brother was released from the hospital without a full recovery.

Because the tube was not inserted properly, the area became badly infected and swollen. Every night he cleaned the area with alcohol, dabbed it with mercurochrome and covered it with gauze dressing. We did not know what to do about his condition. Only a major operation could help him, but he did not want to go through the operation because he knew that it would mean a huge financial drain on his family. So he nursed himself every night, never complaining until his death a year later.

Meanwhile, he was an inspiration to all those around him. He was such a changed person. Complaining had been his forte, but now there was not a hint of that. There was not a trace of anger toward anyone in his voice, even when he talked about the Japanese soldiers who had mistreated him. All was gratitude. Life was a gift. He had seen the darkness. He had endured the loneliness. He had experienced the cruelty of men. Now back at home, he was determined to be in the light.

I can still hear Hi-Seung singing 'Old Kentucky Home,' which was a very popular American folk song in Korea. He sang it while doing household chores; he hummed it while cleaning his wounds. I do not know which part of the song touched him—the melody or the words. Maybe both. Perhaps he sang the song while he was in Japan, yearning for home and picturing himself as a slave being pushed around by the Japanese masters.

The sun shines bright in the old Kentucky home,
　'Tis summer, the slaves are gay:
The corntop's ripe and the meadow's in the bloom,
　While the birds make music all the day;
The young folks roll on the little cabin floor,
　All merry, all happy, and bright,
By'n' by hard times comes a knocking at the door,
　Then, my old Kentucky home, goodnight!

The head must bow and the back will have to bend,
　Wherever the slaves may go;
A few more days and the trouble all will end,
　In the fields where the sugarcanes grow;
A few more days for to tote the weary load,
　No matter, 'twill never be light,
A few more days till we totter on the road,
　Then, my old Kentucky home, good night!

Chorus:
Weep no more, my lady,
Oh! Weep no more today!
We will sing one song for the old Kentucky home,
For the old Kentucky home far away.
(Words and Music by Stephen C. Foster,
Source: http://en.wikipedia.org/wiki/
My_Old_Kentucky_Home)

When Hi-Seung sang, I could feel the sadness in his voice. I did not know whether it was the words or the voice of his singing that made me sad. I just felt sad and felt that something bad was going to happen--not too far away.

A year after his return from Japan, his infection had become too much for him to handle, and he submitted to the operation. During the operation, he lost much blood and passed away peacefully in a hospital bed while holding our hands. Mother's and mine while Father stood next to Mother touching Hi-Seung's shoulder—his head bowed in prayer. My dearest brother was gone, but there were no tears in my eyes, maybe because my sorrow was beyond tears. I could not utter a sound, maybe because words could not describe the feeling swirling in my innermost being. All I could see or feel was emptiness enveloping the universe around me. I saw myself all alone, in the endless space of emptiness.

On the way home in a taxi, I relived the hospital scene—how peacefully Hi-Seung had died. His face was glowing like amber. He whispered that he saw heaven. Excitedly and haltingly he described what he saw: a beautiful park with trees, benches and meandering walkways. Birds were there singing their happy songs. Fields were covered with a brilliant carpet of flowers. Then he described a man in a white robe walking toward him. He said the man was Jesus, and there his heart stopped beating.

His funeral service was filled with emotions. Within a year's period, Hi-Seung had made such an impact on the people who came to know him. His faith in God and his freedom from self enabled him to reach out and touch the hearts of both the old and the young. We found out that in his school—the same high school he had attended before leaving for Japan—he had organized a Christian fellowship group that met twice a week after classes for Bible study and discussions. He shared his lunch with those who could not afford to bring theirs. He gave money to students who needed it, without asking that it be returned. He acted as a big brother to students in need, by listening, giving them a helping hand, and sharing what he had learned from life. As young high school students, in their teens, gave their eulogies with sincerity, detailing what Hi-Seung had done for them, the church became filled with the sound of sobbing.

For Mother, it was a sad day, but she was grateful to have had a son like him. He fulfilled Jesus' teaching, 'He who saves his life will lose it, but he who loses his life for my sake will find it.' Because he was free from himself, he found a bigger self. His body was gone. But his spirit lived on in those touched by him.

It was a very sad and frightening period for me. Not only was the death of my dearest brother a shock beyond description, but also Mother's strange behavior frightened me. Sometimes, she suddenly stopped sewing, staring blankly at the wall in front of her with round eyes—empty of expression— and loudly uttering words that I did not understand. Other times, she jumped out of bed in the dark of the night, rushing to the door, mumbling. I worried that she might end up in a mental hospital and locked up behind metal bars. I worried that she might follow Hi-Seung, leaving me all alone. I walked around the seminary compound, burdened with sadness, and terribly afraid that Mother might also die. I prayed earnestly to God to spare her. For my sake.

In that period, one scene that I will never forget occurred one afternoon. I came home from school. I went to the living room where Mother usually sewed. She was not there. I went to the kitchen. She was not there. Wondering where she was, I walked upstairs and passed by Hi-Seung's room, which was next to mine. Hi-Seung's door was slightly open. Through the opening I saw two people that I loved the most in the world—the cremated remains of Brother Hi-Seung in a wooden box and Mother holding the box tightly to her bosom with her arms around it. Her eyes were closed. I saw no tears flowing down her cheeks, but her face was in deep anguish, pain and helplessness. As I watched the scene, her pain became my pain. Her anguish became my anguish. Her helplessness became my helplessness. I tiptoed to my room, knelt by my bed and prayed, *Oh God, Why? Why? Why does she have to suffer so much? Please help her in her sorrow. I do not know what to do.* I felt totally helpless and alone.

10. Hi-Bum becomes a communist

I thought that the liberation from Japan and the end of World War II would bring not only joy and peace to our nation, but also tranquility to our family. I looked forward to the time when all of us would gather under the loving wings of our parents as in the time of old with joy and laughter. But this turned out to be just a dream. Hi-Seung's death tore our hearts apart. Next, came the sinister and devious arm of communism, waiting to torment us for years to come. Communism came as a peace-loving dove, waving the flag of equality and justice, and snared Hi-Bum, my oldest brother, and devoured him. My family suffered again—this time because of Hi-Bum.

As the Pacific war between Japan and the United States was drawing to a close, Russia declared war against Japan on August 9, 1945, and its forces moved into the northern part of Korea. When the war came to an end on August 15, 1945, the countries that Japan had conquered in the previous decades were returned to their rightful owners. Unfortunately, Korea became a divided country—divided by the United States, Russia, and England at the Cairo Conference in 1943. At the conference, the United States and Russia agreed that until a nationwide election of the Korean people to choose their leaders, the northern half of Korea above the 38th parallel line would be under the Russian supervision, and the southern half would be under U.S. supervision. The nationwide election was to take place in 1948. Meanwhile the Cold War between Russia and the United States started, and the two countries that had helped to defeat Germany and Japan turned into archenemies. The planned nationwide election never materialized, and Korea has remained divided to this day, 2013—North Korea or the Democratic People's Republic of Korea and South Korea or the Republic of Korea.

In the South, the government, under the U.S. supervision, struggled to establish a stable democratic government out of the vacuum left by the Japanese. For thirty-six years, the Japanese attempted to create puppets out of the Koreans. The Japanese wanted to rule, and they wanted the Koreans to follow. They knew that the uneducated mass would follow their ruler without questioning, and the educated few would resist and incite rebellion against them. So the Japanese put leaders in education, politics, and religion in prison. Some patriots escaped to China, America and Europe, and fought for their country's freedom. When the war came to an end, the patriots returned home with a tumultuous heroes' welcome. They came with the hope and zeal to help establish a nation in the Land of the Morning Calm, one that would be strong to defend herself and to be prosperous, independent, democratic and free.

These exiled patriots were an uncompromising, stubborn breed. They were a fearless, determined breed. Their characteristics were essential qualities in men that separated the patriots from the rest. But these same qualities, which had helped them to survive torture, imprisonment and many years of lonely sojourn in foreign countries, became destructive qualities in the process of forming a democratic nation. For these patriots, the word, 'compromise', did not exist in their blood and in their vocabularies. To them only the weak compromised. They talked of a democratic system of government, but their actions pointed to a dictatorship or *democracy my way*. While the people waited helplessly for their leaders to lead them on the path to stability, peace and prosperity, they fought among themselves for power.

While these patriots struggled to gain control of the government, the people suffered from political and economic disorder. Rice was scarce and expensive; its price seesawed from day to day like ocean waves. There were not enough jobs for people with families to feed. Able-bodied people sat around the streets—having nothing to do—playing games, and watching people, ox carts, and street vendors passing by. Streets were strewn with trash. Beggars roamed the streets begging for food. Pickpockets mingled with the crowd looking for their prey. Disenchanted intellectuals mobilized the young to demonstrate on the streets, sometimes inciting riots, and the police brutally responded in return.

In the North, Russia set up a communist government led by Kim Il-Sung, a Korean who had served in the Russian military. With Russia supplying tanks, airplanes and ammunition, Kim Il-Sung quickly established a strong military power with the plan of taking over the South and establishing a unified Korea under his leadership. He sent down his agents to the South to spread the people's discontent and to incite riots among the population who were not happy with the corrupt and incompetent government.

The North Korean communists came not as North Koreans. They came not as communists. They came pretending to be friends of the poor and to be supporters for the discontented intellectuals who had expected greater things from their patriots than the unending factional power struggle. The communists were too shrewd to extol the virtues of communism. They knew that as long as they could fan and spread the fire of discontent against the South Korean government, it would be a matter of time before they could swallow the South under the tight vise of their supreme leader, Chairman Kim Il-Sung.

In this time of disorder and tension, Hi-Bum became acquainted with a group of South Koreans who were disenchanted with their government. Some of them were communist agents, 'wolves in sheep's clothing'. Their job was to amplify his disillusionment and discontent, and to cause him to participate in the disruptive movement to overthrow the existing regime. They succeeded in this regard. The rest is another sad chapter in our family story.

As mentioned in an earlier chapter, Hi-Bum was the smartest one in the family. He was the top student in Kyung-Kee High School, the best high school in Korea. He was so articulate that even his teachers were spellbound when he spoke. Not only was he intelligent, but also, he had a great heart for the poor. Hi-Bum looked after the poor students in his class. If he could not help them financially, he helped them as a tutor, giving his time freely. After his graduation his Japanese teachers sent him to a university in Manchuria, the university that Japan had established to educate bright young people from its conquered countries to serve as its officials after their graduation.

Hi-Bum returned from Manchuria full of expectation and found a position at a university to teach Political Science. He aspired of having a government under which a just society would emerge in the South, and where there would be vitality, wealth and peace.

I heard him lecturing Mother one day.

"I want my country to be a country where there is neither the rich nor the poor, where the country's wealth will be shared equally, and a country where everyone will have an equal opportunity to education so that they can maximize their potential."

"It sounds like Jesus' saying, 'Love your neighbor as you love yourself,'" Mother said.

"Exactly Mother. I knew you were smart." Hi-Bum smiled. "But with one big difference."

"What's that?" Mother asked.

"Christian churches have preached Jesus' 'Love your neighbor' thing for two thousand years," he said. "Where are we now? Do the wealthy share their wealth with the poor? Do the poor children get the same opportunity as the wealthy children?"

"Because of your father's dedication," Mother said, "many are saved, and they try to lead the life of love as Jesus taught us."

"Father's way will take forever," Hi-Bum said. "Only a government with strong leadership can carry it out quickly."

"Did you say a government?" Mother asked looking at Hi-Bum. "Run by a bunch of smart people like you?"

"Yes," Hi-Bum grinned. "Run by a bunch of people like me."

"Poor Hi-Bum," Mother said looking at her eldest son. "Always remember people have heads to think and hearts to feel. Ask yourself what the country will be like if a bunch of people run the government with their smart heads and proud hearts."

Hi-Bum stared at Mother, not knowing how to respond to her words.

"The problems in the world start with 'I want my way people,'" Mother said. "It gets worse when 'I want my way' becomes 'My way is the right way.'"

Hi-Bum remained silent.

"Because of 'My way is the right way' people, who do not respect others' ways, marriages break up; churches break up; governments break up; wars break out," Mother sighed. "Because Japan wanted its way, your family was persecuted and millions of people were killed. Now if Kim Il-Sung gets his own way, I dread to see what will happen to your father, your family and your country."

"I agree with what you have said, Mother," Hi-Bum commented. "But what should we do with the corrupt and ineffectual government? What should we do with the disorder in the country? Hungry people roaming the streets? Beggars wherever we turn our heads? … Just watch and lament?"

"I don't know," Mother sighed. "All I can do is to pray."

"While you pray," Hi-Bum said, "I will try to see what I can do to help my country."

Hi-Bum talked with Mother frequently but rarely with Father. Mother was an easy person to talk to because she was always open and also because he could lecture to her, but not to Father who was as smart as he was and with more life experience than Hi-Bum. He would never be able to lecture Father without being yelled at or being kicked out of the house in the country where Father was king and the children his royal subjects.

A great rift developed between Father and Hi-Bum. Father made a valiant effort to help his son see, without the stained glass of his ideals, what type of company he kept. Without success, Father tried to bring him down from the world of idealism to that of reality. He even tried to send him to America, in the hope that it would prevent his being swept into the communist movement, but Hi-Bum refused to go. In time, there was a complete split between Father and Hi-Bum. He moved out of the house, visiting us only when he missed Mother's cooking. He avoided Father, but he came to see Mother and talked to her, because she was always there to listen. Life was difficult for Mother because she had to maintain a fine balance between the love for her son and the loyalty to her husband.

As the left-wing group became more vocal and violent, and became a threat to the security of the nation, the South Korean government took drastic action, sending the sympathizers to prison. The South Korean police was after Hi-Bum who was in hiding. They questioned Mother. Mother didn't know where he was, but police did not believe her. The police kept visiting Mother and asked, "Where's your communist son, Chai Hi-Bum?"

Her answer was the same, "I don't know." In this period of frequent police visits, Mother began to shake again as she had done with the Japanese police. Whenever the South Korean police banged at our door, Mother started to shake. This banging continued until the police caught Hi-Bum and put him in prison.

Compared to the Japanese, the South Korean police were more thoughtful of us because of their respect for Father, who was not only recognized as a prominent Christian minister but also as an educator. The painful aspect of this episode was that we had to suffer silently the unjust criticism directed toward us. Some people did not distinguish between criminals and political prisoners. Some members of Father's church were very critical of him. Their attitude was, *How can a minister who has a non-Christian communist son in prison preach the gospel of Jesus Christ to us? How can he who can not save his own son be our moral leader?* Some even labeled Father as a communist in preacher's garb. It was especially hard on us when this remark came from those whom we had thought to be our friends. I did not want to go to school because of the way some of my classmates stared at me, the brother of a communist in prison. During all these times, we kept silent because we did not think that they would appreciate our situation even if we explained it to them. We just kept marching on with time, praying for a better day.

11. The Korean War breaks out

June 24, 1950. The North Korean army, with the full support of Russia, broke through the 38th parallel line that divided the North from the South. While the Northern army was rapidly advancing southward, the government informed the public by way of the radio,

Our gallant army is pushing back the onslaught of the northern invaders back to the 38th parallel line. Seoul is safe. There is no reason for the residents of the city to be concerned …

Most of the residents believed the news. We believed the news also, and we carried on our typical routine. Father, reading the Bible in his office. Mother, sewing someone's torn outfit in the living room. I, jumping around with Kwidong, my dog, playing ball. But with each passing day, the rumbling of artillery fire from the northern part of Seoul became louder, and it echoed through the city. By the third day, the sound of battle was like an approaching train. We realized the battle front was moving southward—closer to Seoul, and the radio no longer broadcasted the message, *Our gallant army is pushing back the onslaught of the northern invaders. There is nothing to fear. There is no need for panic …* The day before Seoul was in the enemy's hands, the radio turned silent. But there was nothing that we could do, but wait for the fateful day. On the night of June 27, we heard a thunderous sound of explosion coming from the southwest side of our house where the Han River was located. It did not sound like sporadic artillery shells exploding around the city, but it was much louder, and we wondered what it was. *Has the Northern army already reached Han River?* We wondered. *Is Seoul already under the hands of the Northern army?* We were nervous, and Father told us to go down to the basement to stay overnight.

The next morning the city was quiet except for the sporadic gunfire coming from the center of the city. Out of curiosity, I snuck out of the house to find out what was going on. Our neighborhood, which was a residential area, was absent of people except women with baskets walking toward the market. Further down the road, I heard a rumbling, and I rushed toward it and saw several tanks with red flags rolling along the street. Then I realized that Seoul was in the enemy's hands. I rushed back home and reported my findings to Mother, who was preparing breakfast in the kitchen.

"Go and tell your father what you saw outside," Mother said.

"Will he be upset that I snuck out without asking him?" I asked.

"Maybe," Mother said. "But I think he is more interested in knowing what is going on outside than getting upset. Also tell him that the breakfast is ready."

I somewhat hesitantly walked to Father's office and told him that the breakfast was ready, and mentioned what I found out that morning. Father didn't look upset, but looked solemn. *What is he thinking? Is he thinking of the times under Japan when he was taken to prison by the Japanese police? When he was brought home under house arrest because he had a stroke? Will the Northern soldiers take Father to prison like the Japanese?* I was nervous. Father walked down the stairs without saying a word. I followed behind him. We sat at the breakfast table, and Mother joined us. We bowed our heads for a silent prayer.

"*Yubo*—Dear—I am so worried," Mother said to Father over the breakfast.

"About what?" Father responded.

"About Hi-Bum in prison," Mother said. "Will they harm him?"

Hi-Bum had been in prison close to two years.

"I don't think so," Father said. "They will more likely release Hi-Bum since they will find out that he sided with their cause."

"I hope so," Mother said. "But I am still worried. "

"What I am more worried about," Father said, "is what the South Korean prison guards did to the political prisoners before they fled."

"I was thinking of that too," Mother said. "I guess that's why I'm still worried."

"What I think is that the guards really didn't have much time to figure out what to do with all the prisoners," Father said. "This all happened so fast that they simply left the prisoners in their cells and ran away."

"I just hope so," Mother said.

From the look on their faces and the tone in their voices they seemed to be really worried about Hi-Bum. But for some reason I didn't find myself worrying about Hi-Bum. Maybe some. But not like with Hi-Seung, who was my best friend. Period. When he died, the light went out of my life. Nothing was the same after he died. When he was alive, I looked forward to every tomorrow. To jump around with him laughing and yelling. To learn to be tough and mean like him.

But what about Brother Hi-Bum? I knew he was my eldest brother— fifteen years older than I was. But I didn't have much feeling toward him, maybe because he had never played with me when I was a child. I remembered him slapping my cheek and telling me to act like a normal child because I stuttered and was uncoordinated. He laughed at my walking because my big watermelon head with a thin neck wobbled as I walked. When I recited, "Je..sosu ro...ves me," in front of Mother, she said with a smile, "Say, 'Jesus loves me'." But Hi-Bum laughed and said to Mother, "Poor Mother, you have a problem child here." And I didn't like the way he talked about me.

But he was still my brother. And like Father and Mother, I was also concerned about Hi-Bum in prison, but without much feeling. I just hoped that he was safe, and he would come home for his parents' sake.

Meanwhile, Mother continued to worry about Father.

"I am also worried about you," Mother said.

"Who? ... Me?" Father looked at Mother.

"Yes," Mother said. "You."

"I know," Father sighed. "Maybe, they are going to do the same thing that the Japanese did to me."

When Mother mentioned her worry about Father, I started to worry, too. *Will the North Koreans put Father in jail like the Japanese did? Will they shoot him dead because they are too busy fighting and have no time to care for the prisoners? Or will they leave Father alone since he has a communist son?* I hoped that Hi-Bum would come home. I felt that Hi-Bum living with us would be a safeguard for Father from the communists. We waited for Hi-Bum to come home from prison. After breakfast and our conversation, Father went upstairs to his office, and Mother went into her prayer closet to pray.

Then around ten o'clock in the morning, there was a knock at our door. Mother and I were in the living room.

"Wonder who's there?" Mother asked, looking nervous. "Do you think that the North Korean soldiers are already here to get Father?"

"I will go and check," I said.

"Whoever the person is," Mother said, "be courteous and be honest."

I knew why Mother told me to be honest. If a soldier asked about Father, I would be tempted to tell to him Father was not at home. But the soldier would know right away that I was not telling the truth because I was not good at lying.

"Yes, Mother," I said walking toward the door taking a deep breath and rubbing my hands to stay calm.

Before opening, I quietly peeked through the side of the door. To my relief, the person was not a soldier with a gun but a beggar looking for food. I opened the door, and in front of me was a man in worn and torn clothes. The man had sunken eyes, sunken cheeks and foot-long black hair hanging down his head which reminded me of when Hi-Seung came home from Japan in 1945. A nauseating smell from the man made me pinch my nose. I kept staring at him because he looked familiar.

"Aren't you going to let me in," the man said. "Hi-Dong."

"Brother Hi-Bum," I yelled.

Without asking him to come in, I left the door open and ran to Mother.

"Mother," I yelled. "Brother Hi-Bum is home."

Mother put the needle and cloth on the floor and rushed out to greet Hi-Bum. While Mother cried and led Hi-Bum to the living room holding his bony hand, I rushed upstairs to Father. I saw him reading the Bible at his desk.

"Father," I said. "Brother Hi-Bum is here."

He jerked his head and turned toward me.

"Is Hi-Bum here?" Father asked.

"Yes."

He blankly stared at the door for a while without a word. Then he said, "I will be down in a few minutes," and returned to his reading. I ran down to tell Mother what Father had said. Hi-Bum heard me and said, "Leave Father alone." But Mother rushed upstairs. I heard Mother shouting at Father, which was unusual. Then after a minute, Father meekly came down, his face solemn, greeted Brother in an uneasy manner, and returned to his office.

The first thing Mother did was to take Hi-Bum to the bathroom, and she came out with a bundle of his prison garb with her nose twisted and frowning. She rushed outside and dumped the bundle in the garbage can. She got new clothes and put them next to the bathroom door. Then she hurried to the kitchen to boil rice and to make *tofu* soup for Hi-Bum. While Hi-Bum was taking a bath, Father came down to the kitchen and told us that he would be working in his church office and be home late at night. Mother glared at him in silence, and Father meekly walked out of the house.

After the bath, Hi-Bum looked more like my brother in his new clothes, but he still looked pitiful with sunken eyes and cheeks. When Mother brought a small table with a bowl of steaming rice, his favorite soup, *kimchee*, and side dishes, his sunken eyes turned wide. A broad smile came over his face. He grabbed the chopsticks and was ready to shove the rice into his mouth, but Mother stopped him. "Hi-Bum," she said, "Let us give thanks to our Lord." *Trouble, trouble,* I thought. *He's going to tell Mother not to waste his time with such nonsense.* I looked at him expecting his usual disparaging words to come out of his mouth, but that didn't happen. He bowed his head as Mother gave thanks. As soon as she said, "In Your precious name, we pray," he grabbed hold of the rice bowl and shoved the rice into his mouth, not even saying a word. Watching him eat like a starved beggar, I felt sorry for him even though we had suffered so much because of his political position.

After the lunch Hi-Bum appeared to be satisfied and started to talk about his prison life and his dream for a new Korea, but Mother said, "Why don't you go to your room and have a long rest. We have plenty of time later to listen to your story."

"Father may not like to hear what I say," he said.

"Don't worry," Mother said. "Father will be home late tonight."

"I will take your word for it," Hi-Bum said. "I will go to my room and have a nice rest in my own bed for the first time in two years."

While he was sleeping, Mother and I went to the market and got a fresh mackerel as a special treat for Hi-Bum, who had been starving in prison for two long years. Mother slit open the mackerel along its stomach, removed its bloody, wiggly organs, rinsed it in water, and shook salt on it to grill it. After preparing the mackerel Mother went to the living room to read her Bible, and I went to my room to study.

We waited for Hi-Bum for over two hours, way past five o'clock, but he was still asleep.

"Should I go and wake him up?" I asked Mother.

"No, let him rest as long as he needs," Mother said. "Think about sleeping in a prison cell on a concrete floor with other inmates for two long years. I can't picture myself doing that."

"Let me go up and see whether he is awake anyway," I said standing up.

I tiptoed to his room and put my ear to his door to hear any movement. The only thing that I heard was his snoring. A loud stuttering snore. I rushed down.

"Mother, he must be really tired" I said. "He's snoring loudly."

"Good," Mother said. "Let him rest."

Mother decided to start cooking, and I started the charcoal fire to grill the mackerel. While we were preparing dinner, I heard footsteps by the kitchen.

"It's so nice to be home," Hi-Bum said, "and smell your delicious cooking."

"Poor Hi-Bum," Mother said. "For two years you have been starving."

"It was worse than starving," he said. "It was hell on earth."

I had never heard him mentioning the word, 'hell', before. Mother told me why. Hi-Bum told Mother one day that he had heard so much about Christians going to heaven while non-Christians going to hell that he became allergic to those words. Today was the first time I heard him using the word, 'hell'. *Interesting!* I thought. *Brother Hi-Bum has never used* the word, hell, before. Neither did he use the word, heaven. Did he become a Christian in prison? Father will be so happy when he hears that.

"So you believe in hell after death?" I chimed in.

Hi-Bum looked at me as if I were a dork and turned to Mother ignoring my question. I felt embarrassed, but at the same time I felt insulted. *Who does he think he is?* I thought. *Does he think he is the only smart son in the family? I was a top student at Mee-Dong Elementary School. Now I am a fourteen-year-old high school student—at the top in my class at Seoul High School. Also, not like you—I am more thoughtful of others.* I was angry even though it was his first day out of the prison. I was going to ask him, *Did you become a Christian in prison?* but before I could open my mouth, Mother winked at me—her signal for me to keep my mouth shut. She turned to Hi-Bum and studied his face.

"You sit down," Mother said, "and tell us how it was in prison."

He sat on the kitchen floor and started to talk. Even though he was all bones, his voice was still strong. He did not dwell much on his prison life, but he talked with great excitement of the dawn of a new age in the unified Korea, where there would be neither rich nor poor, neither masters nor servants, and neither landowners nor sharecroppers. Everyone would share the nation's wealth equally. It would be the classless society that Karl Marx wrote about.

It sounded good to me, a fourteen-year-old boy. But Mother did not seem impressed.

"I don't have all the book knowledge like you do," Mother said to Hi-Bum, "but I know human nature."

Then she turned to me and asked with a hint of smile, "Hi-Dong. Why does your teacher give exams to his students?"

Kind a puzzled, I answered, "So that he knows who will get A's and who will get F's."

"Will you be happy if your teacher gives everybody an A regardless how poorly one does in the class?"

"No way," I said, thinking what a stupid question that she's asking, especially in front of her smart son, Hi-Bum.

"Why not?"

"Why should Jong-Jin and Dong-Kyu get A's," I said thinking of my classmates, "when they don't do their homework and don't pay attention to the teacher, while I do my homework and listen to him?"

Mother smiled looking at Hi-Bum.

"I know what you are hinting at," Hi-Bum said. "But Kim Il-Sung is already making it happen in the North."

"Do you think they are happy under Kim Il-Sung?"

"I certainly do."

"Then why did so many Northerners, tens of thousands, run away to the South?"

"They are those rich people who wanted to hold on to their wealth," he said. "And they are those who want to maintain their old ways."

"Do you really think that's the only reason?"

"Yes, I do."

"You wait and see," Mother said.

"Yes, Mother," Hi-Bum smiled. "I'll prove to you that you are wrong."

"By the way," Mother looked straight at Hi-Bum, "Don't ever talk about your views on religion, politics, and philosophy in front of your father. OK?"

"I will try," Hi-Bum responded.

"Father has his views, and you have your own," Mother said. "Father is not going to change his ways, and you are not going to change your ways."

"I know that, Mother."

"As long as Father and you are living under the same roof," Mother said, "honor your father. Don't argue with him. Don't talk back to him."

"Mother, I don't think you will have to worry about that," Hi-Bum said. "From what I saw today, Father will avoid me, and I will do the same."

"So we have a Cold War in our house like the United States and Russia," I chimed in, sounding wise.

"I guess a Cold War is better than a Hot War," Mother sighed looking at me. "Hi-Dong, you go and study. I will call you when dinner is ready."

Within days after his release from the prison, Hi-Bum found a job at the communist Education Office. For the first few days he returned home with a smile on his face, but soon his smile disappeared. One evening I heard Hi-Bum talking to Mother.

"From what I have seen and heard so far," Hi-Bum said, sounding disgruntled, "I think you are right."

"What's right?" Mother asked looking at Hi-Bum.

"Kim Il-Sung's regime," he said.

"What about Kim Il-Sung's regime?"

"It's more like the Japanese," he said. "Not what I studied in books."

"What have you found out?" Mother asked.

"Well, they treat us like kids," Hi-Bum chuckled, sounding dismayed. "Every morning before work, I have to attend the daily ritual—singing the North Korean national anthem, listening to my northern comrades speak of their single-minded determination to push the American imperialists out to the sea and dedicating their lives to bringing South Korea under the leadership of their great leader Kim Il-Sung and they wanting us doing the same thing ... They treat us like kids."

"I hope you didn't show your displeasure," Mother said looking worried.

"Mother, I am smarter than that," Hi-Bum said.

"I am glad," Mother said. "You are not going to change their ways. Just play it safe."

As the days passed, Hi-Bum realized that the just and free society that he had dreamed of under the North Korean regime was just an illusion. He found that a person could not even visit his friend in another town without getting permission from the neighborhood communist office. He found that when a person visited his friend for a few days, he had to report it to the town office. There were meetings at the town office every day and night for housewives, young people, and old people. At the meetings, the people were bombarded by the North Korean officers with propaganda, extolling the virtues of their great leader, Kim Il-Sung, and the evil of the imperialist warmongers, especially the United States. The officers were like walking tape recorders. They had no thoughts of their own. At the push of a button, they played back what was programmed into their brains by their communist doctrinaires.

The officers visited every home, making an inventory of various items such as sewing machines, radios, and furniture. They came and even took count of the number of heads of cabbage, radishes, and egg plants growing in our garden. People were expected at a moment's notice to attend a town meeting or to participate in a construction project with picks and shovels. Anyone who did not obey was punished. Fear and suspicion ruled the society. People became slaves to the state, and the state controlled them at the push of a button. People were just like machine parts, tape recorders, or robots to be used to serve the almighty state which was run by a few of the elite.

Mother knew that it was not the type of society that Hi-Bum had dreamed of. But there was nothing he could do. In a totalitarian state like this one, he knew that no dissent was permitted. It was either obey, or die. He went along with the system, going out to work in the morning and coming home late, bone-tired and depressed. As the communists tightened control over Seoul, we saw a growing frustration on Hi-Bum's face and in his voice.

One evening during the dinner, I noticed Hi-Bum was unusually quiet.

"How was your day?" Mother asked.

"I don't know," Hi-Bum said, slowly tapping his chopsticks on the table.

"Anything unpleasant happened?"

"Today, my boss gave me a list of names of professors," he said, "and asked me to visit and talk with them."

"And?"

"He ordered me to compile a list of professors who may be suspicious."

"Suspicious of what?"

"I guess those who are anti-North."

"What are they going to do with them?"

"From what I have seen," he signed, "they will be either put in prison or get shot."

"How terrible," Mother said. "Do you know any of them?"

"Yes," he said. "Some were my former colleagues."

"Did you say, 'Yes', to your boss?"

"Yes," he said punching his right fist against his left palm and avoiding Mother's gaze. "And I didn't like myself after saying, 'Yes' to him."

"But what else could you do?" Mother consoled him. "It's either your life or theirs."

"That's exactly what I don't like about myself," he sighed. "After saying, 'Yes', I realized that I was a worthless coward. I cared for my life more than others. More than my principles."

Mother reached over the table and held Hi-Bum's hand and bowed her head in silence. I knew she was praying. I looked at Hi-Bum. He did not resist and bowed his head with his eyes closed. I saw a glimmer of tears around his eyes. Even though I was a fourteen-year-old boy, I felt sorry for him because I remembered Mother's frequent advice to my sisters, *Be wary of those well-dressed, fancy-talking boys. Stay away from them. One mistake with them will ruin your life.* Hi-Bum was the brightest in the family, the pride and joy of his parents. Unfortunately, he fell in love with the ideal of Karl Marx. He equated the communism practiced in North Korea with what he had studied in books. Sadly, he realized that the two were not the same. But it was too late. One mistake ended his brilliant career and brought much suffering to his family.

Even as a young boy, I was surprised by the difference between the life under the North Korean government and the life under the South Korean government. The difference was just like day and night. Under the South Korean government, the people complained about their government and their officials in the open. Churches of all denominations were open for worship. People were free to move around from town to town without getting permits. They went about doing their business, without government officials breathing down their necks. Yes, there was poverty. There was wealth. Beggars could be seen on the street. Disorder existed. Demonstrations and police brutality occurred. All those things were possible because there was freedom, and there was respect for the individual.

Under the North Korean government, demonstration was out of the question unless a person was ready to risk his life. Churches were closed, and worship services were not allowed—even in private homes. Streets were cleaner. The wealth was taken away from the rich. Beggars were harder to find on the streets. There were order and discipline. The soldiers marched in perfect unison, their feet moving up and down at exactly the same moment. Unfortunately, there was no freedom. People's lives were dictated by the state. The state programmed the people's thoughts, their movements, and their future. People moved like robots, bound by fear.

There were portraits of the great leader, the great liberator Kim Il-Sung, everywhere people turned their heads—at the entrance to every building, in every classroom of the elementary schools, high schools, and universities, the inside of every bus, on light poles … but not in restrooms. Before every public meeting, we had to raise our hands high toward the sky and shout, "Long live our great leader." Every speech started with the adoration of their great leader. To the communists Kim Il-Sung was their god. For ninety long days, the people in Seoul had to go through the motions dictated by the North Korean communists—if they wanted to stay alive.

Whether he liked it or not, to Hi-Bum his life came first and his principles second. To Father, his God came first, and his life and his family second. To Hi-Seung, his father, who had whipped him the most, came first and himself second.

12. The communists take away my father

The ninety days under the communists were difficult days for us, and especially for Mother. She had a stubborn communist son living downstairs, and she had her stubborn anti-communist husband staying upstairs. They avoided each other as much as possible, and she had to minister to the needs of both. One consolation was that Hi-Bum was out all day, so that Father could come down and move around during the day.

Also, Mother worried about Father's safety. *What will they do to my husband, a Christian minister? I heard that no church was allowed in the North, and the ministers were put in prison. Will they put him in prison also? Or will they leave him alone since his son works for them?* Mother urged him to go into hiding. Relatives and friends urged him the same. But Father refused. He said, "I have served my Lord, Jesus Christ all my life, and I am sixty-one years old now. I don't care what they will do to me. My life is in God's hands."

Why do you always think of your Lord, Jesus Christ first? I wanted to protest. *What about us? Especially, what about Mother? I saw her struggle while you were in the Japanese prison. I saw her struggle while you were under house arrest. I saw her coming home dead-tired after visiting you in the village. You didn't see her struggle, but I did with my own eyes. Day in. Day out. She struggled to feed and lead us while you were in prison. While you were in bed, unconscious. While you were in the village, recovering. She struggled. Without ever complaining. All alone. Now if the communists take you away and kill you, she will be really alone. She will have to work twice as hard. She may die from all the struggles that were caused by you. What about thinking of Mother and your family now?*

I was upset, but too timid to speak up. Also a larger part of me admired and respected Father's courage to put God above his own life. *Will I be able to give up my life for what I believe? For my God? For my country? For my family when I get older?* I wasn't sure.

One day a gentleman, Mr. Lee Sang-Sun, visited us. He introduced himself as the North Korean official who was responsible for protecting the religious freedom of the people in Seoul. He wished to consult with Father to determine the most effective means to maintain religious freedom. He apologized profusely for not permitting church worship in Seoul. He said that as soon as the United States and its puppets were pushed out to the sea, and when the entire Korean peninsula became one nation under the flag of the great People's Republic of Korea, all the church doors would be open. There would be total freedom of worship in the country, not only for Christians but also for the worshippers of other religions.

Mr. Lee stayed with us not just for a few hours but for three days. During that time he exuded such sincerity, kindness, and concern for the religious freedom, that I wondered whether his father was a Christian minister and that he was taught to be thoughtful and kind to others. I thought he was a nice man because he treated me like his brother, but Mother, who had a knack for gauging people, warned me to stay away from him.

"What does a fisherman do to catch a fish?" She asked me.

"Put a worm on his hook," I answered.

"He is a fisherman," Mother said. "And your father is his fish."

"Do you really think so?" I asked.

"I hope I'm wrong," Mother said. "All I can do is to pray and wait."

Also my dog, Kwidong, didn't care for him. When he approached Kwidong with a big smile saying, "What a beautiful dog you are," Kwidong growled. I scolded her not to growl at him, but she wouldn't listen, and I ended up apologizing, "Please excuse me for her bad behavior. She's afraid of people she doesn't know. His answer was cheerful, No problem. I understand. You are lucky to have a dog like her."

It was a beautiful summer morning on August 23rd, 1950, two weeks after Lee Sang-Sun's visit. The sky was clear without a speck of cloud.

94

The air was fresh and dry. Early in the morning Father and I went out to the community garden next to our house. We pulled weeds and sprayed fertilizer around the lettuce, cabbage, and radishes, which were growing beautifully. Father pulled three foot-long radishes and handed them to me.

"Give these to Mother for our evening meal," Father said.

"Yes, Father," I answered, putting the radishes in the basket. "What should I tell Mother to do with these radishes?"

"Leave it to her," Father smiled. "Your mother can make a thousand delicious dishes with anything."

Feeling refreshed, we walked toward the house while Father sang his favorite hymn in his tenor voice:

> *This is my Father's world,*
> *And to my listening ears,*
> *All nature sings and round me rings*
> *The music of the spheres.*

> *This is my Father's world,*
> *I rest me in the thought*
> *Of rocks and trees, of skies and seas*
> *His hand the wonders wrought.*

As we approached the front porch, we saw two men in plain clothes talking to Mother. With full heads of hair and wearing white shirts, they looked like young men in their thirties.

"Are they already here?" Father looked puzzled. "I told them to come and see me at ten this morning."

"Who are they?" I asked.

"They were members of my church years ago," Father said. "They now live in In-Chon."

I ran to Mother to give her the fresh radishes. Listening to my footsteps the men turned toward us. Mother stood next to them looking worried.

"Look, Mother," I said holding up the radishes. "Father picked them for our evening meal."

"Take them inside," Mother said while looking at Father walking toward us.

"Are you Rev. Chai Suk-Mo?" One man stepped forward and asked Father.

"Yes, I am," Father answered with a puzzled look.

He bowed to Father respectfully and said, "I am Officer Kim working for the department dealing with religious matters."

"Oh, Yes," Father said. "You are from the same office of Mr. Lee Sang-Sun."

"Yes, he is my superior."

"How is he doing?"

"He is making good progress," Officer Kim said. "And he wants your presence at a meeting where he can share his plans regarding the opening of the churches."

"When will the meeting be?" Father asked.

"Eight o'clock this morning."

"It's seven thirty now," Father said looking at his watch. "I haven't had breakfast yet."

Father turned to Mother, who was standing by the porch looking nervous.

"It will be a short meeting," Officer Kim said.

"Let me go in and change then," Father said.

"It will not be necessary," Officer Kim snapped.

The cheerful look on Father's face just minutes ago turned dark. He looked at Mother for a second. He turned and looked at me as I held the fresh radishes in my hand. He gave me a little smile. Then without saying a word, Father turned and walked down the steps between the two officers.

Mother and I stood by the porch watching them walking down the street.

"I don't think they were telling the truth," Mother said. "I feel so uneasy."

"About what?" I asked.

"Having a meeting for ministers," she said. "So early in the morning."

"Why would they lie?" I asked.

"I don't know," Mother said. "I just don't feel comfortable."

96

"If they wanted to arrest Father," I said, "they would come in uniforms with pistols by their side."

I was thinking of the Japanese police who had come to our house in uniforms with guns to take Father to prison during World War II.

"I know," Mother said, her voice feeling uncertain. "Let's go in and have breakfast."

When I went into the dining room, I saw our round dining table with three bowls of rice and three bowls of steaming cabbage soup—the cabbage Father had picked from our garden a few days ago—waiting for us. Mother and I sat around the table, and looked at Father's side. His bowl of rice and soup waited for him, but Father was not there to give the grace. I bowed my head expecting Mother to say the prayer. I waited and waited, but she was quiet. I peeked at her and saw her lips tremble and her face in a grimace, but there was no sound. Finally a minute into the silence, I heard Mother's whisper, "Amen." I opened my eyes and looked at her. She was in tears. Mustering a forced smile, she said, "Hi-Dong, let us eat. And pray that Father will come home soon."

Suddenly fear crept into my heart. I recalled Mother's question about Mr. Lee Sang-Sun, "What does a fisherman do to catch a fish?" *Is Mr. Lee the fisherman? And my father his fish? Will the fisherman let the fish back in the river so that the fish can swim back to his nest? Or will he take the fish home for his evening meal?*

Father did not come home that morning. He did not come that evening. Days passed. Weeks passed by. Father did not come home.

We did not know where he was taken. Mother asked Hi-Bum whether he could locate Father's whereabouts. He tried but he couldn't. Our neighbors, our friends, and our church members couldn't provide any leads. No one knew. Father was gone. Never to return.

It was such a strange feeling not knowing where Father was. My head told me that he had been most likely taken to a remote dirt road, shot, and left there to decay under the scorching sun, to be feasted on by swarming flies and crawling maggots, to be drenched in heavy rain, leaving only the bones and his skeleton alongside the dirt road for years to come; and nobody would know his name. Yet, my heart still waited for him, hoping against hope. When I saw a glimpse of a man looking like Father on the street, I rushed toward him, only to find that I was mistaken. I walked away discouraged.

I would prefer to have a deceased father with a known grave so that I could visit his grave and remember him. I did not like this waiting, when common sense told me that it was an exercise in futility. I guessed it was the unfinished business that troubled me. I was sure that it must have been the same for Mother. Fortunately, Mother had absolute faith in God. God was not a being high in heaven, but He was always beside her. She talked to Him in the morning, during the day, and at night. She talked to Him in joy and in sorrow. And she marched on through her trials and tribulations with God beside her.

Mother was beaten and harassed by the Japanese police because of Father's religious stand and his pro-American position. She was tormented by the South Korean police because of Hi-Bum's political leanings. She was harassed by the communists because of Father's religious and educational stature. There was tension, frustration, fear, anger and sorrow in our family during those periods. Under such conditions, a mere mortal would have been crushed, either ending up in a mental hospital or turning into a bitter person, angry at the world and people. But Mother did not buckle. She marched and led us onward with love and wisdom.

Mother gave thanks to God when everything around us was darkness and gloom. She gave thanks to God for His love for us when I saw no love, but instead hate and killing around us. She prayed for the well-being of others even when our own well-being was at stake.

Throughout my growing years, I marveled at the strength of her character, which came from her total faith in God. But often, I wondered how she could praise Him when suffering was all around her. I wondered how she could thank Him when there seemed nothing to be thankful for. I wondered how she could sing about God's wondrous creation when all I saw around me was destruction, scorched hills by the bombs from the sky, corpses on the roadways piled up like trash, and children without parents roaming the streets.

I do not know. I do not know. Maybe, that is what Christ's message is all about. To give thanks. To give praise. In spite of … In spite of …

13. Good by, Kwidong

I remember the day when Mother came to my room. It was two weeks after Father was taken away. I was reading a comic book about a dog trying to save a little boy by pulling the snake's tail curled around the boy's legs. The snake's head was by the boy's knees. It was crawling up toward the boy's head with its tongue sticking out. The boy couldn't move. He cried, *Mother, ... a snake.* I was about to turn the page, anxious to see whether the dog would save his master from the snake. Mother came and sat in front of me. I was going to show her the picture, but she didn't look her usual self. She had a look that I had never seen on her. Maybe, the look of helplessness.

"Are you OK, Mother?" I asked.

She looked at me, and then she lowered her head.

"Is something wrong?" I asked putting the comic book on the floor.

Slowly she turned her head to look at me. Her eyes glistened with tears. My heart sank. *Did someone come and tell her that he found Father's dead body on a dirt road?* I closed my eyes with hands over my chest. Dreading what Mother would say next. Hoping that it would not be about Father but some other bad news.

I waited. And waited. Mother reached out and held my hand without looking at me and without saying a word. I just stared at her dreading to hear her next words.

After a long silence, Mother said, "Hi-Dong, I feel very sad that we don't have much rice left."

I felt relieved hearing the word *rice,* not the word *Father.* I had been hungry since the war, but I wasn't surprised because Mother always worried about not having enough food to feed my growing body.

I was going to say, *What's new?*, but I decided to be more thoughtful and said, "I am sorry."

She reached out and held my hand and looked up at me. I saw tears in her eyes.

She said, "We do not have much rice left, even for the family."

Even for the family ... Even for the family ... Does she mean that we don't have enough rice to share with our neighbor who has been starving? If so, why does she have to tell me? And if so, why does she have tears in her eyes? I studied her face. Then it struck me like lightning that it had to do with my dog, Kwidong, my best friend.

With fear creeping up in my heart, I asked, "Are you going to do something with Kwidong?"

"Yes, we do not have enough rice to last for a week," she said, with her voice low. "Also, I do not feel right, feeding the dog when our neighbors are starving."

Before I could tell her, *Kwidong is a part of my family and my best friend,* she said, "Tomorrow morning, a dog warden will come and take Kwidong away."

Take Kwidong away ... I just stared at her. I felt numb. My shoulders stooped. All the strength in my body seemed to leave like a popped balloon. I just sat speechless staring at her. Holding my hand she started to pray, asking God to give me comfort and strength. Asking God to free us from this pain and anguish. I heard her prayer, but it sounded hollow.

Tomorrow I will have to say, "Good bye," to my best friend. My best friend since I was five years old. Tomorrow I will have to see her walk away with a dog warden like the time when Father walked away with the two North Korean officers only a few weeks ago!

That night I couldn't sleep, because many thoughts swirled in my head. I thought of running away with Kwidong into a forest, and living in the woods as a hunter, catching rabbits and squirrels for food. I thought of becoming a beggar, walking the streets of Seoul with Kwidong by my side, begging for food from street vendors, and sleeping on a hillside under a tree, snuggled beside her feeling her soft hair. I thought of going to the home of a wealthy friend, asking him to keep her until we could afford to have her back. None of these ideas seemed to be realistic. *How can I run away with Kwidong leaving Mother alone? She has already suffered enough. Am I not too selfish to leave her all alone so that I can be with Kwidong? … No way.* Unable to sleep, I tossed around from side to side in bed with many thoughts, including the memory of the first day when we brought a little puppy from a friend's home nine years ago.

The year was 1941, and I was five years old. One afternoon, Mrs. Lee, our family friend, visited us telling us that her dog delivered six beautiful puppies a few weeks ago, and they had been crawling all over the house, wagging their tiny tails.

Looking at me with a smile she said, "Why don't you come over tomorrow and take a puppy home?"

For months I had been begging Mother for a dog, and I jumped at the invitation.

"Is it OK, Mom?"

"Sure," Mother smiled. "Mrs. Lee's dog is a pointer. She is not too big and has short hair. She is very friendly to people, and is smart. Her puppy will make a nice friend for you."

"May I get a puppy now?" I asked Mrs. Lee.

"Oh, sure!" Mrs. Lee said. "It's OK with me, if it's OK with your mother."

"Let's go, Mom," I said.

"Be patient, my *mangnei*—last son." Mother smiled. "Mrs. Lee's been here only a minute."

"How long are you going to talk?" I asked.

"Just a few minutes."

A few minutes is less than five minutes, I figured. I looked at the grandfather clock on the wall, ticking. Tick-tock. Tick-tock. The short arm was on three, and the long arm was on twelve. *Brother Hi-Seung told me that when the long arm moved from one number to the next number, it was five minutes. So when the long arm moves to one, I will remind Mother.* I sat next to Mother. My eyes glued to the long arm. Wishing that the long arm would hurry and go to 1. But it moved so slowly, and there was nothing I could do. I just waited and waited.

As soon as the long arm moved to one, I shouted, "Mom, let's go."
Mother turned and looked at me.

"You talked five minutes," I said. "More than a few minutes."

Mother smiled and explained what she meant by *a few minutes*, and told me to go outside and play. I didn't want to go outside. I sat next to Mother listening to their talk. Hoping that it would be a short one. But they kept talking and talking, and there was nothing that I could do but wait. After two long hours, Mrs. Lee finally was ready to go. Mother and I followed her to her home.

We quietly entered the room where the puppies were kept and found them busily sucking their mama's teats for milk. As we walked close to them and sat down, one stopped sucking, looked at me, and crawled toward me. I put my hands out to touch her, and she licked my finger with her tiny tongue as if she was welcoming me.

"She is your puppy!" Mrs. Lee said. "Look at her smiling at you. You may pick her up."

She had a smiling face with white hair and brown spots scattered around her body. I carefully picked her up and gently lowered her on my lap. She did not resist, and seemed to be happy to be with me.

"Puppies have inborn ways to tell who they can trust and who they should avoid," Mrs. Lee continued. "That puppy already feels very comfortable with you."

"What shall I call her?" I asked, all excited.

She called out about a dozen names, and Mother made comments about several of the names. After few minutes of discussion, they thought that Kwidong –Precious One—would be a good one. So my puppy became Kwidong. As soon as I was home, I made a little bed with an old pillow and blanket in a cardboard box, laid her down, and she fell asleep right away.

For the first few months, I acted like her mother, and it was fun. When she cried, I picked her up in my arms and stroked her while humming a lullaby to soothe her sadness. I warmed her milk in a pan, brought it to her, and lovingly watched her licking the milk with her small, pink tongue. I cleaned up her mess, and later placed a newspaper on the floor near her, and taught her how to walk on the paper to relieve herself. If she didn't, I pointed my finger at her and talked to her in a low tone of voice, pretending to be angry, *I told you not to pee on the floor.* Looking at my finger and hearing my voice, she looked scared and apologetic but still wagged her tail. After a week, it became second nature for her to crawl on the paper to relieve herself.

She grew quickly, and started to walk and run around all over the house, curiously sniffing at everything, and barking when she heard strange sounds. It was so funny to see her barking at the radio—about two feet wide and three feet tall—in the living room when a person talked. I saw her facing the radio in an attack position. Growling and barking in her soprano voice.

When I came home after playing with friends, she jumped all over me, wagging her tail and squealing with joy, wanting me to take her outside. Once outside, she ran around our yard on her four tiny legs, as if she was preparing for a race.

In time she was getting too big to stay in the house. Father and I built a big A-framed dog house with an upside down U-shaped door which was big enough for Kwidong and me to go in. Often, I crawled into her place and lay down to take a nap, lying sideways with my knees bent, while she would sit beside me, watching me sleep. As we both grew older, we took long walks in the neighborhood streets, and climbed up the hill behind our house. When she saw a stranger coming toward me, her face turned serious, and she was ready to protect me from any danger. I knew that she would give her life anytime, to protect me. Thus, she became my constant companion and my best friend.

But tomorrow I will have to say, "Good bye!" to my best friend since I was five years old. Early in the morning, a dog warden will come and knock at the door. Mother will open the door and lead him to Kwidong. The old man will go to her without a smile, put a muzzle on her and take her away. Then my best pal will end up on his family's dinner table.

During the war, people were starving. Nothing was wasted, and all living creatures, when caught, ended up on people's dinner tables. *My best pal, cut to small pieces, cooked in boiling water, put on a plate and placed on the dog warden's dinner table!* My heart ached, but there was nothing I could do but wait for that dreadful day to arrive.

Tomorrow came very quickly. As expected, the dog warden—an old man in a worn, white Korean costume and hat—came, put a muzzle on Kwidong and took her away. I stood and watched Kwidong walking down the steps. As she rounded the corner, she turned her head to look at me for the last time as if to say, *Goodbye.* Without thinking, I lunged forward a few steps toward Kwidong. Then I realized that Mother was behind me, and I made an abrupt stop. I turned around to see her. Her eyes were closed with her folded hands on her bosom.

What should I do? Run and bring Kwidong back with me? My best friend who has given me so much love and joy? Then what about Mother? She said we didn't have enough rice left. I also know she doesn't want Kwidong to go. But she has to.

I slowly turned around, my heart filled with guilt, pain and anguish. I watched Kwidong walking away in helpless silence. I would never see her again. I wished I were dead. Living was no fun.

14. South Korean army returns to Seoul

For weeks I was wrapped up in the thought of Kwidong. I was certain that she was killed and ended up on the dog warden's table. But I still wondered whether she was alive; if alive, I wondered what she was doing. Whether she had enough food to eat. Whether she had a good friend to play with.

Mother and I also worried about Father. We wondered whether he was alive or dead. We wondered whether the communists shot him dead on a dirt road and left him there. We wondered whether the communists put him in a dark, concrete prison cell without food, without water to drink, without any blanket to cover himself on cold nights. Whether he lay in a prison cell, unconscious from the terrible torture—his eyes closed, his mouth open, his hands spread out on the concrete floor like a dead man, his whole body bruised and bloodied. We worried and wondered and prayed. That's all we could do—worry and wonder. Day in and day out. And pray that the war would come to an end quickly and that Father would come home.

On a mid-September afternoon, ninety days into the war, Mother and I were in the living room doing our usual things. Mother was sewing, and I was reading a comic book. There was a pounding knock at the door. *Who's pounding on the door like that? Not Brother Hi-Bum; he has the key. Not a friend; a friend would not pound on the door like that. Is it a North Korean soldier? Why? To take us all away? Mother and me?* I got nervous and looked at Mother. Mother looked nervous too.

"Let me go and see who is there," I said standing.

"Whoever he is," Mother said, "be calm and courteous."

"Yes," I said.

I walked nervously to the door and quickly peeped through the opening by the side of the door. Instead of a soldier, I saw Little Aunt standing, looking somber. My shoulders stooped. I took a deep sigh of relief.

"Welcome, Aunt," I greeted her. "Are you OK?"

Without answering, she rushed to Mother. I followed behind her wondering what she was up to.

"Sister, Sister," Little Aunt said. "Did you hear the news?"

"What news?" Mother said.

"I heard that our soldiers landed in Inchon a day ago," Little Aunt said.

"Oh really?" Mother's eyes widened.

"Not only our soldiers," Little Aunt said, "but the U.N. soldiers led by General McArthur."

"The American general who accepted Japan's surrender document?"

"Yes."

"Your brother-in-law had high respect for the general," Mother said.

"Apparently the Northern soldiers were caught by surprise," Little Aunt said. "They didn't believe that anyone in his right mind would dare to land his soldiers on the muddy beach where the soldiers would be swallowed up by the soggy mud."

"So?"

"That means," Little Aunt said, "our soldiers will be in Seoul within days."

"Wonder what they will do with Hi-Bum," Mother gasped.

"He will take care of himself," Little Aunt said. "Now you have to take care of yourself and Hi-Dong."

"Why us?"

"There will be a lot of anger toward those, ties with the communists," Little Aunt said. "Those who were hurt by them will want revenge."

"Does that mean us?" Mother asked "Because of Hi-Bum?"

"Yes, those who lost their loved ones will not care who is who," Little Aunt said. "They will want revenge."

Mother blankly stared at the wall without response.

"They will be after you and Hi-Dong because of Hi-Bum. I suggest you two come and stay with us until things cool down."

"I don't know," Mother sighed.

"Mother," I said. "Why don't we go and stay with Little Aunt?"

"What about your father if he comes home?" Mother asked.

"Don't waste your time waiting for your husband," Little Aunt said. "The communists are too busy looking after their own lives, and they wouldn't have time to take care of their prisoners. The easiest thing for them is to shoot their prisoners dead."

"I guess you are right," Mother sighed. "But ..."

After minutes of pleading by Little Aunt's *Please come and stay with us* and Mother's wavering response *I don't know ...*, Little Aunt stood up and left.

"I will be waiting for you," she said as walked out of the room.

"Thank you for thinking of us," Mother said following her sister to the door.

Mother's decision was to stay home, and pray and wait for Father.

A day after Little Aunt's visit, we heard a faint rumbling of artillery shells exploding, not from the north, but this time from the west, where the port of Inchon was. With each passing day the sound of artillery became louder. From the balcony, I saw American bombers, flying in formation high in the sky, dropping bombs as they flew toward the western part of Seoul. As days passed, I heard the sound of battle approaching closer to Seoul: machine gunfire, the sounds of artillery shells whistling by and exploding, combat planes diving down, shooting, and flying up. I also saw combat planes flying over our house. One dived down toward an area less than a mile from our house, dropping a bomb. Seconds later I heard the explosion and saw the flames shooting up toward the sky. Mother and I went down to our basement for cover. We were afraid that they might bomb our house by mistake.

That evening there was a lull in the battle sounds, and I saw no airplanes in the air. I was curious to find out what was going on in the streets, and against Mother's advice I walked outside to find out. The street was quiet. Shops were closed. Only a few people walked on the street. I saw Northern soldiers and armored cars rushing by. They looked all tense. I got a little nervous seeing those tense-looking soldiers and rushed back home. When I came home, Mother was sitting by the window looking somber.

"Are you angry at me because I went out?" I asked.

"No," she said. "Hi-Bum is home. Packing."

"Packing to run away?"

"I guess so."

"Should I go upstairs and offer my help?'

"No, leave him alone," Mother said. "A lot of things must be going on in his mind."

While we were talking, Hi-Bum came to the living room with a bag in his hand. He looked sad. Mother stood and walked toward him. Hi-Bum bowed his head, avoiding Mother's gaze.

"Please take good care of yourself," he said in a subdued tone.

"Where are you going?" Mother asked.

"I don't know," Hi-Bum said. "But it's time for me to say goodbye."

"Why don't you stay for a while," Mother said. "I will get something for you to eat."

"Thank you," he said. "But I must go."

Mother lowered her head in silence.

"Mother," Hi-Bum said. "I am sorry for all the problems that I have caused you."

"I know you didn't mean to," Mother sighed.

"Please take good care of yourself," Hi-Bum said looking at Mother with tearful eyes.

Then he straightened himself, turned around, walked toward the door, and marched out of the house. We followed behind him. He walked down the steps as we stood at the porch watching him go. As he turned the corner, he did not look back like Kwidong had done weeks ago. He just walked away.

15. Seoul is free again but not for us

Daihan-mingook, Mansei—Long live, Republic of Korea. The people shouted as they marched on the streets of Seoul. *Our government is back to Seoul. We are free again!*

The marching North Korean soldiers, with their machine-like precision and with rifles on their shoulders, were gone. The pictures of their smiling leader, Kim Il-Sung, hanging wherever we turned our heads were torn down by our young people, who had been holed up in attics and underground hideaways for the last three months. Those pictures were set on fire, were turned into flames and finally into ashes. On the heap of the ashes, and amidst the stench of corpses in the streets, the people walked the streets of Seoul shouting *Mansei*. But their joy was mingled with sorrow for those who had lost their loved ones and those whose houses were destroyed by the bombs from the air and the artillery shells from the ground. There was also great hatred toward the communists who caused this unnecessary tragedy. Those people who had actively supported the North Korean regime during their seizure of Seoul were marked. Soon they and their families would be harassed by the South Korean police and neighbors.

It was a sinister period for us. People's emotions were tense. They had lost family members. Their homes had been destroyed. They wanted revenge against those who had supported the communists. They wanted revenge against those families who had harbored the communist sympathizers. And as Little Aunt had said, we were one of them.

Mother was worried about my safety. I was worried about our safety. Any day, an angry mob might tear down our front door, smash into our house with clubs in their hands, and beat us to death, screaming, *You communist beasts. You are not worthy to live.* Or any day the police might come, put us in handcuffs, and drag us to prison.

"Mother," I said, the day after our soldiers returned to Seoul. "I'm scared."

"I am too," Mother said. "Especially about you. A fourteen-year-old boy. Big enough to be handled like a man by police."

"Why don't we go and stay with Little Aunt?"

"Why don't you go alone?" Mother said.

"Why not together?"

Mother sighed.

"I'm not going without you," I said.

"I know, but ..."

"But what?"

"Your father," Mother said. "How would he feel if he finds no one at home?"

Isn't it better for him to find no one at home than to see our dead bodies? I thought. *Also I don't think he's alive anyway.* I stopped short of telling her that Father had probably been killed and that waiting for him would be useless.

"I just don't feel right going into hiding without waiting for your father," Mother said.

Should I tell her how I feel? Better for Father to find no one at home than to see our dead bodies? It's not the time to act with our feelings, but to act with our heads? But looking at Mother's face, it was not the time to reason but to agree with her way. So we waited for Father. We waited for Father's knocking at the door, saying, *Open the door, Yubo—Honey. I'm home.* We also dreaded hearing the crashing of the door by an angry mob. We dreaded the police banging at our door, like the Japanese police during World War II, and taking us away in handcuffs. But there was nothing we could do, but wait and pray.

We waited for days for Father's knocking at the door, but it did not come. We dreaded hearing the crashing of the door, but the mob did not come and harm us. We dreaded banging on the door by the police, like the Japanese police, any time of the day or the night. The police came, but they didn't bang.

Instead, they knocked only during the day. They came and questioned us trying to find Hi-Bum. We told them that he had left the day before Seoul was retaken, and that he never returned, but they did not believe us. They suspected that he was in hiding somewhere, and we knew his whereabouts. The police came several more times unannounced. They looked in the attic, searched the basement, checked under the floors, scoured the barn, and combed every possible place that a person could hide, but he was nowhere to be found. But they kept asking the same question over and over, *Where is your communist son?* Mother's answer was always the same, *I don't know, Sir.*

One day there was a knock at the door. I went to the door, Mother following me. A man in light-green uniform stood in front of us.

"I am Detective Lee from the Seoul Security Office," the man said. "I am here to find out where Chai Hi-Bum is."

"We don't know," Mother replied.

Detective Lee ignored Mother's reply. Then he smiled and looked at me.

"What's your name?"

"Hi-Dong," I said.

"Is Hi-Bum your brother?"

"Yes."

"Let me talk to you," he said inviting himself into the house.

"He does not know where his brother is," Mother said.

Detective Lee acted as if he did not hear her.

"Let's go to your father's office," he said looking up the stairway.

Apparently someone had told him where Father's office was. As we walked up the stairs, I heard Mother's pleading voice.

"Sir," she said, "Hi-Dong doesn't know where his brother is."

"Lady," he said sounding irritated. "I will soon find out."

"Please Sir," Mother pleaded as I opened the door to Father's office, "please don't hurt the innocent boy. He really does not know."

Once in the room, he closed the door. He also pulled down the window shades. He sat at Father's round table and told me to sit across from him.

"How old are you?" he asked sounding very friendly.

"I'm fourteen, Sir," I replied with my head down.

"Do you know where your father is?"

"I don't know, Sir," I said. "Mother and I have been waiting for him since two North Korean officers took him away two months ago."

He looked at me without saying a word.

"Didn't your brother work for the communists?" He asked.

"Yes, Sir."

"Didn't he find out where his father was?"

"Mother asked him," I said, "but he wasn't able to find out."

"Why not?"

"I don't know, Sir."

"What a worthless son he is," he scoffed. "Where is he?"

"I don't know, Sir."

"So you don't know where your Father is," he chuckled. "And you don't know where your traitor brother is."

"No, Sir."

"OK, young man," his voice turned firmer. "I will not punish you if you tell me the truth."

"Yes, Sir."

"Where is your brother?" His voice turned threatening.

"I really don't know, Sir," I said, my voice trembling.

"You look like an honest boy, but you are lying," he said. "I talked to your neighbors, and one of your neighbors said that he saw your brother sneaking out of your house last night."

"He is lying," I said. "Sir, my father told me never to lie."

He looked straight into my eyes without a word. He reached to his shirt pocket and pulled out a pencil.

"Put your left hand on the desk," he said.

I put my hand on the desk wondering, *What is he going to do?* He put the pencil between my index and middle fingers and turned. It tickled a little, and I thought it was kind of fun. *Funny. What is he doing this for? I* wondered. But when he tightened my two fingers with his thick fingers and started turning the pencil, I cringed. It hurt. Really hurt.

"Please don't, Sir," I pleaded. "It hurts."

"That's good," he said. He squeezed my fingers harder. "Where's your brother?"

The pain was excruciating. I wished I knew where Brother was so that I could tell the detective and didn't have to go through this torture. But I did not know.

"I wish I knew," I said grimacing from pain. "But I really ... really don't know, Sir,"

I started to sweat from the pain. After receiving the same answer several more times, he loosened his grip. I felt so relieved and my shoulders stooped.

"Thank you. Thank you very much, Sir," I said, taking a deep breath.

He looked at me for a few seconds without saying a word.

Then he said with his voice softening, "Young man, I have a son like you, and I am sorry to hurt you. But my job is to find your traitor brother."

He patted my back as if he was really sorry. He told me that as a citizen of South Korea, I had an obligation to report Hi-Bum's whereabouts. Then he opened the door and walked down the stairs.

After massaging my fingers to ease the pain, I came out of the room and saw Mother sitting in the middle of the stairway. Shaking and staring at me with frightened round eyes. Her face was white as a ghost. As I approached her, she tried to say something, but no words came out. I sat next to her, holding her shaking hands. I wanted to pray to God, but I didn't think God would come to our aid anyway. He didn't before. I carefully led her to her bed and sat next to her until she became calm.

After the detective's visit, there was a lull. No police visited us for a week. Instead, three of Mother's church friends visited her, and Mother shared with them what the detective had done to her son, Hi-Dong, a week before. They had pity on me. They asked me to come and sit in the middle of them. One lady put her hand on my right knee, another lady's hand on my back, and the third lady's hand on my left knee. Mother sat in front of me. They prayed their long prayers, each taking a turn.

"Please give Hi-Dong strength to go through this trial ..."

"Let Hi-Dong know that You, who even look after lilies of the field that perish within days, will keep him in Your loving care through this trial ..."

"Let Hi-Dong know that You are training him to be an instrument of Your peace ..."

"Let Hi-Dong learn that by trusting in You that he can go through the valley of the shadow of death and come out strong to face whatever the future has for him …"

I sat there feeling trapped by these well-meaning ladies and hoping that they would stop these long prayers so that I could go out, breathe the fresh air, and jump around.

Mother also worried that the reason why the police did not check on us for days was because Hi-Bum might have been arrested.

"The police must have arrested Hi-Bum," Mother said. "Otherwise, they wouldn't stop banging at our door."

Mother's attention now was on Hi-Bum. She recalled horror stories of how the communists in prison were treated. How they were beaten, hung upside down with their feet tied to the ropes on the ceiling for hours at a time. How the police pricked the prisoners with needles poking between their fingernails and flesh. How the police put their burning cigarette butts out on prisoners' faces. Mother spent much time in her prayer closet. Praying. Praying for Hi-Bum's safety. Praying that Hi-Bum would be treated humanely if he were in prison. Praying that Hi-Bum would finally see the light and turn to God for his salvation.

Then one afternoon a policeman, Officer Kim Sang-Wook, came and asked us to go to the neighborhood police station which was a ten-minute walk from home. We followed behind him, Mother and I glancing at each other wondering what the police were going to do to us. When we entered the station, a policeman with thin eyes and the flat nose sat with his feet on his desk, smoking a cigarette dangling down his small mouth. The smoke from his cigarette gently floated up toward the ceiling. We stood at the entrance behind Officer Kim, wondering what they were going to do to us.

"Captain," Officer Kim saluted to the thin-eyed police with his feet on his desk. "I brought Mother and a brother of Chai Hi-Bum."

"The mother of the traitor and his brother?" Captain said in his squeaky voice, pulling the cigarette out of his mouth. He glared at us.

"Yes, Sir," Officer Kim replied.

"You, two, stand over there." Captain pointed the wall next to the door.

Officer Kim guided us to the wall. I stood there with my head down, wondering. *Is he going to order Officer Kim to give us the pencil torture like Detective Lee did? Or is he going to have Officer Kim to prick our fingers with a needle? Or is he going to hang us on the ceiling upside down with our feet tied to a rope, and scare us to confess? ... Oh God, I prayed. Whatever they may do, please let them do it to me. But not to my mother.*

"So was your husband a Christian minister?" Captain asked Mother with a hint of smile on his face.

"Yes," Mother said looking down the floor.

"And does your Christian minister have a communist son?"

Mother did not respond putting her folded hands over her bosom as in prayer.

"Answer me, Woman," Captain's voice turned loud. "Is your communist son a Christian?"

"No." Mother's soft resigned voice.

Captain's voice turned cynical.

"How can a minister, who can't save his own son, save others to be Christians?" Captain laughed, pointing his cigarette finger at Mother .

"And you told my men," Captain chuckled, "that your husband was kidnapped by the communists?"

"Yes." Mother's answer.

"And your communist son didn't do anything to save him?"

"No."

"And do you think we are that stupid to believe you?" Captain shouted in his high-pitched, squeaky voice. "You ... an old wrinkled liar."

How can he call my mother a liar? I was upset and wanted to shout at him. But I also knew what would happen if I did. I was angry and fearful at the same time.

"She is telling you the truth, Sir," I said.

"Shut up, you, brat," Captain growled at me with his thin piercing eyes. "You, come over here."

As I walked over and stood by his desk, Officer Kim followed and stood next to me.

"Boy," he said. "Look straight at my eyes."

From my childhood, Mother had reminded me not to look straight at elders' eyes as a sign of respect, and I followed Mother's advice. And it had become my habit. When Captain asked me to look straight at his eyes, I just couldn't. I just kept my head down.

"I told you to look straight at me," Captain shouted.

"Captain," I heard Mother speak, "he does that as a sign of respect as I taught him as a child."

"Shut up, you, an old wrinkled liar," the captain said. "I didn't ask you."

He is again calling my mother a liar. How can he say such a thing to the greatest, the most honest human being in the world? I straightened myself, looked at him straight in his eyes, and said in a defiant tone, "She is not a liar, Sir."

"Are you talking back to me?" Captain shouted standing. Then he reached over the desk and slapped me with his calloused hand. The force of his hand made me jerk.

"Please." I heard Mother's pleading.

"Shut up," the captain said sitting down and lighting a cigarette. "You are all communists and liars. Your husband is a communist in a preacher's garb. He is not kidnapped, but escaped to the north. You know where your communist son is, and you don't tell us."

"OK, you brat," Captain said. "Where's your brother?"

"I don't know, Sir."

"I am getting sick of listening to your lies," he said. "Where is your worthless communist brother?"

"He really doesn't know, Captain," Mother spoke behind me.

"Shut up. I didn't ask you," Captain screamed. "That does it."

"Officer Kim." Captain made eye contact with Officer Kim.

I saw Officer Kim pulling out his revolver from the holster. I heard him cock the revolver. Then he placed the barrel against my temple. It felt cold and hard.

"Where's your brother?" Captain asked.

"I don't know, Sir." That's only answer I knew.

"Where's your brother?" Captain asked me again.

Is there something that I can say that will make the captain stop asking the same question? I asked myself.

"The day before the U.N. soldiers entered Seoul," I said, "Brother came home and took a few of his belongings and left us. He didn't tell us where he was going."

"I didn't ask you to explain," Captain yelled. "Now, the last time … Where's your brother?"

I closed my eyes ignoring his question. *What's the use of answering? He's not going to believe me anyway.*

"That does it." Captain sounded final. "Detective Kim … Go ahead."

I heard the pulling of the trigger and the barrel of the revolver jerking on my temple. I imagined the bullet speeding through my head, making holes through my skull and flying out the other side, covered with blood and brain matter. But I felt nothing. I heard no blasting sound of the bullet. Instead, a dead silence.

Then I heard a voice, *Oh my God …* Mother's voice. I heard someone falling. I turned. Mother was on the floor. Slouched. Staring at me with her sunken round eyes. The same eyes I saw when I had walked out of Father's office with Detective Lee a week ago. Her bent arms reaching out toward me. Trembling. I rushed to her, knelt down, and put my arm around her shoulder. She stared at me with round eyes as if she was seeing a ghost.

"Mother, I'm OK," I said. "I'm alive."

She didn't say a word. She stared at me with her mouth drooping open.

"Mother, I'm OK," I repeated. "I'm alive."

I heard a creaking sound of a chair. I turned. It was Captain getting out of his chair, dousing his cigarette butt on the ash tray. He did not look at us. But he looked solemn—not harsh and scornful. He walked to the back door, opened it, and walked out without a word.

That night in bed, I was very depressed. Questions swirled around in my mind keeping me from falling asleep. *Why does the world have to be this way? Why does such a kind and caring person like Mother have to suffer so much?* I was frustrated that I could not help her. I wished that she could unload all her burdens on my young body so that she could have some repose. I was a fourteen year old boy. She was a burdened, weary fifty-six year old woman. It would have been much easier for me to carry the weight of her pain and suffering on my back.

I also wondered why I was born. I did not ask to be born into this painful world, and to see Mother suffer. I was tired of seeing her harassed by the Japanese, South Koreans and North Koreans. I was frustrated at feeling helpless. I also felt sorry for myself and Mother, for we belonged nowhere. I was angry at Hi-Bum, who had brought us so much suffering for his political stand. I was angry at Father for being a Christian minister, who had brought suffering on himself and the family because of his faith in God. I was angry at God for not coming to the aid of His children. I thought that God would reward those who believed and honored Him while punishing those who ignored Him. What I witnessed was the opposite. The communists and the Japanese who scorned Him prospered while those who followed Him suffered. God seemed far, far away!

16. Back home from the police station

After returning home from the police station, Mother stayed in bed for days except when she fixed me breakfast, lunch and supper. I wished that I could cook breakfast for Mother, cook lunch for Mother and cook supper for Mother so that she could rest and recover from the terrible experience. But as a fourteen-year-old boy, I knew how to start the charcoal fire, boil water, and even cut vegetables and skin a fish, but I didn't know how to cook because Mother didn't let me. She said that a woman's job was to cook, and a man's duty was to earn money for his family. When I was a child, she told me if I cooked, my male organ would shrivel to nothing and I wouldn't be able to be a father. I asked her, *What has the male organ to do with being a father?* Her answer was, *You'll find out when you become a man.*

Before the Korean War, my house was like a flea market. People visited us day and night—sometimes from the country sides—to talk to Father for advice and to receive comfort from Mother. But during the war my house turned into a haunted house. People avoided us because of Hi-Bum, and because they did not want to be on the police list as those who visited a home that harbored a communist and that was under police surveillance. But my Little Aunt visited us once a week and kept company with Mother.

When Little Aunt found out our experience at the police station, she walked a mile-and-a-half from her home on Mondays, Wednesdays and Fridays to cook for us and stay over for lunch. She didn't come on Sundays because she didn't want to sit and listen to Mother's Bible reading, a long prayer and a testimonial. Little Aunt said that Christian stuff was for the dogs and Buddhists were lazy bums like her husband who sat on his bottom in a lotus position with his eyes closed for hours at a time. Also, Little Aunt brought news from around the city and the country. Without her we would be in the dark.

In the winter of 1950, the North Korean soldiers marched southward again, this time with the support of the Red Chinese army, over hundreds of thousands strong. Unlike the time when the North had invaded the South on June 24, 1950, the radio provided us with the day-to-day battle report. Unprepared to fight the massive Chinese army, the U.N. forces were in full retreat. Within weeks, on January 4, 1951, Seoul would again be in the iron grip of the communists.

It was early December, 1950. The outside was covered with fresh snow fallen the night before. It was very cold with the temperature hovering around 20 degrees F. Little Aunt visited us. We huddled around the stove in the living room. I wished that Father, the pillar of the family, was with us to guide us in this time of uncertainty. I wished that Hi-Bum would appear and advise us what to do.

"Sister," Little Aunt said to Mother. "What are you going to do?"

"I don't know," Mother sighed. "I'm so weary of living. I don't want to think about it."

Little Aunt reached out and held Mother's hand. With Father gone, all the family's burdens were on Mother's shoulders. I wished I could help her, but I didn't know how. All I did was just sit, listen and watch her.

"Do you think Hi-Bum will ever come home and help you?" Little Aunt asked.

"I don't think so," Mother said. "You know Hi-Bum was not happy with the communists. He's probably in hiding somewhere."

"Do you think we will ever get to see him?" I asked.

"I sure hope so," Mother sighed. "But with the way the North and the South are fighting, I'm not sure."

I felt sorry for Hi-Bum. He had wanted the South Korean government to clean up its act and serve its people. He had thought that Kim Il-Sung's regime in the North represented the true ideals of communism. Unfortunately, he was wrong. He found out that Kim's regime was a repressive dictatorship, not the government that he had envisioned from the study of Marx's writings. Hi-Bum was stuck between two opposing forces. What was he going to do? He didn't belong anywhere, neither the South nor the North.

"Anyway," Mother said, "it's not the time to worry about Hi-Bum. We have to figure some way to go south."

"Why don't you ask Uncle Suk-Moon?" Little Aunt said. "My husband told me the other day his family would be heading to Busan."

Uncle Suk-Moon, Father's cousin, was a successful businessman with many connections. He and Little Aunt's husband had been good friends since high school a long time ago.

"I guess he can," Mother said. "But I'm reluctant."

"Why?" she asked.

"We have not been in touch with them for a long time," Mother said. "I don't feel comfortable to go and ask for his help now ... like a leech"

"Leech or bloodsucker, I don't care," Little Aunt said. "I am going to see his wife after I leave here."

"Don't worry," Mother said. "I'll pray for God's guidance."

"Oh, my poor Sister." Her voice turned loud and her eyes rounded. "Haven't you learned a lesson yet?"

"What lesson?" Mother straightened herself and looked at Little Aunt.

"When you tried to convert me to your Christian god years ago," Little Aunt said with a hint of smile, "didn't you say your loving god rewarded those who believed in him and punished those who didn't?"

"Yes?"

"What happened to you who had turned to the Christian god?" Little Aunt asked. "And what happened to me who had stayed away from him?"

"What?"

"Either your god is taking a long nap," Little Aunt chuckled, "or he is dead."

"Are you trying to make me angry," Mother said, in her usual quiet, but unhappy voice, "like you used to when we were kids?"

"No, Sister, I'm serious. Very serious." Little Aunt said. "Since you turned to the Christian god, he took away your three beautiful babies before they could walk and talk. He took away Hi-Seung. He took away your husband. And your brightest son, Hi-Bum, became a communist and rewarded you with tons of heartache, and he is gone. Now look at me. I stayed away from your Christian god. I still have my five kids. All grown up, healthy and happy. They are also well-to-do."

Mother lowered her head with her folded hands over her bosom. *How can Little Aunt talk that way about God? Isn't she scared to go to hell and sizzle there for eternity?* I thought. *On the other hand, she is right. To me Mother is the greatest Christian, and what she got so far has been pain and suffering. It is not what I learned from Sunday School. The teachers said that God rewarded those who followed Jesus, but punished those who denied Him.*

"I'm sorry, Sister, for being so rude," Little Aunt said. "But I have been so upset to see my sister suffer since you married Hi-Dong's Christian father. Especially when I remember our childhood. We had such a happy and fun time then. But now when I see what is happening to you, it hurts me so much."

Little Aunt's bulldog face really looked sad with her eyes drooping when she spoke.

"Thank you, Kyung-Ja." Mother raised her head and looked at her sister. "My reward is in heaven. That's my true home."

"I sure hope so," Little Aunt said. "You have been my close friend since my birth. You have given all your life in service for others. I hope there is really heaven and hell and that God will reward you abundantly."

Doesn't Little Aunt believe in heaven and hell? My curiosity got roused.

"Little Aunt," I called.

She jumped and turned to me with her round eyes. Apparently she wasn't aware that I was in the room.

"Yes, Young Man?" She said, a smile returning to her face.

"Don't you believe in heaven and hell?" I asked.

She looked at Mother and turned to me.

"I don't believe in heaven and hell," Little Aunt said. "But your mother believes in heaven and hell."

"Who's right?" I asked. "Mother or you?"

"When it comes to believing," she said, "there's neither right nor wrong since nobody knows."

"Your Little Aunt is right," Mother chimed in. "But to those who believe, God gives them power to overcome life's trials and tribulations like I have been going through."

"How did we get on this subject?" Little Aunt chuckled. "It's getting too deep for my knuckle-head, Sister."

"We were talking about going South," Mother said.

"That's right. About Uncle Suk-Moon," Little Aunt said, standing up. "I'd better hurry and see his wife on my way back home. We don't have too much time. Those Red soldiers may come down here any day."

"Thanks, Kyung-Ja," Mother said. "But don't insist."

"You know who I am," Little Aunt said walking out to the door. "I will let you know as soon as I find out."

We followed behind her to say goodbye and thanks.

Little Aunt came the next morning looking a little sad. She said that Uncle Suk-Moon could have only one more person because the boat he had rented was already way over its capacity. He feared what would happen to the overloaded boat in a storm on the Yellow Sea, hugging the west coast of Korea. Little Aunt and Mother talked a while and decided to visit friends to find one more spot. After lunch, they left the house. While they were gone, I studied the map of Korea hanging in my room, trying to figure out how far Busan was from Seoul. On the map I also saw Cheju Island, the largest island located in the southwestern part of Korea. I figured out that the direct distance from Seoul to Busan was 200 miles; Seoul to Inchon, 20 miles; and Inchon to Cheju Island, 260 miles. Since the boat would travel from Inchon southward along the western coast and then eastward to Busan, I figured that the boat would have to travel more than 300 miles to Busan, but a train would travel 200 miles. I wished that I would be able to ride on a boat so that I could see fishing boats catching fish and sandy beaches along the way.

In the evening Mother returned home with a smile.

"Guess what?" Mother said.

"What?" I replied.

"Yung-Suk's mother wants you to go with them to Busan," Mother said.

"Me alone?"

"Yes," Mother said.

"On a boat?" I asked, excitement rising.

"No," Mother said. "On a train."

I was disappointed, but I was glad that I would travel with Yung-Suk's family. Yung-Suk had been my friend since childhood. His father was a minister, who had also been kidnapped by the communists like my father. And for all my years Yung-Suk's mother had loved me as her own. Now she volunteered to take me along. How nice to be going with my good friend and his sister Yung-Ja.

"Can we go together with them?" I said.

"It would be nice," Mother said. "Unfortunately, she has just enough space for her family, but she will squeeze you in with them."

"What about Little Aunt?" It suddenly dawned on me that I didn't find out what her family would do.

"Poor Kyung-Ja," Mother said. "She has to stay behind to look after her in-laws. They are in their seventies and can't even walk outside without someone helping them."

I felt sad leaving my favorite aunt behind. I hoped that she would be more careful with her mouth in front of the communists if they entered Seoul so that I could see her often when peace returned to our country and when we were back in Seoul.

As days passed, the news on the war front became more ominous. The massive Red Chinese army was steadily pushing southward toward Seoul. South Korean and U.N. soldiers were in full retreat. Within weeks Seoul might be in the hands of the communists, but Mother did not seem to be concerned. She just went about her daily chores: cooking, sewing, reading the Bible, and going into her prayer closet for prayer. I wondered, *Has she decided to go south for my sake when she'd prefer to stay home and wait for Father and Hi-Bum? I am sure she doesn't want to leave her house, where she has raised her children and has lived through joys and sorrows. I am sure that she wants to stay until God calls her Home. But she is leaving because of me.*

I knew that a lot of things were going through Mother's mind. I decided not to bother her with my questions. Instead, I decided to let her be while I waited for the departure day when Mother and I would be separated for days until we would be together again in Busan.

17. Getting ready to go south

It was late December, 1950.

"I hear the Northern army is closing in on Seoul again," Mother said, "with the help of hundreds of thousands of Red Chinese soldiers."

"I know," I said.

"I am sure your father is with the Lord in heaven now," Mother said. "Now my job is to keep you safe."

I agreed with her that Father was dead because the communists were too busy for their own lives to bother to look after their prisoners.

Since Father was taken away, I had been feeling guilty for not giving my life to save him. I thought that Father walked down the steps between the two North Korean officers to attend a ministers' meeting that morning. I thought that Father would return home. Still, the feeling of guilt had dwelled within me since then. *Suppose I knew the truth, that he was kidnapped. Could I save him? There was no way I could knock those two officers down, but at least I could have tried. They would have knocked me down and shot me in the head with their pistols. But I could die feeling good knowing that I tried to save Father like my brother, Hi-Seung. Remember, Brother volunteered to join the Japanese army to save Father from the Japanese prison. I could have done the same thing. Given my life for Father. Anyway, the past is past. I cannot go back to the past and do things over. Think about what I have to do to help Mother to get ready to go south.*

What should we do with the house? What should we do with all the furniture? All the things that we have accumulated over the years? What should we take with us? How much can we take? All these questions burdened us, and we had to resolve them in three days.

House? There was nothing we could do but let it stand, hoping for the best. If the house turned to flames and then to ashes from a bomb from the sky, we would have to rebuild it on our return. Furniture? If the house stood, but vandals entered it, broke the windows and tore down the furniture, let them be. We would have to get new windows and buy new furniture. But what about the grandfather clock? Father's books? His clothes? What about the dear koi fish in the aquarium? My first impulse was to take the two koi fish—one gray and the other orange—to the river and let them swim away, but I didn't have the time for such a noble act. Mother and I agreed to let them swim in the aquarium as long as they could. Mother said to leave Father's office untouched, regardless of what might happen to it.

"Even his Bible?" I asked.

"Yes," Mother said. "That's my way of honoring him."

I didn't understand her. *Why not take his Bible? Why not take his pen and pencil set? Why not take his leather strap that he used to discipline us? Why not take his gold watch that the American missionary gave him? They are all small things. Why not take them with us in remembrance of him? I can read his Bible daily and remember his Sunday services: Father standing at the pulpit with the Bible in his hands, looking down at us with a smile, and reciting with a warm and clear voice, "God so loved the world that He gave His only begotten son. Whosoever believes in Him should not perish, but have everlasting life." I can keep his pen and pencil set at my desk and use them to write clearly—like his sermons—without wasting a word. I can wear his watch, and remember and follow his punctual nature. Ten o'clock is ten o'clock. Not a minute less. Not a minute more. Also, I can save his whip to discipline my kids when I get married and raise children. Like Father, I will tell my kids, "If you play with the electric fuse box, I will whip your calves three times."* All these things made good sense to me, but this wasn't the time to argue with Mother. Her feelings were more important than mine.

As Mother wanted, first we went to Father's office. I moved back Father's chair to the front of his desk. This was the chair where the detective sat to interrogate me weeks ago. I opened Father's closet to check whether everything was in order. I saw a necktie lying on the floor, picked it up and put it back on the necktie hanger. I saw the punishment whip lazily hanging down by the side of the closet. My right hand reached toward the whip to take it with me, but my left hand slapped my right hand saying, *Don't*. Mother dusted off Father's bookshelves with a rag. She knelt down in front of his shoe rack, picked up each shoe and wiped it off gently as if she was caring for a little infant. Then Mother went to Father's desk, picked up his Bible, and opened to chapter eleven in the book of Hebrews. Father's favorite chapter.

Now faith is the assurance of things hoped for, the conviction of things not seen. For by it the men of old received divine approval. By faith we understand that the world was created by the word of God so that what is seen was made out of things which do not appear. By faith ...

She laid the open Bible back down on his desk. We both stood in front of his desk silently with our eyes closed, Mother holding my hand. After a minute or so, we quietly closed his door and walked down the stairs.

Mother looked sad. She said that she was going to the market to get some fresh air. I thought it was a great idea.

"Mother," I said. "Why don't you go and have a bowl of ox tail soup so that you have energy to travel next Monday?"

"Maybe."

"Please do," I said. "I will do the moving while you are gone."

"I will bring a bowl of ox tail soup for you also," Mother said going out the door.

While she was away, I looked out the living room window reliving my happy childhood with Father, Brother Hi-Seung and Kwidong. But now Brother passed away from his injury. Father was taken away by the North Korean Communists. Kwidong was given away to a dog warden because we didn't have enough food—even for people. Tomorrow I would be saying goodbye to my home. My home, sweet home.

I had known all along that I had to leave home. But when Mother returned with a steaming bowl of ox tail soup and a bowl of rice, and put them on the table with a dish of *kimchee* for me, I felt sad. I realized that this would be my last meal at home. After the meal when Mother said, *Get ready*, my shoulders sagged. My heart cried out, *I don't want to leave home. My home, sweet home. Also I don't want leave home not knowing, for sure, whether Father will come back to us. What will he do, if he ever returns and finds no one home?* But my brows frowned, *Don't waste your time dreaming. Father's not going to return. He's in heaven with God. Don't pain your mother. Go to your room and pack.*

I trudged up the stairs. The tick-tocking of the grandfather clock echoed through the hall way. I would be leaving home, but the grandfather clock would stay behind tick-tocking with no one listening. I opened the door to my room. Tomorrow I would hold its round door knob with my hand, and close it, maybe for the last time. I looked around my room. The drawing of Tarzan, my hero, that I had drawn with a crayon hung on the wall facing my pillow; monkeys looked down at Tarzan with their scared eyes. The sling shot that Hi-Seung had made for me hung on a hook by my desk. I saw a small black and white picture of Hi-Seung holding my hand in one corner of my desk. The family picture was next to Hi-Seung's. *What should I take tomorrow? Certainly the slingshot. Certainly the pictures of Hi-Seung and the family. Should I take the drawing of Tarzan? No. I can draw another one sometime.* I opened my closet. I saw comic books stacked up in one corner hidden by my pants. *Should I take them with me? Just a few? No. I am a high school student now. Read short stories, novels, and biographies of famous people instead.* Then behind my clothes, a brown leather collar and leash hanging down on a hook caught my eyes. Kwidong's collar and leash. I pulled them out and held them in my hand. *Should I take them?* My head said, *Don't look back. March on with time. You have much to do ahead of you.* But my heart said, *Why not keep them in memory of my best friend?* I looked at them, recalling the fun times I had with Kwidong. *Should I take them or leave them?* I couldn't make up my mind.

Day after day, the communist soldiers, with tanks and artillery on the ground and planes in the air, were closing in on Seoul. Soon they would enter the city in mass with tanks rumbling through the streets and houses going up in flames from the bombs from the sky, and the second cycle of the communist siege would unfold. But this time the government-run radio told us the truth. *The Red Army is moving south ...* And we had time to plan and escape from their ruthless grip. We would be in the south waiting to return home.

It was a cold, dreary December morning. Before dawn, I said goodbye to my home and Mother. I walked toward Yung-Suk's home with a backpack on my back and a bag in my hand. In the bottom of my backpack, I put the brown leather collar and leash. I wished that I had a picture of Kwidong to keep with me for the rest of my life, but I had none.

It would be my first journey all alone without Mother. Mother said we would be together in Busan in a week. But I was worried. Mother would come in an LST, landing ship tank, an easy target of the enemy air planes and torpedo boats. She would be sailing along the coastline of the Yellow Sea for the four-hundred mile journey that might take days or weeks depending on the ocean weather. In December the waves were high, and the wind strong. *Will the winter storm swallow a big ship like the LST? I don't think so.* But I was still worried.

While walking toward Yung-Suk's house, I wondered what would happen to my house, furniture, the grandfather clock, the koi fish, clothes, the kitchen utensils, many games, the desks and comic books. They were all left in the house with the doors and the windows tightly shut and the curtains drawn. Mother would lock the front door with a heavy steel lock before she left.

Will the North Korean soldiers smash into the house, throw everything out on the yard, pile them up, light a match, watch the flames turn our belongings to gray ash, and use my house as their office space like the Japanese police had done? What about the bombs from the sky? Will the U.N. planes bomb our house, reducing it to rubble? I kept turning back to look at my house. Maybe, for the last time. Then I thought of Hi-Seung. His words, *You are Tarzan in the human jungle. Strong and unafraid.* I also remembered the words of my high school math teacher, who not only taught us math but also peppered us with the words of wisdom, *Remember, time moves only in one direction—to the future. Do not look back, but always march forward with time.*

I walked with my body upright and my eyes looking straight ahead. I hastened my pace. As I was turning a corner, my feet felt like two icicles. They didn't move. My head said, *Don't act like a boneless bean curd. You are Tarzan in the human jungle. Don't look back. Move forward.* But my body thought otherwise. My head turned toward my house. My two-story brick house. I looked at the front door. It was shut tightly. I looked at the windows. All the curtains were drawn clear to the bottom. The curtains that Mother had made and was very proud of. I looked at the balcony where I used to look out at the changing scene of the seasons. From spring to summer. Summer to fall. Fall to winter. Back to spring. Year after year. I remembered Mother's words, *Man's life is like seasons …* I wondered, *When will I be able to stand at the balcony and look at majestic Mount Nam San, the persimmon trees, and the golden forsythia in full bloom as in the times of old? Maybe never.* I resumed my walk toward Yung-Suk's house. With my body upright and my eyes looking straight ahead. I hastened the pace.

When I came to Yung-Suk's house, his mother welcomed me.

"Oh, Hi-Dong," Mrs. Park said. "I'm glad you're going with us."

"Thank you, Mrs. Park," I said.

"Are you nervous" she asked, "Not going with your mother?"

"A little," I said.

"Everything will be OK," she said. "You'll be with your mother in a week."

"Thank you."

"We should be ready to go in an hour," Mrs. Park said. "Go and see Yung-Suk. He's in his room."

When I went to his room, he was busy packing.

"Where are you going to stay in Busan?" I asked.

"Dr. Lee's house," he said. "He's my father's friend. He offered us one of the rooms in his hospital."

"Do you think there will be enough room for me?"

I thought the one room with Yung-Suk, his mother, his sister Yung-Ja and myself would be too small for four of us.

"We'll find out when we get there," he said. "But don't worry. It'll be only a week before your mother will be in Busan."

As we were talking, his mother called, "Are you ready?"

"Yes, Mother," he replied shoving in few books in the bag.

"Hurry up," she said. "We're ready to go."

Yung-Suk picked up his duffel bag and a backpack. We walked to the front door.

"I'm glad you are going with us," Yung-Ja said.

"Thanks," I said.

"I'm going to sit next to you in the train," she said teasingly. "Then I'll get to see your cute bow legs."

Over the years I had felt Yung-Ja, two years older than I, liked me, and I felt close to her like a sister. Whenever she saw me coming, she teased me saying, *There comes Hi-Dong with cute bow legs?*

"Do you like them better than your straight legs like arrows?" I responded. "I'll be happy to exchange."

"Me with your bow legs?" She said looking down at her legs giggling.

"Children, it's not the right time to make fun at each other," Mrs. Park scolded us. "We have a long journey ahead."

"I'm sorry," I apologized.

"Let's get going," Mrs. Park said while walking out to the door.

"Yung-Suk, lock the door," Mrs. Park said handing him the keys. "Be sure to lock both the top and the bottom locks. We may never get to come back, but who knows."

Never get to come back. What a terrible thought. Never get to come to my home. Never get to come back to the place where I had so much fun with Hi-Seung, Kwidong and friends. I turned my head toward my house for one more time, but the trees and houses blocked my view.

18. On a train to Busan

When we arrived at the Seoul Train Station, we hurried past the crowd and rushed to the platform. A coal-fired black locomotive with half a dozen freight cars, that had been used to haul cows and pigs, waited for us. I saw people climbing upon the roofs of the train. A swarm of people sat on the roofs with belongings on their sides. *Aren't they afraid of falling down? I was nervous. Especially when the train moves? What are they going to do if it rains or snows? What are they going to do if a strong wind blows? Do they have handrails that they can hold onto? What are they going to do when the train enters a tunnel? I hope they keep their heads low so that no one will get his head smashed by the concrete wall.* As I was worrying about the people on the roofs, I heard Yung-Ja's voice.

"Which car should we ride in?" Yung-Ja asked.

"There's less of a crowd in the rear," Yung-Suk said.

We rushed to the rear train. A swarm of people were at the entrance elbowing to get in.

"Push," Yung-Suk said, using his elbows like spears as he tried to carve a path for us to the front.

"No," Mrs. Park chided Yung-Suk. "Everyone's in the same boat as we are. We must wait for our turn."

"Mother," Yung-Suk said, "there's no line. It's everyone for himself here."

"We wait," Mrs. Park's voice was firm, and Yung-Suk stood back, his eyes focused on the door.

Our turn seemed to take forever, and not everyone was as thoughtful as Mrs. Park. People pushed in front of us one after the other. Finally, there was a breathing space where we could get on board. We showed our boarding passes to the train attendant standing at the door. Yung-Suk and I helped Mrs. Park step on board. Yung-Ja hopped up by herself. Yung-Suk let me go up first, he following behind and pushed me forward. Inside the train, I saw families huddled together in little circles with their belongings as walls. To our surprise the place wasn't full. Mrs. Park looked around from one end to the other.

"Mother, I see a space by the wall over there in the middle," Yung-Suk said. "We'd better hurry and pick the space before the mass of people rush in."

Mrs. Park was not in her usual commander-in-chief mode. She did what Yung-Suk suggested and followed him. We followed behind her to the middle to the empty space that was more than big enough for several families. Yung-Suk eyed a pretty girl in a high school uniform in one corner. With her sat an old wrinkled woman with gray hair, an old man with a long white beard, and a middle-aged lady.

Yung-Suk said, pointing to the group "Let's sit over there."

We followed Yung-Suk and put our bags around as a wall next to the group and sat. Yung-Suk, a typical fifteen-year-old, sat where he could have a nice view of the pretty girl.

"Thank goodness, we made it." Mrs. Park breathed a sigh of relief as she sat down. "Glad we came early."

Yung-Suk turned his head toward the pretty girl. Yung-Ja looked at him with scolding eyes and squeezed Yung-Suk's hand, but he ignored her. He kept looking at her. I turned around to see the pretty girl and saw her head bowed, probably to avoid Yung-Suk's stare.

Finally Mrs. Park whispered in a low voice. "Yung-Suk," she said. "Stop."

Yung-Suk sheepishly looked at his mother with a grin.

"It's cold, Mother," Yung-Ja said.

I nodded my head in agreement. It was cold. I could see my breath coming out of my mouth. Yung-Suk snorted air from his nostrils, making puffs of vapor. It reminded me of the captain in the police station glaring at me with a cigarette between his fingers. I wondered what Yung-Suk would say if I told him about the captain.

"The body heat from the people will get this place warmer when the doors are closed," Mrs. Park said. "Get a blanket out of your bag and wrap it around you."

The train must have been used to transport cows. The cold air mixed with the smell of the cows' dung filled my lungs.

"It stinks in here," Yung-Suk blurted out, flopping down on the floor next to the metal wall.

I flopped next to him.

"Why don't you plug your nose with cotton?" Yung-Ja said. "I'll get it from my bag."

"Then I'll have to breathe this foul smell with my mouth," Yung-Suk said in his usual loud voice. "This place smells worse than an unflushed toilet."

The pretty girl glanced at him with a hint of a smile. I said to myself, *Oh. Oh. He is going to be slapped by his mother speaking so crude in front of the girl and all these strangers.* I eyed Mrs. Park. Her eyes had narrowed and her right hand was in the air. I waited for her hand to come flying, at the speed of sound, smack onto Yung-Suk's right cheek at any moment. I knew her quick temper. Much quicker than my father. I had seen her many times beating Yung-Suk in her room with a wooden rod and slapping him with her calloused hand and Yung-Suk begging for mercy. Scared as a child, I used to run away home in bare feet with my shoes in my hands.

"Where are we going to pee and poop?" Yung-Suk blurted out.

I looked at Mrs. Park. Her eyes turned narrower. *Oh, oh, any time now.*

"I'm sure the train will stop along the way," Yung-Ja said.

"Why do I have to be cooped up in this train all day long?" Yung-Suk asked.

"Shut your mouth," Mrs. Park broke her silence and shouted aloud, glaring at him with her thin eyes.

All the heads around us turned toward us, including the pretty girl. Yung-Suk cringed. My body also tensed. *Mrs. Park, Please don't slap him in this crowd. In your house it's OK, but not here.*

"You are my man," the old man with the long white beard said looking at Yung-Suk with a broad smile. "I was just like you. Tough and crude."

"You were worse than that young man," the old wrinkled woman chimed in looking at Yung-Suk. "Much worse."

"Now look at me," the old man said with a broad smile. "Wise and gentle."

"Oh Lord, have mercy," the old wrinkled woman responded, rubbing her hands.

I watched Mrs. Park wondering what she was going to do next. Her narrowed eyes turned soft. She glanced at the old man. She seemed sad. Maybe, the old man reminded her of her husband who was—liked the old man—gentle and humorous. Maybe, she was thinking of her husband who was taken away by the communists. Like my father because he also was a Christian minister.

"You children," Mrs. Park's voice became gentle. "Close your eyes. Give a silent prayer of thanks. We made it this far. "

Yung-Suk rolled his eyes. Yung-Ja and I closed ours. I thought of Mother who would be sailing soon along the coast line. I prayed, *Please God, protect my mother from any danger as she sails southward. Thank you God that we have made it safe so far and without Yung-Suk being slapped by his mother. Please keep Mrs. Park calm till we arrive at Busan.*

The place had quickly filled up with people. No more space to spare. Not even space to walk without bumping into the hunched backs of people, making little islands. Cacophonies of voices filled the room: babies crying, high pitched women's talking, and men growling as if they owned the place, squeaky voices of wrinkled men ordering their young.

We waited for the train to start rolling. Minutes passed. We heard no sound of a whistle blowing. Instead, a train attendant in a black uniform and black hat walked in.

"hello, everybody," he shouted.

The place became quiet.

"We still have a lot people on the platform waiting to get in," he said. "Please squeeze together so that we can accommodate a few more."

"We are already squeezed in here," a middle-aged man shouted, "like sardines in a can."

"You're a lucky, man" the attendant said. "Sardines in the can are dead. You are still alive."

Yung-Suk opened his mouth to say something. I scooted my foot over, ready to kick his. I was sure this time his mother's calloused hands would grab him by the neck and throttle him in front of us all.

"Please," the attendant said. "Move your belongings so that we can accommodate a few more people running away from the Northern army ... Just like you."

The people mumbled and pushed their belongings closer to them. Looking around the room, the attendant smiled.

"Thank you for your cooperation," he said pointing his finger at the door.

More people walked in.

"In a few minutes, the train will depart," the attendant said as he was walking out. "Please enjoy your trip."

"Enjoy the trip?" The the middle-aged man grumbled. "This is no time for humor. I want to punch that guy in the mouth."

"Shut your mouth." I heard a sharp woman's voice sitting next to him.

"Ouch. Don't ..." The man pleaded.

After a few more minutes, the whistle blew. The long journey was about to start.

"I have to pee," a little child shouted.

"Go. Quickly," his mother said. "Before they close the doors."

The mother pushed the young boy to a door. A tiny stream of urine flowed out the door and down on the platform. When the stream of urine stopped, a worker waiting outside by the door closed the metal door with a loud bang. The place became dark like being in a deep tunnel with only the lights filtering through the dusty windows on the two ends of the compartment. The final whistle blew, and within seconds I heard the heavy coal-fired locomotive chugging. The creaky wheels rolled along the track. I felt the train crawling forward picking up its speed. The air filled with the noise of the passengers seconds ago turned to a hush.

Trapped in four dark rusty steel walls, the steel floor, and the steel ceiling, I felt I was being whisked away to a slaughter house like a herd. I wanted to run away. Run away to Mother. Run away to my home. To breathe the fresh air. To hear the grandfather clock tick. To watch the birds fly in the open space. But how could I get away from this cell? The metal door was too strong to kick open with my tender foot. The opening in the corner was too small to squeeze through.

I saw the herd of people huddled on the floor with their heads sticking up like match sticks in the dark. I saw Mrs. Park, Yung-Ja, and Yung-Suk sitting around me, speaking not a word. They were in the same cell as I was. They were kind enough to have me join them in their journey toward freedom, freedom from the communist grip. I closed my eyes in a prayer of gratitude, gratitude of being in a train for the journey to Busan to join Mother. In a week.

As I sat in the corner of the unlit compartment, I recalled the night before my trip to Boopyung with Father. I was seven years old. It was my first train ride, and I was so excited that I could not sleep. In comic books I had seen pictures of a train rolling up steep hills in a jungle with animals watching in awe. I had heard grownups, all excited, talk of their first train ride. Often in bed I dreamed of riding in one of those black trains choo-chooing near my house. But tomorrow my wish would be fulfilled. I tried very hard to sleep to be prepared for the first long trip. I counted the numbers from one to twenty, twenty to one, and back. I breathed deeply over and over. I lay on my tummy thinking it would help me to sleep. But the picture of my riding in a train kept me awake. I could even hear the chugging sound of the locomotive with its wheels rolling on the steel tracks and the train whistling at the station signaling its departure. I saw myself looking out the window, seeing people and trees speeding by. I spent a sleepless night, waiting for tomorrow.

Tomorrow came very slowly. I skipped to the train station next to Father, whose steps were twice as long as mine. Father handed a train attendant two tickets. His and mine. Father lifted me up on the steps and walked up behind me. I ran into the compartment and took the first seat by the window as Father followed behind me with a smile. I waited and waited to hear the whistle blow. When the whistle blew, my heart went pitter-patter. I heard the wheels squeak. I heard another whistle. Then seconds later, I felt the train move. I put my hands on the bottom of the window looking out. Spell bound. I looked out to the street. Shops and men smoking as they sat by their shops moved away from me. The train gathered its speed, and houses and people sped away in a blur. As the trained entered farm land, I saw fields with green vegetables, rice paddies surrounded by majestic mountains far away. Farmers in straw hats worked in rice paddies with their knees deep in mud. Cows roamed in green pastures, some looking at the train with their round eyes. I waved to them. They seemed to smile at me. Clouds floated away in the opposite direction in the sun-lit sky. It was my first trip and the most memorable one.

But on this trip, I wasn't excited. Instead, I worried. *What will I do if Mother's boat gets hit by an enemy torpedo and sinks? What will I do if the boat gets torn up by heavy wind and flips over and sinks to the bottom of the sea? Then I will be the only one left to spend the rest of my life all alone.* I wished that I had been like the train chugging along without a thought and without feeling. Like the grandfather clock tick-tocking day and night, in joy and in sorrow, in war and in peace. Tick-tock. Tick-tock.

The train chugged along. The only way I knew that the train was moving was from the chugging sound of the locomotive and the rattling sound of the wheels on uneven rails. There were no windows to look out and see the passing scenes of people, fields, cows, and mountain ranges. All I could see were the people in the dark, some sitting cross-legged, some with their eyes closed, and some leaning against their belongings looking blankly at the ceiling. *What are they thinking? Thinking of their homes in Seoul? Happy memories that they left behind? Or of their uncertain future waiting for them?*

After about two hours, the train stopped and the door opened. The cold winter air rushed in and brought us back to the present. The sky was clear. I saw a mountain range far away covered with snow. The people rushed out to the frozen field. Women in long skirts scattered around on one side of the field and crouched down. Little girls doing the same, next to their mothers. Men stood on the other side doing their *business*. Mrs. Park motioned for us to go, too. Out we went to the field. The field where the cows roamed far away. I hesitated. *How can I unbutton my pants with people are all around me? Men. Women. Young children. Especially girls. Maybe, I should wait until the next stop. But what am I going to do if I have to go and the train doesn't stop?* I walked away from the crowd toward the hills far away. Further away, ignoring the cold, cows roamed with their heads to the ground, picking up straw and chewing. Some turned their heads to watch the scene. I pictured a male cow asking a female cow, *What are those humans doing over there? Some crouched down. Some standing up. Sure looks weird,* and the female cow responding, *They are doing what we also do. We don't bother whether I am she or you are he. We do it the same way.* I didn't mind cows looking at me. I unbuttoned my pants and exposed my private part in the freezing air. My hand shook.

"Hurry up," Yung-Suk yelled behind. "You don't want to get left behind."

"Sorry," I said.

"I hate to go back into that cow barn," Yung-Suk said. "It's like sitting on an unflushed toilet."

"I agree," I said. "It's so nice to breathe the fresh air and pee."

After a few minutes the whistle blew. The people rushed back toward the train, some mothers with children on their backs. We followed them.

The train chugged along. The smell in the train no longer bothered me, but sitting for hours on the metal floor was uncomfortable and boring. Those lucky ones by the tiny windows were, at least, able to see the changing scene. Some ladies babbled. Next to me, an old man with a long white beard sat on his mat cross-legged with his eyes closed as in meditation. Others lay down over their belongings, some with their eyes closed and some blankly staring at the ceiling. My thoughts turned to America where I could study hard and be a great inventor like Thomas Edison. I wanted to invent something that would be used by every household in the world, like Edison's electric light bulb. I thought that the sooner I mastered English it would be easier for me to study in America. I pulled out the book, *Fundamentals of English* and opened it. But there was not enough light. I could only see dark lines on a page, not separate characters. The lines shook with the shaking of the train. I felt dizzy. So I closed my eyes, like the old man next to me, and recalled the pictures of America that I had seen in magazines. Tall men with long faces, long noses, and long legs, in tuxedos. Tall women with skirts exposing their slender legs in high heels. A man and woman, holding hands, walking on a street, a scene that I had never witnessed in Korea. A man standing proudly next to a Model T with a cigar in his mouth. The majestic Empire State Building reaching toward the sky.

The above pictures that I had seen in magazines were all in black and white. So I imagined the people having blond hair with blue eyes and long pink noses like the missionaries that I had met. I pictured myself, a five-foot six-inch tall boy with black hair and brown skin, walking along the Empire State Building surrounded by a crowd of six-foot blonds with long noses and blue eyes. I couldn't see the cars passing by, and I couldn't see the displays through windows along the street because those giants blocked the view. I wiggled through the crowd to the Empire State Building and ran up the stairs all the way to the 104th floor without huffing and without sweating. I looked down on the city. I saw blocks of buildings stretching miles away with ribbons of streets separating the blocks. Cars crawled below with people walking along the sidewalks. I imagined myself jumping from the building, gliding down like a seagull and flying along Broadway between rows of buildings watching the scene below.

As I was enjoying the scenes unfolding in my head, I heard the train slowing down and screeching to a stop. I heard Mrs. Park saying, "It's time to get out and stretch again."

The people rushed out to a field like the last time. They formed groups as before, women squatting down on one side and men standing further away from the train. Unlike the first time, I heard women talking, some giggling. Men stood with their heads bent without saying a word. Unlike the last time, I felt less timid. I joined the men. I unbuttoned my pants and let the stream streak down on dry chaff and straw on the ground. After feeling relieved, I walked further away from the train and bent down to stretch my legs, my fingers touching the ground. Then I lifted my arms and turned sideways back and forth. Back and forth. Up and down. Up and down. The sky was clear. The cool breeze woke up my senses. With my mouth wide open, I gulped down the cold, fresh air. Over and over. And it was refreshing, indeed. Then within minutes the whistle blew, and I followed the crowd back to the train.

As the hours passed by, my bottom turned numb from sitting on the steel floor. I kept changing my position, but it didn't help. I looked around. Like me, the people looked weary and bored. "When will we be in Busan?" I heard a little girl ask. "Soon," a lady said. "Why don't you lie down and sleep?" "I can't," she said. "It's too bumpy and noisy." I wished that the train would speed up like a bullet and take us to Busan, which would be our new home. But it just chugged along. Slowly as a turtle.

As I was trying to think of something that would free me from boredom, I saw a chubby, gray-haired lady in gold-rimmed glasses with a hunched back and wrinkled face standing by the entrance. She waved her hand.

"Hello, everybody," she said in a loud, husky voice, "I know you are all bored, frustrated and tired. Let me introduce myself. I'm Kim Hae-Ryun. As you can see, I'm an old woman with wrinkles all over."

She pulled up her shirt sleeves to show the wrinkles on her flabby arms. People stared at her. *Is she a clown from a circus?* I wondered. *Or is she going crazy from the train ride?*

"Also I am chubby with a hunched back," she said. "My grand kids call me Grandma Hunch."

I saw Yung-Suk turn toward the old lady. *Uh, uh, trouble, trouble.* Before Yung-Suk could say anything, Mrs. Park tapped his shoulder.

"Yung-Suk," Mrs. Park said, "Keep your mouth shut."

Then I heard the old man with the long white beard mumbling, "Oh shut up, old woman. Act your age."

"When I walked nude toward my husband a couple years ago," Grandma Hunch said, "he ran away screaming."

How can she say such thing in front of children? I was horrified. *My mother would never do that.* Then the old man chuckled and said to the old lady next to him. "*Yubo*—Honey—you are a beauty queen compared to that woman."

"Now you know," the old lady whispered, "how lucky you are."

"Now I hear no more screams from my husband because he is up there," Grandma Hunch sighed, pointing her finger toward the sky.

"I will be happy to be up there with the angels," the old man chuckled, "if you were my wife."

"*Yubo*, behave," the old lady chided her man. "She may hear you."

"My husband may be looking down at me wondering what his big-mouthed wife is up to," Grandma Hunch said.

"Your husband wouldn't be wondering," the old man chuckled. "He would be running to God asking Him to stop your antics."

I looked at the old lady. Her eyes were like a threatened cat ready to pounce on her attacker. I saw her hand reaching out toward the old man with her fingernails pointing toward his knee.

"OK, OK," the old man said pushing her hand away. "I'll shut up."

"Anyway, you may not believe me," Grandma Hunch said. "Forty years ago, I was a beautiful woman. Straight back. No wrinkles. No fat."

The old man grinned.

"Also I had a beautiful singing voice," Grandma Hunch said. "My students at Ih-Wha College called me *Nightingale.*"

"Oh my God!" I heard the woman scream sitting next to the pretty girl and the old man with the beard. "Professor Kim!"

The woman jumped up with her hands on her chest. Every head in the compartment turned to her in unison. The old man with the beard looked up to her with his eyes wide and with his mouth open. *Is Grandma Hunch really a professor?* I wondered. *She doesn't look or act like one.*

"I am Lee Hae-Ja," she said. "I sang solos in your choir twenty years ago."

Professor Kim looked at Hae-Ja through her gold-rimmed glasses.

"Hae-Ja. Hae-Ja," Professor Kim tapped her head. "See what old age does to you?"

"Do you remember the time when you came over, and congratulated me for winning the city-wide vocal competition?" Hae-Ja said.

Professor kept tapping her head, her eyes glued to Hae-Ja. Then I saw a broad smile over Professor Kim's wrinkled face.

"Didn't I give you voice lessons one semester?" Professor Kim asked

"Yes, yes," Hae-Ja said.

"I remember," Professor said. "You know, when you reach my age, the first thing that goes is memory. Hae-Ja, come over here."

Hae-Ja hurried to Professor as if she was crossing a stream, hopping from one rock to another. Professor Kim opened her arms and welcomed Hae-Ja in her embrace.

"You got a little older, but you're still the same Hae-Ja," Professor Kim said looking at Hae-Ja with a broad smile.

"We have here a lady with beautiful soprano voice," Professor Kim said. "She will melt your boredom and give you a lift."

"That was a long time ago," Hae-Ja said smiling.

"Never mind," Professor Kim said. "Why don't you sing one of your favorite songs? ... No. No. I have a better idea. Sing *Arirang* instead. The second time around, we can all join you."

"Professor, I haven't sung since I graduated," Hae-Ja said.

"That's all right. This is not a concert hall. Let's all have some fun here, even for a few minutes."

"But ..."

Hae-Ja frowned, ready to protest. Then she closed her eyes, pulled her shoulders back, and opened her mouth to sing our most popular Korean folk song about a lover sighing over his mate's departing.

Arirang, arirang, arariyo,
    An expression of sigh
Arirang kokarul nermer kanda
    Arirang hill he goes over
Narrul beriko karshinoon nimoon
    He who forsakes me and goes away
Sipnido motkarsuh, balbyung nanda
    Before he reaches a mile, he will have aching feet.

"Doesn't she sing beautifully?" Professor Kim said, her finger moving back and forth keeping time. "Ready. Everyone. Let's join her."

A few women nearby mumbled the words. Others grinned and looked away.

"Oh, don't be shy," Professor Kim said. "You, men, don't act like shy little girls. Let's all sing with our hearts open. This is not a concert hall. This is a cow barn."

Everyone laughed. More people joined in singing. Professor Kim waved her two chubby arms high and low as if she were conducting a choir in a concert hall. Hae-Ja stood straight with her eyes open and sang as if she were giving a recital.

"Good," Professor Kim urged us. "Louder."

In time everyone joined in the singing. Even the bearded old man sang with his eyes closed. The old man didn't sound bad at all. Yung-Suk, whom

I'd never heard sing in the church, joined the group. Our cow barn had turned into a concert hall. We sang *Arirang* over and over. Then another familiar song. Then another. When it was over, all were smiling. Singing helped us to wash away our boredom, loosen our hearts and tense bodies. For a brief moment, we were able to forget our stench-filled surroundings.

19. Refugee life begins

It took a day-and-a-half to arrive at Busan—thirty-six hours to travel two hundred miles. When we got off the train, the evening sun lighted the city of small two-story buildings, private houses and narrow streets. Street vendors packed up their merchandise to go home for the evening. I felt free. Finally I was on the ground. I could stand, walk, breathe the fresh air and feel the breeze from the sea. All I had to do now was just wait. Mother would arrive here, and we'd all be together again.

"Let's hurry," Mrs. Park said, hurrying out of Busan station, "before it gets too dark."

Mrs. Park was small with short legs. For every two steps she took, Yung-Suk and I took one step. While she hurried, we leisurely followed her. The streets were filled with people walking in all directions, like in an amusement park. Garbage was piled up like a mound on a street corner, soaking wet from the frequent rain. The streets were slippery, covered with mud. Muddy water trickled down the drain along the gutter. An old man in a straw hat stood facing a brick wall, and I saw a yellow stream flowing out from his midsection splattering against the wall. Mrs. Park walked by the old man as if nothing was unusual while Yung-Ja turned her head away from him.

"He's like an old dog peeing by the street," Yung-Suk snickered. "At least he doesn't lift his leg."

"That's why it smells so bad here," I exclaimed. "People peeing all over the street like dogs."

"Boys," Mrs. Park stopped and glared at us. "Don't make fun of that man. You are not going to be any better when there are no restrooms around."

"These boys need to grow up," Yung-Ja chimed in.

145

I saw Yung-Suk open his mouth ready to bark at Yung-Ja, and I quickly tapped his side. I did not want to see Yung-Suk getting yelled at and slapped by Mrs. Park on the muddy street with people watching. Fortunately, he kept his mouth shut and walked with his eyes on Yung-Ja in the front.

As we passed the buildings to a more open space, I saw the hills in the north. The barren hills were dotted with shacks. The shacks glowed in the setting sun, their roofs covered with flattened ration cans, their walls made from cardboard boxes. I wondered how the refugees survived the cold winter nights when the freezing wind from the sea slapped against the cardboard walls. I wondered how the roofs—made out of flattened cans—would hold up against the pounding summer rain.

But soon I realized that the refugees living on the hills were the luckier ones than the masses roaming the streets. Disheveled old men with sunken cheeks roamed the streets begging for food. Little children in dark torn clothes holding empty metal cans followed people asking for food. Women with their long uncombed hair, their children following behind, begged for food with pleading voices. One-legged young men limped along in the crowd.

Instinctively, my thoughts turned to God, whom I had been taught to be all-loving, all-caring to all people, Jews and Gentiles alike. *How can an all-loving God allow so much suffering for these people? Does God discriminate? Letting some children roam the streets without parents, while others live at home with their parents? Letting young mothers without husbands beg for food with their hungry children, while others with husbands live in their homes with full stomachs? Letting some young men without limbs walk the streets, while others with both legs and arms pass them by?* Some elders had told me that it was not God who caused such suffering but the Devil. *Then doesn't God have power over the Devil?* I did not know the answer. I just felt uneasy knowing that I had both feet and arms; I had food to eat, even if the portion was meager; I would have a place to stay, thanks to Yung-Suk; and I would be with Mother soon. I felt sad and uncomfortable, passing these people by without being able to help.

I followed Mrs. Park down a narrow street lined with shops. *So many shops. Just like Seoul. Mother will like it here. I can already see her haggling with these merchants for pennies.* I and Yung-Suk followed his mother while looking around. At the end of the block stood a gray, two-story building.

"That's Dr. Lee's house," Mrs. Park said.

A short while ago I'd rejoiced at the chance to stand and move. But with my shoulders and arms drooping from carrying heavy bags on muddy streets and the sweat pouring down my cheeks, I thought that the train ride had not been that bad. Now seeing a marble sign *Dr. Lee, Myung-Sik* by the door, I closed my eyes and breathed a big sigh of relief.

We stepped up to the doorway, pushed open the door, and walked in. A middle-aged man in a long white coat stood talking to a woman.

"Dr. Lee," Mrs. Park bowed. "Have you been in peace?"

"Oh, Mrs. Park," the doctor said, leaving the woman and walking over to us. "We've been waiting for you.

"How was your trip?" he asked.

"We had a safe trip down," Mrs. Park said.

"That's good," he said. "Who do you have with you?"

Doctor Lee looked at us standing behind Mrs. Park. We stood with our heads bowed in respect.

"This is my daughter, Yung-Ja," Mrs. Park said, "and my son, Yung-Suk. And this is Hi-Dong, the youngest son of Reverend Chai Suk-Mo. His mother will arrive in a week."

"Welcome, welcome," he said. "You people have grown like weeds since I last saw you in Seoul two years ago. You must be all exhausted."

"*Yubo ...Yubo,*" Dr. Lee called his wife.

"Wait a minute." I heard Mrs. Lee's voice—a sharp soprano voice with a southern accent. "As soon as I put the soup pan on the stove, I'll be there."

"*Yubo,*" Dr. Lee said. "Mrs. Park is here."

"I told you to wait a minute," she shouted.

How can she talk back so disrespectfully to her husband? I wondered. Especially in front of people? I never saw ladies acting that way in Seoul.

"*Yubo,* Mrs. Park from Seoul is here," Dr. Lee said again.

A door opened and a short, chubby lady marched out like a general in front of his soldiers. Her cheeks were red and plump like a tomato. She greeted us with open arms in her high-pitched voice.

"Oh, Oh, Mrs. Park," she said bowing, "Welcome, Welcome."

"Thank you," Mrs. Park bowed.

Mrs. Park introduced us to Mrs. Lee, and we bowed.

"Welcome, welcome," Mrs. Lee said. "Why don't you come to the dining room for something to eat?"

"*Yubo*," Dr. Lee said, "They must be exhausted from the long trip. First, let them go up to their room and have some rest."

We followed Mrs. Lee upstairs. The wooden stairway was steep and just wide enough for one person to walk up. Holding our bags in front of us, we followed her up the stairway to the room where we would be staying.

"Here we are," Mrs. Lee said.

She opened the sliding door to the room. My immediate reaction was, *How can we stay in this tiny room? Its smaller than my room at home.* Six *tatami* mats covered the floor. The room was brightened only by the light filtering through the paper-covered sliding door. *I know I will stay here only for few days, but this room is too small even for three. They need space for all the bags they have. They will need a table to eat on. They will need a place for pans and dishes. Then at night how can they sleep without bumping into each other?* I thought of Yung-Ja. *What will Yung-Ja think, sleeping with me in this small room? Even for a few days? How is she going to change in front of me?* I felt uncomfortable being a burden to Yung-Suk's family, but there was nothing I could do.

"I wish I had a bigger room for you," Mrs. Lee apologized. "Unfortunately, this is the only one we have."

"This is more than enough for us," Mrs. Park said. "We deeply appreciate your opening the room for us."

"It's an honor," Mrs. Lee said. "Please settle and rest a while."

"This is like a chicken coop," Yung-Suk blurted as Mrs. Lee left. "Big enough for four chickens."

I cringed. With one less chicken, they would have more room.

"Shut your big mouth," Mrs. Park glared at him.

I cringed wondering what she would do next. I sucked in my breath.

"Learn to be grateful, big boy," she said. "Without Mrs. Lee's kindness, we would be living in shacks on the hills."

I shifted from one foot to the next feeling uncomfortable.

"Sit down, Children. Let us pray," Mrs. Park said regaining her composure.

Dear heavenly Father, thank you for keeping us safe through our travel to Busan. And thank You for providing us with this room while many shiver in the streets.

She paused.

Please open the hearts of those who have rooms to spare so that the refugees do not have to roam the streets, especially mothers with little children. We pray for the well-being of my children's father and Hi-Dong's father. Wherever they may be, please give them courage and peace in the knowledge that You are with them. Also we pray for the safe journey of Hi-Dong's mother to Busan. Amen.

I wished that Mrs. Park did not mention my father's name because whenever I heard his name, my heart ached. I wondered whether he was shot along a dirt road and left there. I wondered whether he was still alive in a prison, longing to come home. I felt so guilty because I didn't give my life to save Father. Like Hi-Seung did.

"I'm exhausted," Mrs. Park said. "You all must be exhausted too."

"Oh poor Mother," Yung-Ja said, helping her lie down on the *tatami* floor.

"Oh, it's so nice to lie flat on the floor even with sweat all over my body," Mrs. Park let out a deep sigh of relief stretching her arms out with her eyes closed.

"I'll be right back," Yung-Ja said going out of the room.

"Do we have to sleep with Yung-Ja?" Yung-Suk said.

"You don't have to," Mrs. Park said.

"Good," Yung-Suk said. "Where do we sleep?"

"Find any place you like," she said. "On the street. In the train station. Up on the hills. Without you, we'll have more room here."

"Oh, Mother," he said. "You're joking."

"You're fifteen years old now," Mrs. Park said. "It's time for you to act and think like a grownup. Think before you speak. Don't spill out what is on your mind like a barking dog."

Yung-Suk glanced at his mother, who was lying on the floor with her eyes closed and her arms stretched.

"In Seoul you had your own room, and Yung-Ja had her own," Mrs. Park said. "But here, we will be together in this room twenty-four hours a day,

day after day, week after week. We'll all have to be patient and be mindful of each other's feelings. You understand?"

I gave my head a shake looking at Yung-Suk.

"I'll try," Yung-Suk said.

"That's not a good enough answer," she said, her voice irritated. "Do you understand?"

I nodded more vigorously.

"Yes, I understand, Mother," Yung-Suk said.

"That's better," she said.

"Hi-Dong," she called, her voice gentle, "you must be tired from the long trip."

"I'm fine," I said.

"You must be tired and sweaty," she said, "like I am."

"I'm fine, Mrs. Park," I said even though I was tired and sweaty.

I pictured myself sitting in a bathtub with warm water up to my neck. I pictured myself humming with my eyes closed feeling the gentle heat from the water soaking through every inch of my tired body and loosening up my tensed muscles. I saw myself slowly getting out of the tub, rubbing all my body with a soapy wash cloth, and rinsing off by pouring a bucketful of cold water over my head. As I was picturing the cold water pouring down my head and splashing on the floor, the door opened, and Yung-Ja came in.

"Mother," Yung-Ja said, "I brought two wet towels for us to clean up.

Mrs. Park sat up taking the towels from Yung-Ja.

"The pink towel is for me and Yung-Ja," Mrs. Park said. "And the green towel is for Yung-Suk and Hi-Dong. That's the only towel you'll have. Take good care of it."

One towel for Yung-Suk and me? How disgusting. Who's going to use it first? Of course, Yung-Suk. I am just his friend. I pictured Yung-Suk wiping off his sweat-soaked hair, his face, and his neck. When I pictured him wiping the sweat off from his armpits, I felt nauseated. *What am I going to do? Run away? Ask Mrs. Park for my own? But she already said that those were the only towels she had.* I felt like throwing up, but I sat quietly as if nothing was going on inside me.

Then she handed me a towel and said, "Hi-Dong, why don't you wipe off the dry sweat? Around your neck, arms and feet."

I had an urge to grab the towel and follow her order. Then I remembered Mother's advice, *Always think of others' needs first.* My reaction was, *Forget her advice this time. There's plenty time to think of others' needs first.* I held the wet clean towel in my hand debating what to do. Then an inner voice said, *How can you expect to be Tarzan when you worry about the little thing like who's going to use the towel first? How can you expect to be a fearless person who will do anything that he sets his mind to?*

"Yung-Suk, you use it first," I said handing the towel to him.

"No," Mrs. Park said, "you're the guest. You clean yourself first. Then give the towel to Yung-Suk."

But I couldn't. *How can I wipe off my head with full of sweaty black hair, my face and neck, my sweaty armpits, and give the sweat-soaked towel to Yung-Suk? Without me, he would have used it all by himself.* But I didn't want to go against Mrs. Park. I took the towel. I wiped myself with one end and handed the towel to Yung-Suk.

"Yung-Suk, use the other side," I said.

"Hi-Dong, you are smarter than I am," Mrs. Park smiled. "Why didn't I think of that? Yung-Ja and I will do the same thing."

"I'll sew the names on the towels," Yung-Ja said, "So that we know which side belongs to whom."

Good boy, I told myself. *You helped to solve the two-towels-for-four people problem.*

As the week drew to a close, Yung-Suk and I walked to the dock where boats of all sizes arrived with refugees from the north. Day after day we went to welcome Mother, but she did not walk off the ramp from the LST. Ten days had passed, but Mother did not come. Dread filled my waking hours. Dread kept me awake at night. I dreaded the day when someone would bring me the tragic news: Mother's boat sank in a stormy sea. *What am I going to do then? Brother's gone. Father's gone. Kwidong's gone. Now Mother's gone. I will be all alone.*

While I worried about Mother, Yung-Suk met one of his high

school classmates from Seoul who told him of a study group formed by his classmates; he joined them and spent more and more time with his classmates, and I was left alone. I could not find any such group from my school. So I went to the dock alone. Waiting and waiting.

One night I was in my sleeping bag trying to sleep. It was around 11:00 P.M. A dim light from the hallway filtered through the sliding door covered with rice paper. Mrs. Park snored in her usual high-pitched staccato. Yung-Ja and Yung-Suk were fast asleep. My mind was still with Mother. *Is she still sailing toward Busan? Or is she on the bottom of the sea? What will I do if she is dead?* I tossed around. I tried to divert my attention to the comic book about Tarzan in an African jungle, that I had loved reading before going to bed as a child. But it didn't work. I recited, *The Lord is my shepherd, I shall not want. The Lord is my shepherd, I shall not want.* Over and over as Mother had told me when I had a hard time sleeping as a child. It didn't work. I kept telling myself, *Don't act like a nervous chicken. Act like a fearless tiger.* It didn't work.

Then out of nowhere my brother Hi-Seung showed up, who had been dead more than three years ago. He looked as if he had been standing in front of me in broad daylight. He seemed to say, *Have you forgotten what I taught you when you were a child? Didn't I tell you to tell yourself, "I believe in myself. I can do anything that I set my mind to?" I didn't teach you to worry. Worrying is not going to help Mother arrive safely in Busan. Worrying is not going to make your day a happy one. A person who believes in himself does not get bogged down in worry. A person, who believes he can do anything that he sets his mind to, does not walk around worrying day after day. He moves on with life confident that he can handle whatever the future brings to him. So Hi-Dong, you are a fourteen year old young man with a big future ahead of you. Sooner or later you'll have to face life alone. Remind yourself again that you can handle whatever the future brings.* Then he was gone. I opened my eyes. The room was still dark. Mrs. Park continued to snore. Yung-Suk and Yung-Ja were sound asleep.

Does man's spirit live forever even though his body dies? Was that Hi-Seung's spirit who just talked to me? I wondered. *Or was it my mind reminding me to be strong?* Anyway, worrying was not going to bring Mother to Busan. Worrying did not make me happy. Instead, worrying made everything around me look gray. Even the fresh ocean breeze did not smell refreshing. The morning sun rising from the eastern horizon on a clear day did not look beautiful. I also realized that doing nothing everyday was not going to keep me free from worrying. The best thing that I could do was to find a job. But who would hire me, a fifteen-year-old boy with no work experience? I told myself, *Brother Hi-Seung taught me not to be afraid of the dark, not to be afraid of the water, not to be afraid of the bullies. I am going to be tough like he was. Tomorrow morning, I will go out, walk from shop to shop and ask for a job until I find one.*

The next day while Yung-Suk was with his classmates, I told Mrs. Park of my plan.

"Hi-Dong," she said. "Don't feel you are a burden to us. You know I love you like my own son. Yung-Ja and Yung-Suk think you are their brother. There's nothing for you to feel uncomfortable about staying with us."

"Thank you, Mrs. Park," I said. "Working will help me stop worrying about my mother."

"You are too young," she said. "I don't even ask Yung-Suk to get a job."

"But I want to try, Mrs. Park," I said in a determined voice.

She studied me with the look of concern.

"How are you going to find a job?" she asked.

"I can go to shop owners and ask," I said.

"They'll look at you. Smile at you. And tell you in a Busan accent, *You, too young*," she said.

"I'll keep trying until I get one," I said.

"You are really serious?" she said.

"Yes," I said.

20. I become a fish cleaner

The next morning I walked through the downtown of Busan toward the shore. I saw, far away, cargo and military transport ships docked along the pier. Along the shoreline I saw wooden shacks lined up displaying a variety of catch from the sea. Abalone, clams, slimy squid, and fish of all shapes and colors.

"Please come and check the fresh mackerel caught last night," a merchant shouted in his Busan accent.

"Fresh squid," an old wrinkled woman shouted waving a dried squid in her hand, "Please come in and taste this tender squid dried only three days ago."

After passing the open market, I saw a number of stores selling fish of all kinds. I walked into the first shop. A lady was busily sorting a pile of fresh fish on a table. Mackerel into one rack. Smelts into another rack. Long gray-scaled ones into another. *What do I say?* I wondered. *Can I work for you? Do you need a person to help you? Would you hire a fifteen-year-old boy? Or please give me a job; I can do anything you tell me to do, and I will do it well?* I stood by the front door feeling nervous. She looked at me while sorting.

"What do you want?" Her voice was abrupt in a heavy Busan accent.

"Do you have a job for me?" I asked with a halting voice.

"A job for you?" She stopped sorting and stared at me.

"Yes," I said standing straight. My voice firm.

"You are from Seoul. Seoul boys don't know how to work," she said, and she returned to her sorting.

I stood there trying to figure out how to respond. But she was talking to the fish instead of me. I couldn't hear what she said to the fish, but her lips moved fast. Sheepishly I stepped out of the shop and walked across the street to another one. The shop owner looked very much like the old man with the long gray beard in the train, except the owner looked younger with his long beard darker and his white Korean clothing splattered with blood. Probably from chopping fish. The owner sat on a beat-up wooden stool smoking a thin, foot-long Korean pipe made out of bamboo. I stood in front of him. He looked up blowing out the smoke at me and said, "What do you want?" I said to myself, *This man has no manners, blowing the smoke at me. I don't want to work with a person like him.* I quickly turned and walked across the street. I decided to check out the owner before going into a shop the next time. If I didn't feel comfortable with the way an owner looked or acted, I decided to pass the shop for another one.

The first several *No's* from the shop owners were discouraging, but as the morning turned into afternoon, and as I got more *No* responses, I realized that I was turning into a thick-skinned boy, not the innocent, fearful child that I had once been. I felt proud, and thought of my brother, Hi-Seung. *Look at me, Brother,* I said while walking to the next shop. *I'm becoming tough. Like you.*

It was late afternoon. Still no one hired me. I was getting tired, hungry without any food in my stomach. I was discouraged even though I had been reciting as I walked the streets, *I am becoming tough like my brother. Even monkeys fall from trees. Don't be afraid to fail if I want to succeed.* I wanted to quit and go back home. Feeling weary I passed by a store along the shore. It was bigger than the stores where I had stopped. In front of the store, metal containers filled with fish were on display. Some fish were silvery and long. Some were dark blue and round. Some were pink. Water-filled buckets of live clams and abalone were placed on the ground next to the fish containers. A middle-aged lady wearing an apron sat on a stool in the far corner reading the Bible. She looked up, and she seemed nice. I walked up to her and bowed.

She smiled and asked in a Seoul accent, "What can I do for you?"

"I'm looking for work," I said. "I'll do anything."

She closed the Bible, put it on the stool, and walked over.

"Are you alone?" she said.

"I live with my friend's family," I said, "waiting for my mother from Seoul."

"When will she arrive?"

"She was supposed to be here in a boat two weeks ago," I said.

"In a boat?"

"Yes," I said. "In a boat."

She put her fingers on her mouth, pacing the floor. What was she thinking? Was she going to give me a job?

"How old are you?" she broke the silence.

Should I tell her I was sixteen? Then she may give me a job. I was tempted to tell her a lie. But I remembered Mother's words, *Do you want to be a wealthy liar or a person of integrity?*

"I'm fifteen years old," I said.

"Fifteen," she mumbled, "and all alone, worrying about your mother."

How did she know that I was worrying?

"I wish I could hire you," she said. "But I don't make enough money for my own family."

"You don't have to pay me," I replied thinking that working would be better than worrying about Mother twenty-four hours a day.

"No pay?" A questioning voice.

"Yes," I said. "No pay is fine."

I stood straight like a soldier in front of his superior.

"Well, then," she said pacing the floor back and forth.

I waited for her next words. After a few seconds her pace slowed.

"When do you want to start?" She asked looking at me.

My heart raced. *How nice. She is offering me a job!*

"Right now," I said.

A smile came over her face.

"You are a determined young boy," she said. "Let's get started."

I looked up the sky. I wanted to yell aloud, *Brother Hi-Seung, I got a job. All by myself. Without help from anybody. All by myself.*

"Thank you very much," I said bowing low.

The lady smiled. Like Mother's smile. Warm and gracious.

"Now what's your name?" she asked.

"My name is Chai Hi-Dong," I said.

"I'm Mrs. Kim," she said. "Today I'll show what we have and what you'll be doing starting tomorrow."

"Thank you."

She walked around the racks filled with fish.

"Do you know the names of the fish we have here?" she said.

"Well," I said. "I know some."

"Tell me," she said.

The first items that caught my eyes were sea shells in the buckets.

Pointing to one bucket, I said, "Those are clams."

"Good," she said. "What about others?"

"Abalone and oysters in shells," I replied.

She pointed to the fish.

"Those are mackerel," I said pointing to the ones with dark wavy bars on the back, and silvery bellies. "And those wiggly things are squid and octopus."

My taste buds rose. I liked to eat squids. Mother used to buy them by the dozen, boil them in hot water, and slice them into small pieces. The white meat was tender, and I dipped the meat in a hot sauce mixed with some vinegar. I also like to chew dry squid, that were cooked in salt water and then dried.

"What are the names of the others?" she asked.

"I'm sorry," I said. "I don't know."

Mrs. Kim smiled.

"They are lady fish, sea bass, snapper and flounder," she said pointing to each. "Every morning fishermen will come with their catch. Your job is to separate the fish in groups and place them on the racks. Also I'll pick out the fish for restaurants nearby. First, you cut off the head. Remove the scales. Slice along the belly and removed the inside. Rinse them off in water and deliver them to the restaurants."

I remembered cutting open the koi fish in the aquarium in our living room, splattering blood all over the bathtub. Worrying about being punished by Father for killing the fish that he loved. Rushing out to a market with Mother to buy koi fish that looked like the ones I killed. Putting them in the aquarium. Father saying that the fish had grown. Now I didn't have to worry about being punished. It was my job to chop their heads with a big knife, remove the scales, slice their belly. Then remove the insides with my fingers. Blood would be all over. I would rinse them in water and delivering them to restaurants.

"Have you ever cleaned a fish?" she asked.

Should I tell her my koi fish story? How I cut open the koi fish belly? Better not. She may say, "God was preparing you to be a fish cleaner from your childhood."

"Not really," I said.

"Do you think you can handle the job?" she said.

"No problem," I replied.

"Good," she smiled. "Today you just watch me work. All right?"

"Yes," I said.

I was proud. I found a job all myself. Also this was my first job. I didn't care even if my family and friends frowned on me for working as a fish cleaner and delivery boy—a job fit only for low-class boys. I didn't care even if Mrs. Park thought that I put myself so low to work for such a menial job. To me there was neither a higher-class nor a lower-class job. A job was a job. My responsibility was to do my best. I decided to be the best fish cleaner in the world, the best fish cleaner that Mrs. Kim had ever had.

As days passed, I found that I enjoyed working for the lady. She treated me like her nephew. Eating lunch together. Giving me dry squid to chew while cleaning. Asking me whether I received any news from Mother. And letting me take frequent breaks. Often during the break, I walked along the shore looking toward the piers where the LST approached, wishing that Mother was on one of the ships.

At the end of the day, the lady always gave me fish to take home. Mrs. Park looked forward to seeing me come home with a fish dangling down in my hand, for it provided a good portion of our evening meal. I also felt good that I could contribute something in return for their caring for me.

One evening I was walking home with half a dozen dry squid in one hand and a box of left-over cooked fish in the other. The sky was covered with the dark clouds. A young woman stopped in front of me. She had a baby on her back. Her dark uncombed hair fell on her shoulders. Her eyes sunk into her skull. Her unwashed cheekbones stuck out through her skin.

"Can you share a couple of those squid," she pleaded. "My baby is starving. My *jut*—mother's milk—is dried up."

She did not have the Busan accent. Most likely a refugee from the north. Her voice, though weak, sounded like Mother with me on her back years ago. *Has she been roaming the streets every day? For how long? Sleeping under an eave, caressing her baby on her bosom so that the baby will not catch cold. Did her husband go to fight the enemy and get killed, leaving his wife and the baby to be cared for by themselves?* I lifted my arm toward her with the dried squid in my hand. Then I remembered Mother's saying, *A dry squid is just a snack. Not a meal.* Also I remembered Mother's advice, *Always put others' needs ahead of yours.* I moved the box toward her.

"Please take this," I said handing the box to her. "It has cooked fish inside."

"Oh, thank you," she said, her voice cracking. "Thank you. Thank you."

She bowed over and over.

"Please don't bow," I said. "I'm just a young boy."

"Thank you," she said. "I hope my body will make enough milk to feed my baby."

"Please take these too," I said handing her the dry squids.

She looked at me. I saw her in tears.

"Thank you," she said. 'But you take the squids."

She refused.

I put the squid in her hands and walked away. As I walked, I turned around. She stood looking at me with the baby on her back. Tears welled up in my eyes. Then the same question that had dwelt within me since my childhood resurfaced. *Oh God. Why? Why? Why? If You are so loving, why do You let this mother and her baby suffer so? And why do You continue to make me worry about Father and Mother? Making me wonder whether Father was shot by the communists along a dirt road and left there to decompose under the scorching sun? Making me wonder whether Mother was drowned and sunk to the bottom of the sea to be nibbled to the bones by fish swarming around her* water-soaked body? Oh, God where is Your love? The Bible says that You care for even the lilies of the field that bloom one day and die the next day. Why don't You care for the lady and the baby? Why don't You care for me?

Weeks passed. There was still no news of Mother. Yung-Suk's family were concerned and said comforting words to me. But those comforting words made me more worried. I could not let go of the fear. The image of Mother drowning on the sinking boat haunted me. *What should I do if Mother drowned along the way? I am sure Yung-Suk's family will take care of me. But I don't want to be a burden to them. Should I ask Mrs. Kim whether I can stay with her in return for my service? She has treated me like her family and will most likely have me stay with her. Then what will Mrs. Park think? Will she let me go? Probably not. She will tell me to stay with them as her adopted son.*

I scolded myself thinking such a thought. *You are lucky to have a job. Pay attention to your job and try to be the best fish cleaner in the world. Chop its head off with one clean blow. Cut open its belly with one stroke of the knife. Take its insides out with one grab, instead of groping around feeling nervous. Clean as many fish as you can in a day. Always remember Hi-Seung's words, "I'm in charge of my future. I can do anything that I set my mind to."*

A few weeks had passed since becoming a fish cleaner. It was a late cloudy afternoon. The shack where I cleaned the fish turned dark with the sun behind the clouds. The air was hot and humid. The sweat dripped down my cheeks from my head onto the chopping board. Dozens of chopped fish heads in a pail looked up at me with their round eyes, covered in blood. My hands moved like a robot. I picked up a fish. Chopped its head off with a sharp knife in one blow. Threw the head in a pail on the floor. Removed the scales. Chopped off its tail and fins. Cut open up its belly. Removed the inside. Rinsed off the blood. Put the clean fish on a rack. Picked up another fish. Repeated the cycle. Over and over.

I was tired and weary of working. I was tired and weary of worrying about Mother day and night. I was tired and weary of the endless battle going on inside me since childhood: the battle between my tender nature and my desire of becoming fearless Tarzan. I was angry at my cowardly thoughts filling my days with worry. I was angry at myself unable to take total control of my emotions. I was angry. Very angry. I picked up the biggest slippery mackerel in the bin.

"I'll show you," I uttered, "I can cut your thick head with one blow."

I cocked my hand and lifted the knife high in the air. I aimed the sharp edge of the knife at its neck and let go of my hand down as if I was hammering a nail. The sharp edge of the knife sped down and slid into its neck. But it did not cut thru. The fish looked up at me with its big round eyes. It seemed to laugh at me.

"You dumb fish," I yelled. "I'll show you who I am."

I lifted the knife back up and hammered down at the fish. It didn't cut through. I tried again. Didn't cut through. Tried again. Didn't cut through. I pounded at the fish with the sharp edge making multiple cuts. The blood oozed out of the cuts. The big round eyes of the fish still looked up at me. Never blinking. Instead, those eyes seemed to sneer at me. With the knife slashing at the fish, my yelling turned to scream. I repeated, *I'll show you who I am. I'll show you who I am.* I threw the knife on the floor. It bounced off the floor making a ping sound to a corner. I picked up the mackerel with its head dangling down. I threw it against a wall. It hit the wall with a thud and fell on the ground leaving blood stains on the wall. I kicked the pale that was filled with the fish heads. The heads jumped out scattering around floor with the bloody water making pink trails. My scream turned to a groan, coming from somewhere deep within. Words flowed out of my mouth mixed with a groan. The words that I did not understand. Tears flowed down my cheeks like a stream.

"Hi-Dong. Hi-Dong." I heard Mrs. Kim uttering my name and the door opening with a bang. She rushed over toward me. Suddenly I realized what I had been doing. I stopped groaning. I stopped yelling. My body still shook violently. I put my blood-covered hand on my cheeks to wipe off the tears. The tear drops dripped down on my cheeks mixed with the blood, and to the ground.

"I'm sorry," I said avoiding her eyes.

Mrs. Kim held my hand without words, feeling my shaking hand. She closed her eyes as in prayer, and then led me to the back of the store. She brought a wooden chair for me to sit. She brought a pale of water and knelt down in front me. She put a towel in the water, squeezed it and wiped off my tear-stained, bloodied face. She took the towel around my neck and head, and wiped off the sweat. She put my hands in the water and washed off the blood with her hands. Then she held my hands, looked up at me with teary eyes, and closed her eyes. I knew that she was praying for me. Like Mother wherever she might be. I closed my eyes feeling her gentle hands. Fresh tears filled my eyes, streaming down my cheeks.

21. I go to Masan to find Mother

Every morning I went to clean the fish and came home exhausted. Mrs. Park kept busy inquiring into Mother's whereabouts. She asked the people from my father's church who fled from Seoul. They did not know. She visited the church ministers who had known or studied under my father. They did not know. Then one evening I came home from work and was greeted by Mrs. Park with a smile on her face.

Instead of her usual greeting, *How was your day?*, she said excitedly, *Hi-Dong, I have good news for you.*

Has she found a better job for me, like working for a U.S. general as his houseboy? I had known that Mrs. Park felt sorry seeing me come home looking worn-out. Also I had felt uncomfortable coming home and filling up the room—the only room—with the fish odor soaked into my clothes. Yung-Ja often covered her nose when I came into the room and said, *That fish odor's killing me. Why don't you get another job?*

"Yes?" I said looking at Mrs. Park.

"Today I met a lady from your father's church who remembers you," she said.

"And?"

"I told her you were with us and waiting for your mother," Mrs. Park said. "She had heard from her friend that your mother was in Masan."

"Masan?" I said, my voice rising. "The small town west of Busan?"

"Yes," she said. "It's only a several hours boat ride from here."

Why Masan? Mother has never mentioned about stopping at Masan. Did Uncle decide to settle there instead of Busan? More business opportunities there for him?

163

"Do you think it's true?" I asked.

"She seemed certain," she said.

What do I do now? I wondered. *Go to Masan? But where do I get the money to buy a train ticket? All I get from my work are fish, fish and more fish. Not a dime in my pocket. Borrow from Mrs. Park, who's struggling to feed her family and me? No, I will not do that. Find a job that pays me? But where? Who will hire a fifteen-year-old boy whose only work experience is cleaning fish? The best thing I can do is just wait. Mother knows I'm in Busan, and she will send someone to contact me.*

"I'm so happy to know that she is alive," I said.

"I'm so relieved," Mrs. Park said letting out a deep sigh of relief. "I have prayed for you and your Mother every day."

"Thank you very much," I said with my heart filled with gratitude.

Mrs. Park had taken care of me just like her son. Yung-Suk and Yung-Ja treated me just like their family. Even when Yung-Ja complained about the fish odor, she didn't sound offended.

"Tomorrow," Mrs. Park said, "go with Yung-Suk to Masan and find your mother."

What? Tomorrow? Tomorrow, I will be with Mother? My heart raced.

"Tomorrow?" I blurted out. "With Yung-Suk?"

"Yes, with Yung-Suk" Mrs. Park said. "He's very excited too."

I looked at Yung-Suk. He grinned.

"What about my job?" I asked.

"I'll take care of that," she said.

The dread and gloom in me were replaced by excitement and anticipation. Everything looked bright again. I couldn't wait. Tomorrow I would be together with my dear mother. Then a part of me felt uneasy. Masan had tens of thousands of people. I didn't know where she lived, and how could I find her without her address? Mrs. Park told me to go find the Bright Light Holiness Church and ask for Mother's whereabouts since the church minister had studied under Father in Seoul, and he would have heard about Mother being in their city. But what would I do if the minister didn't know? Stay there until I find her? Or just come back to Busan?

The next morning I woke up earlier than usual and tossed around in bed, thinking of the exciting day ahead of me. I kept waiting for the family to wake up, but they kept on sleeping. So I decided to wake them by snoring. I snored as loudly as I could. Mrs. Park smacked her lips and turned on her side. I snored again.

"Stop it, Hi-Dong," Yung-Ja called out.

I pretended that I didn't hear her, and decided to let out one more loud snore.

"Hey, Hi-Dong," Yung-Suk nudged my side. "Stop snoring."

"What did you say?" I squirmed as if waking up from a deep sleep.

"You snore like a bear," Yung-Suk said.

"Who?" I asked. "Me, snore?"

"Yes, you," Yung-Suk said. "You're worse than Mother. I'm amazed the ceiling is still holding up."

"That's the first time I've heard you snore," Yung-Ja said half asleep.

Mrs. Park was awake too. She sat up and rubbed her eyes.

"Hi-Dong must have been tired from work and excited about joining his mother today," Mrs. Park said. "Let's help him get going."

I took out a clean pair of underwear, clean shirts, pants, and socks from my bag, hurried down to the bathroom to brush my teeth and wash. I changed into a whole new outfit from the inside out. I looked at the mirror saying, *How do I look, Mother? Pretty good?* I was ready to be embraced by Mother's welcoming arms, saying, *You have grown into a handsome young man.*

After breakfast, Yung-Suk and I rushed to the pier. I looked up to the sky. A typical Busan sky. Covered with dark clouds, threatening to rain. There were a half dozen boats lined up on the pier, and people walked up the ramps.

"Which one is for Masan?" I asked Yung-Suk.

"Let's ask one of the ticketing agents standing by the ramps," Yung-Suk said walking toward an agent.

The agent pointed his finger toward the boat behind him. We rushed to the boat. About a dozen passengers were in front of us.

"Do you have the money?" I asked nervously.

"Don't worry, Hi-Dong," he said. "Mother gave me enough money for the round trip and lunch for us."

"Round trip?" I got nervous again. "Do you think we may not be able to find my mother and need to come back to Busan?"

"You have cleaned thousands of fish by now," Yung-Suk chuckled. "Do you think you can find a blind fish among hundreds with your eyes closed?"

"Finding the churches shouldn't be too hard," I said. "I'm sure there aren't many churches that belong to my father's denomination."

"I just hope so," Yung-Suk replied.

On the boat we found the cabin was nearly full. We decided to stay on the deck and enjoy the view around us. Drops of rain started to fall from the sky which was blanketed by the dark clouds. So we chose to stay under the eave by the stairway.

Within minutes, the horn blew and the boat started to move toward the open sea. This was my first ride on a passenger boat, and the excitement of the ride put my worry, *What am I going to do if I don't find Mother?*, aside. The boat moved at a snail's pace. And when we were on the open sea, it was moving up and down by the waves and did not seem to move at all. Only the slow-changing scene of the coast line told me the boat was moving. As the boat sailed westward toward Masan, the rain turned heavy making a splashing sound on the deck, and water from the eave splattered on the wooden floor making our pants wet. I watched the coastline dotted with houses with thatched roofs partially blanketed by the downpour. Fishing boats swayed by gentle waves like fluttering leaves in the wind. The rain continued to fall for over an hour. Then I saw the blue sky up ahead of us, and the dark clouds moving eastward.

"We're lucky Hi-Dong," Yung-Suk said. "We'll not have to walk in the rain."

"Wonder how many more hours it'll take to be in Masan?" I said.

"Mother said it usually takes two to three hours," he said. "We should be there in an hour or so."

Looking at the same scene for over an hour and feeling my pants soaking wet made me feel uncomfortable and bored like on the train ride to Busan from Seoul. Also my stomach started to churn with the swaying of the boat.

"Yung-Suk," I said. "I feel like vomiting."

Yung-Suk's eyes turned round.

"Can you control it for an hour?" he said.

"I'll try," I said.

I closed my eyes and took a deep breath to relax, but it made me feel worse. I recited the words, *I am enjoying the scene. My stomach feels fine. I'm not going to vomit.* It didn't work. My breakfast was creeping up to my throat.

"It's coming," I mumbled, my hand on my mouth.

Yung-Suk nervously looked around.

"Go to the back," he said. "And do it there."

I rushed to the back of the boat. No one was there. I bent over the rail reaching far out worrying that it might splash on the sideboard and let go of the food rushing out of my mouth. It dropped down on the sea and disappeared from my sight.

"Do you feel better?" Yung-Suk asked when I returned.

"Now I have a headache," I said, wishing that the ride would soon be over.

An hour seemed like an eternity. No more excitement on my first boat ride. Too sick to worry about Mother. My attention was on my churning stomach and the aching head. As I was praying that the boat would soon arrive at Masan, the rain stopped. The sky was turning from dark to gray. I saw the blue sky ahead of us. From the boat I saw the panoramic view of the town with a lot of houses. There were no high rise buildings but only houses with straw-covered roofs. Fishing boats lined the shore. Sea gulls glided in the sky riding the gentle breeze. I looked at my watch. We have been in the boat more than two hours.

"That must be Masan," I said.

"I think so," Yung-Suk replied. "Are you excited?"

"I sure am," I said.

Gazing at the tranquil scene and the excitement of meeting Mother calmed my churning stomach and aching head. *Mother must be in one of those houses. In a few hours, I'll be with her.* I felt the excitement building up and was ready to begin the search. The search for Mother.

It took three hours to arrive at the city of Masan. As soon as the boat came to stop at the dock, we rushed out of the boat. When we arrived there, the first thing we planned to do was to find the Bright Light Holiness

Church. But how? There was no information booth. There was no street map. There was no telephone. The only way was to ask people.

"Hello," I stopped a middle aged man in straw hat, in straw sandals, and in a torn white Korean costume, walking toward us carrying a live pig tied to a wooden A-frame on his back. "Do you know where the Bright Light Holiness Church is?"

He looked at us as if we were foreigners and uttered some words, but his southern accent was so strong that we did not understand.

"Excuse me?" I said.

The pig on his back grunted. The man looked at Yung-Suk. Then at me. He said something in a loud voice and walked away with a broad grin.

"Did you understand what he said?" I asked Yung-Suk.

"If I did, I would have talked back at him," Yung-Suk said. "I feel like we're in a foreign country."

As we walked further, we saw a wrinkled old lady with gray hair. She stood in front of the door pouring dry red beans into a large wooden bin.

"Excuse me," I said."Do you know where the Bright Light Holiness Church is?"

She did not respond, and I tapped her back. She stopped pouring and turned to look at us. Her eyes grew wide as if she were seeing a couple of foreigners. She frowned and cocked her head to the other side.

"Do you know where the Bright Light Holiness Church is?" Yung-Suk shouted.

She looked at us with an uneasy smile.

"I'm deaf," she said turning around to continue her work.

"I'm very sorry for bothering you," I said.

As we resumed our walk, a man with a dark long beard, wearing a white Korean robe and a straw hat walked toward us. He looked like a village chief.

"Excuse me," I said bowing low.

The man stopped in front of us, holding a long bamboo pipe in his hand.

"Do you know where the Bright Light Holiness Church is?" I asked.

"The Bright Light Holiness Church," the man mumbled in Masan accent. "Holiness Church ... Holiness Church."

"Yes," I said. "The Bright Light Holiness Church."

"I know only one Holiness church in town," he said. "It is on a hill about half an hour walk from here, but I do not know whether it is the Bright Light Holiness Church."

"Thank you very much," I said. "We will go there anyway and check."

Following his direction, we rushed toward a church on a grassy hill surrounded by trees. It was a small church with a triangular roof covered with the straw. A wooden cross stood above the roof. The walls were dirt red. We meandered up the road to the church and found that the door was open. We walked in. The place was dark. There were no electric lights hanging down from the ceiling. Instead unlit oil lanterns were set on wooden stands along the walls. The varnished floor was empty of chairs. One lectern stood in the front with a wooden cross hanging behind.

We took our shoes off and sat in the back to rest for a while. The sanctuary was filled with stillness. Not even the sounds of chirping birds could be heard. I wished that my heart was at peace like this surrounding, not like being on a boat in a stormy sea.

While we sat there resting our tired feet, we saw a man about forty years old walking in from the front. He carried with him a mop and a bucket.

When he saw us, he asked, "Can I help you?"

"May I speak to the minister please?" I said.

"I am he," he said with a smile.

"I am sorry, Sir," I said.

"In Christ there is neither janitor nor minister," he said. "We are all one in Christ."

I looked at Yung-Suk, not knowing how to respond to the minister's fancy words.

"You speak with the Seoul accent," he said.

"Yes, we are from Seoul."

"Are you refugees looking for the church?"

"No," I said. "I'm looking for my mother."

He looked at me for a second. Then he came over and introduced himself as Reverend Kim, and I introduced myself as the son of Reverend Suk-Mo Chai from Seoul.

"Reverend Chai," he exclaimed in surprise. "He was my teacher at the Seoul Seminary."

"Who is this young man?" Reverend Kim asked turning to Yung-Suk.

"My name is Yung-Suk," he said. "I am the son of Reverend Park Hung-Shik, who taught at the seminary with Hi-Dong's father."

"Oh, I know your father also." Reverend Kim tapped his hands with a smile. "I took his course on the New Testament. You both have parents who were wonderful and dedicated professors."

Reverend Kim asked me about our fathers but I didn't want to talk about my father. It was too painful. I was sure Yung-Suk felt the same. We stayed quiet, both looking down at the floor.

"Are they in good health?" Reverend asked.

"Well ... Well ..." I stammered and couldn't finish the sentence.

"The communists took them away," Yung-Suk blurted out.

"What?" he said as if he did not hear Yung-Suk. "The communists?"

"Yes," I said.

Reverend must have sensed our pain. He closed his eyes looking toward the heaven. He did not ask further about our fathers.

"What has brought you here?" Reverend asked.

"I came to find my mother," I said.

"Your mother?" he said raising his eyebrows.

If he knows Mother's whereabouts, why does he raise his eyebrows? I was scared.

"Do you mean you don't know?" I gasped.

Reverend's answer was *No.* Mother had never visited him. No one had ever told him of Mother living in Masan. *Yung-Suk's mother felt certain that Mother was in Masan? Maybe, there is more than one Holiness church in town.*

"Are there other Holiness churches in town?" I asked.

"Yes," Reverend said. "We Holiness church ministers get together every two weeks for lunch. But none of them mentioned about your mother being here."

Where is Mother then? Not in Busan. Not in Masan. Where? On the bottom of the sea? Am I the only one left in my family? Father's gone. Brother

Hi-Bum's gone. Brother Hi-Seung's gone. My best pal, Kwidong's gone. Now Mother's gone. My breathing slowed. My heart seemed to stop. All the energy seemed to be draining out of every cell of my body. Yung-Suk nudged closer. Reverend reached out to hold my arm.

"Hi-Dong," Reverend said. "I helped three refugee families from Seoul to stay with my church members. Let's visit them and ask whether they know where your mother is."

I didn't feel like continuing the search. I just wanted to go back to Busan and work as a fish cleaner, hoping that God would take me away soon so that I could join my family.

"Thank you," I said. "But I just want to go back to Busan."

"Hi-Dong," Yung-Suk said pushing my side. "Do you mean to give up even before trying? The boat leaves in the evening, and we have all day to look for your mother. She must be waiting for you somewhere in this town."

"Yes," I said, my voice weary. "I just want to go back."

"Do you really mean it?" Yung-Suk said, his voice firm. "Just give up and go home?"

Just give up and go home? Is that what Hi-Seung taught me? Do I want to stay as being a mushy bean curd instead of fearless Tarzan? … I don't care whether I am called bean curd or Tarzan. I feel tired. I just want to go back … Then how will Yung-Suk feel? He didn't have to come. But he came here as a friend, not only to locate Mother but to support me. Also what will Mrs. Park think? She paid for my boat ride when she didn't have enough money even for her family. I must continue my search. Search for Mother. At any cost.

"I'm sorry for what I have said." I apologized.

"I understand," Reverend said, lifting me up from the floor. "Let's get some lunch before we start walking."

After treating us to a steaming bowl of noodle soup and hot *kimchee*, Reverend took us to his church members, who had housed refugees from Seoul. We went there, and they did not know who Mother was. Reverend wanted to continue the search with us, but I refused.

Like my father, I knew that Reverend had a busy schedule. Visiting his church members, who were sick or distressed. Preparing his sermons for the Wednesday evening service as well as the Sunday service. Going home to be with his family in the evening. Yet, he had spent the whole morning for me. He even bought us lunch. *How can I expect him to help me more? No way.* But he insisted on coming with us, and I declined saying over and over, *Thank you very much for spending your precious time for me. I am sure that you have a lot of things to do like my father did. Yung-Suk and I can look for Mother. Thank you.* Finally he gave in. Before leaving, he gave us the directions to a refugee camp nearby and suggested that we go and check.

We walked on a winding dirt road leading to the refugee camp on the outskirts of Masan. There were dozens of small tents scattered around the field. There were hundreds of unkempt, unsmiling people walking around, and they all looked weary. I felt they didn't want to be bothered. Clothes fluttered on the lines held by two wooden poles around the tents. The only smiling faces were the children kicking a rubber ball, playing soccer between two goals made of rocks as their goal posts.

We walked around from tent to tent asking, *Have you seen a gracious-looking lady, around sixty years old, with gray hair? She has a warm, gentle voice, and a Seoul accent. Her name is Lee Kyung-In.* The answer was a polite *No.* Some gave us leads that were outside the camp. We walked back to the town visiting the houses that the people at the camp suggested. But Mother was nowhere to be found.

By the time we exhausted the leads, the sun was inching toward the western horizon. We walked to a market place. Merchants and farmers were packing up their goods to go home. Yung-Suk looked at his watch. It was five-thirty. We had to be on board by six-thirty. The dock was a twenty-minute walk. It was getting dark. Yung-Suk looked at me.

"Yung-Suk," I said. "Why don't you go to the dock and wait for me? I'll go to the market and look for Mother."

"No," Yung-Suk said. "I'll go with you."

"I'll be fine," I said. "I'll join you at the dock. You go there and rest."

"No, I'm coming," he said, his voice firm.

The market was still crowded with people. I stopped at the first store.

"Excuse me, Sir," I asked the merchant. "Have you seen a gracious-looking lady, around sixty years old, with gray hair? She has a warm, gentle voice, and she has a Seoul accent."

The merchant looked at us and smiled. He rubbed his hand on his pants.

"I see dozens of women stopping here everyday," he said. "Some, native and some, refugees."

I realized that I was really asking a dumb question. *Of course he must have seen a lot of women shoppers each day. Old and young. Some with babies on their backs. Some with teenage daughters. Those haggling over prices.* But I wanted to find Mother. Yung-Suk felt the same. We scouted the market. A place where merchants sold produce. A place selling fish. A place selling meat. A place where they sold clay pots of all sizes. I rushed, Yung-Suk following close behind. To get a glimpse of Mother in the midst of the crowd. To rush to her. And to hold Mother's hand. But Mother was nowhere in sight.

"What time is it?" I asked Yung-Suk, leaning against a wooden wall for breaths. I wiped sweat from my cheeks.

"Six o'clock," he said.

"Why don't you go to the dock?" I said. "I'll join you before the boat leaves."

"No," he said. "Four eyes are better than two."

We decided to spend ten more minutes looking for Mother and one more place to check. Fabric stores. Mother might be there to buy clothing material to make dresses to sell like she did at home.

"Where are fabric shops?" I asked an elderly woman.

"Are you—a young boy—going to buy dress material?" she said.

She covered her mouth with her hand suppressing her giggle.

"No," I said. "I'm looking for my mother."

"Did you get separated from your mother while shopping?"

"No," I said. "I am from Busan trying to find my mother."

"Dear lady, can you just tell us where the fabric stores are?" Yung-Suk shouted.

She pulled her head back as if she'd been slapped. She pointed down the street. But for once I was grateful for Yung-Suk's direct nature. We rushed in the direction she'd indicated, the whole time scanning the street for Mother.

"Hey, look," Yung-Suk said.

A woman in a store was talking to a merchant waving her hands. I could only see her back, but the way she stood with a thinning gray hair looked like Mother. But then maybe it wasn't. I ran to the store. The woman turned as I approached her. She was not Mother.

"Excuse me," I said to the lady and walked back to Yung-Suk.

Turning to Yung-Suk, I asked, "What time is it?"

"It's ten after six," he said.

"Is it time to go?" I asked.

"Yes," Yung-Suk replied.

It was getting dark. The boat was not going to wait for us. We left the market and headed to the boat. People were going home. There were houses along the road. *Mother may be in one of these houses*, I thought. *If she hears my voice, she'll rush out and welcome me.*

As we hurried to the boat, I yelled aloud, "Mother! Mother! This is Hi-Dong."

Yung-Suk walked beside me without saying a word.

"Do you hear me, Mother?" I yelled. "It's me, Hi-Dong. I am looking for you."

Mother did not rush out.

Maybe, if I sing the song that Mother taught me when I was three years old, she may hear me and rush out. I don't think anyone knows this song. Except me.

I took a deep breath and started to sing the children's song as loudly as I could while my head turned from side to side, hoping to see Mother rushing out from one of those houses along the way.

Rabbit is hopping one, two, three.

I am a-jumping one two three.

Mother's clapping one, two, three.

Look at me people.

I'm now three.

Children holding their mothers' hands looked at me as they walked by.

A beggar turned to look as he was begging for something from a merchant. Drunks wobbled by. But Mother did not rush out to greet me.

As I stepped onto the boat, my voice was hoarse. I was exhausted and drained. Yung-Suk put his arm around me. Warm tears welled up in my eyes. I tried to control the tears by taking deep breaths. I did not want to cry in public. I bowed my head, and bit my lip to curb the flow. But tears fell as if a huge dam had been broken. I sobbed with my hands on my chest. I tried again to take a deep breath to stop the sobbing. But it did not work.

I was not aware of the passing of time. Then I heard the sound of a horn. I felt the boat move, rocking gently by the waves. I felt the gentle breeze.

"Hey, look!" Yung-Suk said.

"What?" I said wiping my eyes.

"There's the North Star," Yung-Suk said.

"Oh," I said.

"We'll find your mother," Yung-Suk said. "We will."

I lifted my head and opened my eyes toward the night sky. The round moon graced the eastern sky with its gentle rays brightening the sea. The twinkling stars looked down at me as if they wanted to spark a light in the dark chamber in my heart.

Yes, with the North Star as my guide, I will find Mother. I will find her, if not today, then tomorrow.

The next day I wanted to stay in bed because the trip to Masan seemed to have taken away every ounce of energy in my body. I just didn't want to get up. But how could I not? Four people slept, ate, played and prayed in this small room. Day and night. Week after week. But also I was a Yung-Suk's friend, not a part of the family. They were kind enough to have me stay with them. How could I stay in bed when the others were up and ready to start their day?

I got out of bed pretending as if nothing had happened yesterday.

"Good morning," I greeted Mrs. Park, my morning ritual. "Have you slept in peace?"

"Yes, Hi-Dong" Mrs. Park responded. "You must feel let down after the trip."

"Oh, I'm fine," I said with a forced smile "I'm sure God will take care of her wherever she may be, and God will help me to find her one day."

I glanced at Yung-Suk to see his reaction. He just smiled.

"Yung-Suk, did you hear what Hi-Dong has said?" Mrs. Park said. "Trusting in God?"

"Oh, Yes, Mother," he mumbled, "I trust in God just like Hi-Dong."

Thanks, Yung-Suk, for not blurting out and telling her how I acted yesterday. That I yelled out calling for Mother in full view of the crowd in the street. That I sang the child's song as loud as I could while the people stared at me. That I broke down and cried like a baby on the boat.

As days passed, I found that I didn't want to talk to anyone. I didn't want to look at people's faces. Even in hunger, food had no taste. My hearing was muffled. My seeing was out of focus. My sensations were numb. All I wished for was sleep, sleep, sleep with a blanket over my head. Not just for that day but also the next day. Day after day. I just wanted to be alone. But where? There was only one room shared by four people, and I was just an uninvited guest. So during the weekdays, I kept busy myself chopping fish heads, removing their organs, flushing them with water and delivering them to restaurants. During weekends I walked the streets of Busan aimlessly mingled in the crowd, feeling all alone and oblivious to what was going on around me.

22. Good news—Mother is alive

Two months had passed since my visit to Masan. The memory of Masan still lingered. The haunting image of the boat tearing apart in a storm, and Mother sinking down to the bottom of the sea kept me feeling uneasy. But I pretended to be cheerful. Smiling, even though I wanted to cry. Mingling with people even though I wanted to be all alone. Mrs. Park knew what had been going on inside me. She took an active role in locating Mother. She visited my family friends and Father's church members living in Busan. When she heard rumors, she crosschecked so that I would not experience the trauma that I had from the Masan trip. But her search was in vain.

Then one Saturday afternoon we were all in the room. Mrs. Park was peeling potatoes for the evening meal. Yung-Ja sewed her torn socks. Yung-Suk and I were engrossed in a game of chess. Yung-Suk was trying to trap my queen, and I was trying to save the queen.

A lady called out, tapping on the sliding door.

"Yes," Mrs. Park responded.

Yung-Ja opened the door.

"Are you Mrs. Park?" the lady asked. Her voice was loud like a drum. "The wife of Reverend Park in Seoul?"

"Yes," Mrs. Park said. She seemed to be wondering what this lady was up to.

"I'm Mrs. Hong," she said. "I attended Reverend Chai's church in Seoul."

I looked at her. *Did I see her in Seoul?* I did not recognize her.

"Oh, did you?" Mrs. Park said, seeming surprised.

"Now I live in Cheju Island with my family," she said. "My husband is in the import-export business and he comes to Busan often."

"What does he ship?" Mrs. Park said.

"The island is hot and humid. Tons of rain year round," she said. "There is an abundant supply of oranges. He brings oranges to Busan and takes grain to Cheju."

Please don't talk so loud, lady. I said to myself. *I'm concentrating to save my queen.*

"How did he get into the shipping business?" Mrs. Park asked.

"He was a business man in Seoul," the lady said. "He got bored living as a refugee. Then he saw the opportunity to supply oranges to the mainland."

"He's a smart man," Mrs. Park said.

"Yes," the lady said. "He has a sharp eye for business opportunities."

"There must be a lot of refugees on the island," Mrs. Park said. "Doing nothing."

"Yes," she said. "Many want to work, but there aren't many jobs to go around on the island. And islanders complain because the refugees are depleting their limited resources."

"I don't blame them," Mrs. Park said.

I found a move to save my queen. I held the queen in my hand and made a final check to decide whether the move was the right one.

"I hear Reverend Chai's son has been living with you," the lady said.

I jerked my head toward the lady.

"Yes," Mrs. Park said, looking puzzled.

"There he is," she said pointing at me. "He's Hi-Dong."

"*Eigo*— Hallelujah." Mrs. Hong exclaimed turning to me. "Your mother has been wanting to contact you for months."

Mother is in Cheju Island? Abruptly I turned, my hand brushing through the chess pieces. The pieces scattered on the board, some dropping on the floor. Yung-Suk did not yell for my messing up his winning game. Instead he turned to Mrs. Hong. Yung-Ja stopped her sewing.

"Mother is on Cheju Island?" I blurted out.

"Yes," Mrs. Hong said, "The military command directed the LST your mother was on to Cheju City instead of Busan."

"She's alive?" I said. "Are you sure she's alive?"

My heart pounded. Like a drum.

178

"If your mother were dead," she smiled, "she wouldn't be able to think of you."

"Are you sure you are talking about Mrs. Chai, wife of Rev. Chai Suk-Mo?" Mrs. Park asked.

"I'm certain," Mrs. Hong said.

She opened her hand bag and pulled out an envelope.

"Who's it addressed to?" I asked her to be sure.

"Let me see," Mrs. Hong said. "She looked over the envelope.

"Is the name on the envelope?" I asked feeling anxious.

"Yes," Mrs. Hong said. "My eyes are getting old and the writing is so wiggly that I can not read it too well."

Wiggly? That must be Mother's writing. I know Mother's writing is wiggly and hard to read. With excitement mixed with fear I asked for the envelope, and Mrs. Hong handed it to me. I closed my eyes, and with the envelope in my hand I prayed, *Please God, when I open my eyes and look at the envelope, let me see my name, Chai Hi-Dong, written by my mother.* The room turned quiet. I opened my eyes. My hands shaking, I looked at the envelope. It read. *To my mangnei—youngest son—Hi-Dong.* It was Mother's hand writing. I held the envelope over my chest with my hands, and with my eyes closed. Tears filled my eyes and ran down my cheeks. *Thank You, God. Mother's alive. She is waiting for me on Cheju Island. We will be together again.*

Mrs. Park came over and held my hand and joined me in tears.

I heard Yung-Suk taking a deep breath. I heard Yung-Ja whisper, *How wonderful.*

"We are so happy for you," Mrs. Park said. "Soon you'll be with your mother."

"Mrs. Chai will swoon," Mrs. Hong said, "when she sees Hi-Dong."

"How long will it take to go to Cheju?" Yung-Suk asked.

"It'll take several days on an LST. It all depends on the weather." Mrs. Hong said. "My husband already arranged for Hi-Dong to leave on an LST."

"When will it be?" Mrs. Park asked.

"Next Monday," Mrs. Hong said.

"Four days from now?" Yung-Suk said, rubbing his knees.

Next Monday? I felt Mrs. Park's hand jerk in mine. Yung-Ja looked

179

at me across the room. My heart sank. In four days I would have to say *goodbye* to Mrs. Park, Yung-Suk and Yung-Ja. They were like my second family. I slept with them listening to Mrs. Park's snore. I ate with them. I went to church with them. Yung-Suk and I played and roamed the streets like two brothers. Yung-Ja teased me like she had done in Seoul. Then in four days, I would say *goodbye* to them, not knowing when we would meet again.

Mrs. Park broke the silence. "I am going to miss this young man," she said patting my hand. "He has been like my son."

I wanted to hug her and say, *Thank you.* But I couldn't because I was timid, and it was not the custom to hug anyone in public. I gently squeezed her hand in mine.

"By the way," Mrs. Hong said pulling out a thick envelope and handing it to Mrs. Park, "it's from Mrs. Chai."

What is in that envelope? A letter of thanks for taking care of me for all these months? But the envelope is too thick just to have a letter. A pretty handkerchief that Mother sewed? Who would need a pretty handkerchief in this time of war? Mrs. Park held the envelope in her hand. Her fingers moved slowly up and down, her eyes looking at the envelope.

"Please open it," Mrs. Hong said.

Mrs. Park turned the envelope and slowly tore open the flap. I saw a thick packet of money with a folded white paper. Did Mother send money to thank Mrs. Park for having taken care of me?

Mrs. Park pulled out a folded white sheet. Her eyes scanned the paper. Then her eyes turned downward in silence. Slowly she straightened herself, her hand with the envelope moving toward Mrs. Hong.

"Please return the envelope to Mrs. Chai," she said. "Please tell her that it has been a pleasure to have Hi-Dong with us even for a short while. We will all miss him."

"But …," Mrs. Hong hesitated.

"Please, please," Mrs. Park said, reaching toward Mrs. Hong and dropping the envelope on her lap.

Then Mrs. Park turned her eyes toward me with a smile. Our eyes met. I swallowed the tears welling up in my eyes. *Thank you Mrs. Park. Thank you!*

23. On a boat to Cheju Island

On the day of my departure, Mrs. Park prepared a special breakfast. Steaming white rice in a big bowl. A snapper—I had brought home from work the night before—broiled on the charcoal fire. Several side dishes that were absent in our normal meals. After breakfast, the whole family accompanied me to the boat.

"My dear Hi-Dong," Mrs. Park said holding my hand, "Everything will be fine this time. I'm sure."

"Thank you, thank you very much," I said bowing. "Please take good care of yourself. Thank you very much again."

"Hey, Hi-Dong," Yung-Suk said, shaking my hand, "I hear Cheju has beautiful beaches all around. Enjoy swimming, and stay healthy until we see each other again."

"Thanks, Yung-Suk," I firmly held his hand and shook it. "Take care."

Then I turned to Yung-Ja.

"Thanks, Yung-Ja," I said. "I'm going to miss you calling me Bow-Leg."

"I'll miss you too," she said, looking sad.

After bowing at them one more time, I walked up the ramp and stood at the rail looking down at Yung-Suk's family. I tried to smile. Instead, my eyes twitched. My heart felt numb. I tried to lift my hand in the air to wave, but my arm felt stiff.

"God be with you," Mrs. Park shouted.

"Thank you very much," I responded.

"Hi-Dong," Yung-Suk shouted with a grin, "be sure to learn to protect your queen next time."

"Don't worry," I shouted back, "I'll show you."

In minutes I heard a dreadful sound. The LST blew its horn making a deep groaning sound. Not once but twice. Mrs. Park looked up. Yung-Suk and Yung-Ja waved.

I waved back shouting, "Thanks a lot! Take care!"

The ship started to move. With each passing minute, the ship moved further and further away from the dock. Yung-Suk and Yung-Ja still waved. Their fluttering hands becoming smaller. I looked over at Busan, which had been my home since leaving Seoul. From the boat, the city and its surroundings seemed like a scene in a painting with the dark blue water in the front and the gray sky above. Soon my life in Busan would become a memory, one of searching and longing for Mother and the memory of refugee life with Yung-Suk's family. Four grownups living in a tiny room, sleeping like sardines in a flat can, eating with whatever we could gather for that day, laughing, crying, worrying …

The deck was filled with families huddled around forming small circles—like the scene in the train compartment coming down to Busan. With a bag in one hand and a duffle bag on my shoulder, I meandered through the crowd, and found a space by the corner of the captain's deck at the stern of the LST. I pulled out a blanket from my duffle bag and spread it on the floor. I put the other bag on one end as a pillow and lay down. It felt soft like a real pillow, but the steel deck felt as hard as concrete. But I was used to sleeping on a hard floor, and I figured the sleeping bag would provide enough cushion to sleep at night in reasonable comfort. I looked up to the sky; it was covered with gray clouds. I hoped, *The night sky will be clear so that I can gaze at millions of twinkling stars above. It's chilly but not too cold. This will be my home for the next several days. Unlike Yung-Suk's place, here I can do whatever I want. Without being a bother to anyone, I can lie down. I can stretch. I can read. What freedom I have. Let me enjoy.*

As the ship moved further away from the land, it swayed sideways and moved up and down by the waves. I thought that the ship's swaying was kind of fun. Then within a few minutes, I felt dizzy. The delicious morning breakfast in my stomach followed the motion of the ship giving me the feeling of nausea. Instead of enjoying the freedom that I felt in the beginning, I ended up flat on the floor with my head on the bag, being tortured by seasickness. Fortunately, unlike the time when I went to Masan in search of Mother, I did not vomit and the seasickness began to subside by noon. I got up and walked to the rail. Far away on the horizon the gray clouds in the sky touched the dark blue water forming a giant arc. Huge waves tossed the boat up and down like a toy. I walked around the deck feeling the cool wind. People were all around. Some looked at the sea. Some, lying on the floor, stared at the gray sky. Some slept leaning against their belongings.

In the afternoon the sky cleared; the sea became calm, and the boat sailed toward Cheju Island, hundreds of miles away. I found that sitting on the deck of an LST on the open sea all day doing nothing was a good way to learn to handle boredom. All I saw around me were the refugees in groups on the deck looking bored, the vast water around the ship making a giant circle, and the endless sky with dark gray clouds floating aimlessly. I got out my Robinson Crusoe novel to read. How he survived the shipwreck and managed to live, as the only white man, on a tropical island with cannibals, who hunted humans to eat. I read it for an hour or so. I looked at the sky. It was still cloudy. I walked around the deck glancing at the people huddled in circles. I watched the billowing waves of the sea. Returned to my place. Read some more. Looked at the sky again. Walked the deck again. Watched the waves again. Read some more ...

The night turned cold with the February wind blowing from the north. I kept myself warm by wearing several layers of underwear and socks. I was no longer seasick and found myself enjoying being on the open sea in total darkness. I lay down with my head on the bag gazing at the cloudless sky filled with millions of twinkling stars and the round moon journeying toward the west.

My mind wandered. *What is beyond the stars? Endless space or a huge wall? If a wall, what is behind the wall? Heaven where God and angels live, and where Father and Brother Hi-Seung live? Do animals, like Kwidong, live in heaven with people?*

Brother Hi-Bum said that heaven and hell were man-made stuff. They didn't really exist. When we died, we just turned to pounds of dirt supplying nutrients for plants. It will be so nice, though, if there is heaven. Then I will see my loved ones when I die.

But how am I sure that God will send me to heaven instead of hell? I am pretty sure He will send me to heaven because the Bible says, "Those who believe in Jesus as their Savior will be saved." And I believe. Then what is the meaning of believing? Just because I say, "I believe Jesus is my Savior" guarantees me a place in heaven? Does a murderer go to heaven just because he says he believes in Jesus as his Savior. What about those good people I know—like my Little Aunt—who openly tells Mother that she doesn't believe in Jesus? And what about those Koreans who have never heard of Jesus? Will they go to hell?

I hear hell is a hot place. Very hot. There is a mile-long track filled with red hot charcoal where the sinners walk around and around not just for a day but forever. The bottoms of their feet sizzle. They can hear the sizzling sound. They can feel the pain. But they can not jump off the track because horned devils are all around them, watching their every move. Anyone who jumps off the track will be pierced right away by the devil's darting spear, and he will be placed back on the track. Bleeding. I sure don't want to end up in hell. I sure hope that my favorite Little Aunt doesn't end in hell.

Where is hell anyway? Elders say, "Those who believe in Jesus are lifted up to heaven when they die, but those who don't believe in Him will descend into hell." Is hell at the center of the earth where it is very hot and filled with molten lava? I don't want to think about. It's too gruesome.

Some elders say that our bodies turn to soil like Hi-Bum said, but our spirits live forever with God in heaven. Then what is spirit? I know that my head does the thinking and my heart does the feeling. I know where my head is, and I know where my heart is. But where is my spirit? Inside me or outside? And what does it do? Does one's spirit get old when the person is alive and stops getting old when the person dies? If that's true, when I die at the age eighty-eight, I will meet eighteen year old Hi-Seung's spirit and sixty-one-year old Father's spirit. They will have to bow down to me since my spirit is much older. That will be fun. But do the spirits recognize each other in heaven? Will the spirits of Father and Brother Hi-Seung recognize me and welcome me? If not, what good is there about going to heaven? ...

Oh, it's getting too complicated. Let me sleep a little.

184

A lot of questions and no answers. But it was fun to think. Time flew by fast, and it kept me from boredom.

I spent two nights on the deck. The third morning I saw an island over the horizon. A mountain stood in the middle. Mount Hala, the tallest mountain in South Korea, loomed before me. I read in my Geography book that Mt. Hala was 6,400 ft high. People crowded against the railing facing the island—the island where Mother was supposed to be. I joined the crowd thinking, *Before night falls, I may join Mother. No. No. Don't say, "may." Instead, say "I will see Mother." She will cry when she sees me. She will pray holding my hand. She will rush into the kitchen bringing something to drink. Then she will want to know how I have survived since leaving Seoul.*

Mt. Hala seemed so close, but the boat seemed to take forever to reach the island. The people returned to their groups and sat down. Waiting. I stood watching the scene changing ever so slowly, hoping that the boat would speed up and get to the pier of Cheju City. But in the vast sea, the boat seemed to be standing still. It took an hour or so before I could see civilization: fishing boats, tiny houses, beaches, and a port. As we approached the pier, the giant ocean waves subsided into ripples. The refugees scurried to pack up their belongings and to get ready to debark. I saw a line forming by the exit. I quickly picked up my bags and rushed to the front of the line. As soon as the metal hit the concrete pier, I rushed down to the gate to be the first one off. It took another *forever* before the steel gate opened and the boat's ramp lowered. A soldier stood on the dock by the ramp talking to a crew member. I waited and the people behind me waited to get off the ramp. Then I heard a man's voice through the ship's intercom. Loudly and clearly.

This is the captain speaking, the man said. *I have just received an order from the naval command headquarters that our ship be directed to Seogwipo from Cheju City. I apologize for this change. Please be patient. As soon as we unload the cargo and replenish the boat with supplies, we will depart.*

When I heard the announcement, my heart sank. *To another port? Where's Seogwipo? Walking distance from here? Or the opposite side of the island? Will there be buses to take us back to Cheju city? But I don't have any money for the bus fare.* My mind raced. *What should I do? Stay on the boat not knowing where it is heading for? … No, I'd better find a way to get off the boat rather than getting lost at another place and spend days or weeks to find Mother. But how? A soldier is standing at the bottom of the ramp with a rifle on his shoulder. I am afraid that he may shoot me if he sees me running away. Then what should I do? Just stay and go to Seogwipo and try to find a way to Cheju city?* My mind raced to find the solution. Hi-Seung's words flashed by mind, *I can do anything that I set my mind to.* Finally I made the decision. To jump off the ship.

I looked down the ramp. The soldier was talking to the crew. Four workers were unloading tall cargo in a wooden box, the size of a large automobile, on wheels. Two workers in the front leaned their backs against the cargo as they guided it slowly down the ramp; the other two in the back held the cargo with straps so that it wouldn't roll down too fast. The wheels creaked against the steel ramp. This was my chance to get off. I stepped behind the worker furthest away from the soldier. The cargo moved down ever so slowly that it seemed to take forever. I felt the crowd behind me watching my move. My hands became sweaty. My shoulders tensed, fearing that at any moment someone in the crowd might yell and get the soldier's attention. I whispered to myself, *Hurry up, workers. Hurry up. I want to get down and find Mother.* After interminable minutes, the cargo was finally down on the dock. I sped away like Kwidong, running to catch a fleeing rabbit. I ran toward the crowd nearby, fearing that the soldier would chase after me with the bayonet on his rifle. But nothing happened. Either he did not see me or he couldn't be bothered with a young boy running away. In the midst of the crowd, I stopped to take a deep breath. *I did it. I did it,* I whispered. *Brother Hi-Seung, I did it. You told me that I could do anything that I set my mind to. Today I set my mind to jump the ship, and I did it. Thanks, Brother. I am the Tarzan of the human jungle, not the mushy bean curd anymore.*

24. Finally, I am with Mother

Cheju harbor was in a recessed portion of the coastline with a concrete wall. It had no concrete pier where a big cargo ship could dock sideways. A round walkway made of rocks and gravel protected the harbor from the sea. At the end of the walkway was a small lighthouse.

Along the dock, fishermen spread their catch and yelled at passersby to stop and buy. I walked along, watching their displays. I saw a woman pick up a fish and wave it at a fisherman. I figured she was haggling. I moved closer. I could not understand whether she was haggling or yelling because of her accent. I wondered, *Who can I ask for the directions to Sea-of-Galilee Church when I don't understand the natives' accent? Or will they understand me? I should find a refugee to ask for the directions. But how can I tell a refugee from a native?*

I walked towards the town, studying the passersby. The people wearing laborers' Korean costumes walked slowly while the people wearing westernized dresses hurried. I saw an elderly man in a suit and a hat walking toward me.

"Excuse me, Sir," I said. "Do you know where the Sea of Galilee Church is?"

The man stopped. He smiled. Surely he knew.

"Me Chinese," he said in broken Korean. "Me speak Korean very little."

How strange. I thought the Chinese wore blue outfits with blue caps as in Seoul. Perhaps he is a diplomat. Chinese, Koreans and Japanese all look alike anyway. Maybe, I should I ask a lady with a Korean hairdo.

I walked by the shops looking for a person speaking without the accent. All the women spoke in Cheju dialect with a strong accent. Customers and shop owners talked very fast and loudly as if they were arguing. Then at one fish shop I heard a lady talking with a merchant, with her back facing me. She had a big rock cod in her hand.

"I saw the same size fish in another store at half the price," the lady said.

How nice. I have finally found a lady whom I can understand. The voice sounds familiar too. Where did I hear her voice? Busan? No ... Seoul? Yes, Seoul. Then whose voice? I poked my head in as if I was checking on a fish to buy.

"This fish was caught by my husband last night," the merchant said "You can't buy fish any fresher than this one. But I'll sell it to you at twenty *won*."

"Since I don't want to walk back to another store," the lady said, "I'll take it for ten *won*," the lady said.

"I'll lose money then," the merchant replied.

"You got the fish free from the ocean," the lady said.

"We have to make a living," the merchant responded. "I have five children to feed."

The merchant put her hand out toward the lady with her fingers spread wide and pointing up. The lady was quiet for a second. Her haggling tactic reminded me of Mother. When Mother haggled for anything she started with a half of the asking price and negotiated up to the middle in a gentle tone of voice.

"Alright, I'll take it home for fifteen *won*," the lady said.

"I can't," the merchant said. "Selling fish does not give me enough income to feed and clothe my five children. But since you are a nice lady, I'll sell it to you for seventeen *won*."

The lady examined the fish in her hand. She lifted it up and down, as if she was going to say, *This fish is a small one. Not worth seventeen won.*

"Well, I'll have to walk back to the other shop," the lady said.

She slowly turned around to put the fish back on the wooden rack. I knew from my trips to market with Mother that this was a trick. She was hoping that the merchant would give in to her asking price. She looked up towards me. She looked very familiar. *Isn't she Cousin Suk-Moon's wife?* I mumbled. *The cousin whom Mother traveled with from Seoul?* Suddenly her eyes turned round. She dropped the fish on the floor.

"*Eigo,*" she cried out, "Are...n't you Hi-Dong?"

"Ye...s, Sister," I said, my voice cracking.

My whole body felt a jolt of life I hadn't known for months. I knew the voice sounded familiar, but I had never thought that the lady was Min-Ja, Uncle Suk-Moon's wife.

"Your mother has been worrying and praying for you every day," Min-Ja said.

"Let's hurry. Your mother will be in high heaven. "

Let's hurry. Let's hurry. Those were the happiest words I'd ever heard. The heavy weight that had dwelt within me since we said, *See you in Busan,* dropped from my chest. I felt so light I could have jumped ten feet high.

"Okay! Okay, lady. Fifteen won," the merchant said. "It's yours."

Min-Ja handed the money to the merchant and came out of the store. We rushed toward home on a dirt road, Min-Ja holding the fish by its tail. With each step, the fish moved back and forth. The roads were big enough for two ox-driven carts to squeeze through. Houses along the road were all one-story with thatched roofs and rock walls alongside the road. People wearing Seoul dress mingled with the natives.

"How far yet to go?" I asked Min-Ja as we walked uphill toward Mount Hala.

"Five more minutes," she said.

In five more minutes, I will see Mother. My steps quickened.

"Slow down, Hi-Dong," Min-Ja said smiling. "I have short legs."

After passing a dozen homes, Min-Ja stopped at an unvarnished wooden gate with double doors. I heard a familiar rhythmic sound of wooden bats pounding clothes on a wooden block—an old traditional way of smoothing out the wrinkles on dried clothes after washing.

"Here we are," Min-Ja said pushing open the door.

As we walked into the dirt courtyard, I saw Mother sitting on the wooden floor open to the courtyard. She was busy pounding a white folded sheet laying on a block with bats in her hands. Her arms moved up and down in rhythmic motion.

"Is it Min-Ja?" Mother said without turning to look.

"Yes," Min-Ja said. "Guess who I brought home?"

"Who?" Mother said.

Finally. Finally I see Mother right in front me. I see her face with my own eyes. She looks old and tired. More deep wrinkles on her face. Her hair all turned gray. Her voice is weak but still warm. Is Mother ill? Has she been having enough food?

"Mother," I said holding the tears welling up inside. "Hi-Dong's here."

The pounding suddenly stopped. She turned, the bats still in her hands. She looked at me as if she was seeing a ghost. Her eyes in shock. Her mouth open.

"I'm Hi-Dong," I repeated.

"My *mangnei*," Mother gasped.

Mother dropped the bats on the floor and rushed across the courtyard in bare feet.

"Oh, my *mangnei*," Mother said holding my hands. "You've come home to Mother. You've come home."

Mother is in front me. This is not a dream. This is real. Tears fell down my cheeks. I bowed my head and sobbed.

"My dear *mangnei* is home," Mother said caressing my hands in her bosom.

Then she turned to Min-Ja and asked, "How did you find him?"

"I was at a store haggling for fish," Min-Ja said. "I saw a boy with bags standing in the store. I looked at him. He was Hi-Dong."

"Thank You, Lord," Mother said. "Without you, he would have spent all day looking for me. Let's all go in."

"Aunt, I'll leave you alone," Min-Ja said. "You must have a lot to talk about with Hi-Dong."

"Thank you again," Mother said.

Mother turned to me and said, "You go in. I'll join you as soon as I clean my feet."

I stepped upon the floor, set my bags on the corner and sat down. Mother rinsed off the dirt and dried her feet.

"My *mangnei*," she repeated. "You are home."

"Mother," I said looking at her pale face. "Are you all right?"

When I was a child, I often worried that Mother might die from all the pain and suffering that she had gone through. That same fear crept into me.

"I'm all right," she said.

190

"Are you really?" I asked.

"Don't worry, my son," Mother said, hobbling out to the kitchen. "I'm just getting old."

I knew she was going to bring some fruit as she had done at home for her guests.

"Mother, you don't have to get anything," I said. "I'm your son. Not a guest."

"You are my most precious guest," she said.

Mother brought in several locally grown oranges on a plate. She peeled one and handed the slices to me, all the while asking me questions about how I had survived the last few months.

"What happened?" I said. "How did you end up in Cheju?"

Mother chuckled. She said somewhere along the southern coast their ship was ordered by the military command to change its course to Cheju Island instead of Busan. When the naval command post sent an order, *Captain, steer your ship to Cheju Island,* the captain simply followed the order. He did not argue with the naval command about how the refugees would feel if they found themselves in Cheju—not Busan, their original destination. The captain just said, *Yes, Sir,* and turned the boat southwest toward Cheju Island. Within a day the ship reached the island and docked at Cheju city, the capital city of the island, and the refugees were escorted by local volunteers to the refugee camps dotting the hillside of Mount Halla. There were no trucks. The old, the young, mothers with children, all walked up the dirt hill with their belongings on their backs, on their heads, or pulling with their hands. Mother did not know how long she would be staying at the camp. With no telephone and mail delivery, she had no way to correspond with me. She did not know anyone at the camp except Suk-Moon's family whom she came down with.

"Did you live alone at the camp?" I asked.

"Suk-Moon's family wouldn't do that," Mother said. "They made a space between us so that I could have some privacy until I moved down here."

"How did you get to move to this house?" I asked.

"Suk-Moon found a place for me," Mother said. "I owe his family a great debt."

Suk-Moon found a distant relative who had been living on the island for years, and the relative found a place for Min-Ja's family and Mother.

I looked around from the floor where I sat. To my right, I saw a room with paper-covered sliding doors. To my left, there was another room with the sliding doors. Next to the room, I saw space with a gray blanket hanging down like a curtain.

"Which room do you stay in?" I asked.

"Which room do you think?" Mother said with a glimmer of a smile.

"I don't know," I said. "Which one?"

"That one," Mother said pointing at the curtain. "Go and see."

Mother opened the blanket so that I could walk in. The room Mother stayed in was not a room but a passageway between the kitchen and the living room. I stepped on the floor. It was uneven and made a creaking sound. The passageway was the size of a car. There was no window. No electric bulb hanging down from the ceiling. The door to the kitchen had cracks big enough to spy through. A gray blanket curtain hanging on the side of the passageway provided some measure of privacy. In the hot and humid climate of the island, the room stunk with the *kimchee* odor. It was a depressing sight to see and learn that Mother, who had lived in a two-story brick house with a large room of her own, stayed in this dark hole. But I did not want to show her my disgust. I wanted to act positive and jovial.

"This room is bigger than your prayer closet," I joked thinking of the closet at home that she had frequented for praying.

"I'm so grateful," Mother said, "to have a room of my own where I can pray and sleep."

She mentioned thousands of refugees on the hillside living in green military tents without dividers among the families. Gusty winds often tore the tents apart. Rains flooded the tents. And those affected had to resettle in other tents. But she had four walls to shield her from heavy winds, a roof to keep her from the sun and the rain, and a floor to shield her from the flood rushing between volcanic rocks. She was the same mother I had always known. Never complaining. Always accepting whatever life brought to her. Praying without ceasing. Maybe, that was why she had been able to survive through so many travails.

"Mother, I am a fifteen-year-old boy." I grinned. "Will you feel comfortable having a grown son sleeping next you?"

"You are always my baby, no matter how old you are," Mother reached over and held my hand with a smile. "You can keep me warm at night."

I covered her hand with my mine. Her hand did not have much flesh; it was bony and dry, like a dried squid. But it was Mother's hand. The hand that bathed me and clothed me when I was a baby. The hand that sewed my torn pants as a child. The hand that checked my pulse and my temperature when I was sick. Now her hand was in mine. Mother was in front of me. *Thank You, God. I don't have to search for her any longer.*

"Hi-Dong, you had a long trip. Why don't you lie down and rest a while," Mother said. "I'll go to a market and get a fresh mackerel for dinner."

"Yes, Mother, I will," I said. "Since I have finally found you, I can rest a while."

I felt limp like a creature without bones. All the tension was gone. Now I could relax and rest. I walked into Mother's room, and put my knapsack and bag on one side. The room was dimly lit by the light coming through the openings around the curtain. I saw a neatly folded mattress and pillow in one corner and the Bible next to them. In another corner by the kitchen door was a small eating table with a couple of bowls, a spoon, and pair of chopsticks. Two small clay pots were set by the wall. I opened one jar, and it contained the *kimchee* that stunk up the room. In the other jar was rice. It was almost empty. *How has Mother been surviving for all these months without money? Has she been eating only one meal a day? Has she been surviving just with rice and kimchee?* When I thought of those questions, my heart ached. *Well, whatever hardship she has gone through till now, it will be over soon. I'm here now. I will get a job and take care of her. I will not let her work. She can sew for fun, but not to feed me.* I flopped down with my bag as a pillow, feeling good to be all alone in the room and rest. *I won't be wakened up by Mrs. Park's constant snoring. I won't lose sleep worrying that I may expose myself with Yung-Ja in the same room. Here the only person I will be sleeping with will be Mother. And if I happen to expose myself and Mother wakes up and sees me, she will smile and say, "Thank You, Lord. My son is now a young man."*

I did not know how long I slept. A warm hand in mine wakened me. It was Mother looking down at me with her gentle smile. The smell of freshly broiled mackerel whetted my appetite.

"Lunch time already?" I said.

"A table is set for my long lost son," Mother said. "There is a pan of water out in the courtyard for you to wash."

"I'm hungry," I said sitting up. "Let me eat first."

Mother brought the meal table and placed it in front of me. On the table were two bowls of steaming rice, *kimchee*, mackerel, and seaweed soup. Mother gave grace, her voice teary. I looked at my rice bowl. It was filled to the brim. I looked at Mother's bowl. It was as small as a coffee cup. It was filled just to the top.

"Mother," I said reaching over to pick up her bowl. "Let me give you some of my rice. You don't have enough."

"Don't do that," Mother said. "A young growing body needs a lot of food. I'm an old woman, and I don't need much."

"You are just saying that," I said.

"Don't worry and eat," she insisted. "You haven't had your mother's cooking for months."

Yes, it was the first time since leaving home that I could enjoy Mother's cooking. It was the first time that I could eat without feeling like a parasite encroaching on the meal that was not enough even for Mrs. Park's family. But looking at the cup of rice in front of Mother, my heart sank. *Has Mother survived with two cups of rice a day because she did not have much money? Is that why she looks so old and tired? With me here, the rice pot will be empty within days.* I was hungry for Mother's good cooking, but my heart felt heavy. I had an urge to exchange the rice bowl, but I decided against it. It was a joyful day, and I did not want to argue with Mother over the rice. *Tomorrow I will look for a job. I will take care of her.*

Over the lunch table, I heard Mother's story. Her unending prayer for my safety and her longing to have me beside her. Her struggle to survive without anyone supporting her. She had supported herself by doing what she knew best. Sewing. Mother sewed for a lady who owned a dress shop. It was not a steady job with a steady income. When the lady needed help, she called Mother. When the lady did not have enough work, Mother was not called. Then Mother had to do something she had never done before. Make rice cakes and sell them on a street corner.

After lunch I walked out to the court yard to look around. Like the farm houses on the mainland, I saw a heavy wooden gate, a courtyard, clay pots of various sizes on one side of the house for storing rice, dry beans, soy sauce, soy bean sauce, and hot bean sauce. One big clay pot was without a cover. Facing the courtyard were two rooms separated by a wooden floor. A kitchen was next to a bedroom. On one side of the house was an outhouse. Next to the outhouse was a swine cage where pigs grunted. The thatched roofs were tied down with heavy ropes. The walls were built with rocks. Plenty of rocks. The courtyard was laid with flat rocks. The dividing walls between houses were also made of rocks.

"Mother," I said. "Rocks are all over."

"Yes, Hi-Dong," Mother said. "This island is famous for rocks, wind and women. Do you see the roof?"

"Yes," I said.

"You'll soon find that on this island the wind is so strong that without the roof being tied down with heavy ropes, you'll wake up in the morning and see the dark clouds in the sky," Mother said. "And it rains and rains."

"A few days of rain will fill up the water pot," Mother said, pointing to the large clay pot, without the cover, that came up to my chest.

Mother said that water was scarce, and the people on the island had been using rain water to supplement the well water which had been getting low because of the additional refugee population. I thought it strange that water was scarce on the island surrounded by miles of water. Unfortunately, it was undrinkable salty sea water.

"Mother, you said that island women are famous," I said.

"Sure, they are," Mother chuckled. "Don't mess with them."

"Why not?"

"Let's go out to the street," Mother said. "I'll show you."

We opened the entrance gate and walked out.

"Can you tell refugee women from islanders?" Mother asked.

I stood by a street corner watching people, especially women. After a few minutes I could tell the difference.

"Refugee women are dressed like those in Seoul and walk like women," I said, " and Island women are dressed in a plain traditional costume and walk like wrestlers."

"Yes," Mother smiled. "Also they are very tough. They push their men around as if they are their servants."

"So the island women are tougher than their men?"

"Yes."

"How come?"

"I heard that for generations the women worked in the sea as divers to get clams, oysters and abalone that were in abundance on the seabed while the men worked in the fields."

"And?"

"In time, these women, braving the sea, diving in and out of water for hours a day, year after year, developed stronger lungs and muscles than their men working in the fields. The men could not outfight their women, and eventually they buckled under."

"It would be fun to wrestle with one of those women," I chuckled.

"You give it a try," Mother smiled. "But don't come home with a bloody nose. Looking ashamed."

We passed the main street lined with shops and walked on a nearby pier. The narrow pier was built with rocks to keep boats in the inlet from the heavy waves. A group of husky women in swimsuits and caps sat around a fire on the pier with their clasped hands around their knees. Oval-shaped wooden baskets with shoulder belts were next to them. Half a dozen wooden baskets floated in the water a few hundred feet away.

"Mother," I said pointing to the baskets in the water. "What are they?"

"Those are baskets for abalone," Mother said. "Those women are called sea maidens. They dive down to the sea floor and collect abalone. Some can stay in the water for many minutes."

I saw the water splashing and saw a sea maiden coming out of the water and putting her catch in the basket.

"It must be fun," I said.

"Yes, if you do it for fun," Mother said. "But making a living by catching abalone is a hard life."

We walked to the end of the pier and sat on a rock. The sky was overcast, but the sun's rays turned the clouds light gray and pink. Young boys swamed along the pier diving down and up like trout. I saw a sea maiden disappear in the water. I waited for a minute and saw the water bubble, and up came the sea maiden with an abalone. Then she swam toward her basket and dumped the abalone into the basket. She disappeared into the water. It seemed so much fun.

"Do you think that they will let me swim next to them?" I asked Mother. Mother looked at me with a broad smile.

"Do you want to try and see what those husky women will do to you?"

I thought of what Mother said of the island women. How they pushed their men around. I pictured the chief sea maiden seeing me swim next to them and the chief ordering her girls. *Soon-Ja, go grab his right hand. Min-Ja, grab his left hand. Kyung-Ja, grab his right foot, and lastly Nin-Ja, grab his left foot. While you stretch him flat out on the water, I will go under him and show him what we can do to a boy from Seoul.* I decided that swimming next to them wasn't a good idea. But it seemed like so much fun.

"I'll have fun living here," I said.

"You will," Mother said. "Unfortunately you don't have a future living on this island. You are at an age where you can soak up knowledge like a sponge under able teachers. Here, there aren't such teachers.

"By the way, did you bring your English books?" Mother asked.

"Some," I said.

"Good," Mother said. "Learn as much English as you can while on Cheju where you have plenty time to study. God has given you a good mind. I don't want it to go wasted."

What is Mother thinking? Is studying English the only way not to waste my good mind? What about studying other subjects like science, mathematics, and philosophy?

"Why English?" I looked up to Mother.

"I am going to send you to America," Mother said, without blinking her eyes.

197

Send me to America? She must have had too much time on her hands to think such a crazy thought. She doesn't even have enough money to eat and yet she talks about sending me to America that will cost hundreds of dollars. Anyway, I am not going to leave her alone. I am going to take care of her. I am sure I can find a fish-cleaning job that I am an expert at.

"Thank you, Mother," I said, my voice firm. "But I'm not going to leave you alone."

Mother looked at me with a smile. Then she turned to look at the waves splashing over the rocks. Her thinning, gray hair fluttered in the breeze. The hazy sunlight through the dark clouds highlighted the deep wrinkles etched on her face. The wrinkles. Gifts of life. Suffering. And more suffering.

"Hi-Dong," Mother said. "Let's pray about it."

Since Mother's mention of sending me to America before leaving Seoul, I dreamed of going to America. The country that I heard of and read about. A dreamland, where the highways were paved with *gold*, where cars sped fast like bullets, and where buildings were taller than mountains. The country where no one starved because everyone had a *money tree* in his backyard where dollar bills grew like leaves. The country where Henry Ford introduced automobiles, where the Wright brothers flew their first airplane, and where Thomas Edison, my hero, invented the light bulb. I wanted to go to America, to study hard. Very hard. And return home as a world-famous inventor. When a huge crowd would gather at the airport to welcome me, I pictured myself standing behind Mother, and shouting at the crowd, *It's not me who you should welcome, but my mother standing in front of me. She is the one who should get all the accolades.* But now, Mother came first, and my dream second.

When I woke up the next day, Mother had been outside cooking. Since leaving Seoul, it was the first night I slept in the same house with Mother. Free from worry. Feeling secure. Feeling comfortable even when sleeping in a hallway with a squeaky floor. The uneasy feeling of being a burden to Yung-Suk's family wasn't there. I felt free.

"Have you slept in peace?" I said walking out to the courtyard and stretching.

Mother was fanning a charcoal fire on the stove to start the morning meal. The black charcoal was turning red sending its gray smoke upward. The sky was blue like the ocean. The air was dry and mild.

"Yes," Mother said with a smile. "So nice to have you home. Even the sky and the air are welcoming you. The clear blue sky and the dry air—not the usual dark clouds and humid air."

"What are you cooking for breakfast?" I asked.

"A real treat," Mother said. "I will fix you an abalone dish. I went to the pier and got it from a sea maiden this morning. You can't get it any fresher."

Mother's already spending too much money because of me. I thought. *A mackerel will be much cheaper than abalone. Probably more healthful.*

"Oh, Mother," I said, "you don't have to do that."

"This is the Island specialty," Mother said. "I want you taste it."

"While you are cooking," I said, "I'll set the table."

"That's a woman's job," Mother said.

"Mother, you are too old-fashioned," I said. "It doesn't matter who sets the table. A man or a woman."

"I guess you're right," she said. "We are so bound by tradition."

When breakfast was ready, I sat across from Mother at the black table with the aroma of the abalone dish filling up the room. Her ever gracious face, etched with wrinkles. Her gentle receiving eyes. Her caring voice. Mother who didn't squelch my inborn curiosity about the world around me but allowed me to explore. She was sitting across from me for the first time since I had left Seoul. I felt the warmth spreading throughout my body. *Thank You, God, for keeping my mother alive so that I can sit in front of her and look at her again with my own eyes. Help me to become a person that Mother will be proud of.*

She picked up a piece of abalone with her chopsticks and brought it to my mouth for me to taste.

"Is it delicious?" Mother said.

"Yes, very much so," I said.

I picked up the rice bowl filled with steaming rice. Then I saw again that her rice was in a cup about half the size of my bowl. The same question rose up in my mind. *Has she been surviving with a cup of rice a meal for all this* time? Is that why she looked so pale and weak? With me here, how is she going to survive from the money she's making from sewing? I will look for a job right away. But it is the first morning that Mother and I are together. It is the time for celebration and the beginning of a new life, not the time to argue about my working, knowing that Mother will strongly disapprove. "Your job is to make use of your God-given mind to serve people's well-being," Mother will say. "Not to stoop low doing menial work to support your mother."

"So nice to have you with me," Mother said picking up another piece for me.

"Mother," I said. "Please eat."

"Yes, I will," Mother said. "But having you in front of me, I feel full."

About halfway through the breakfast, I decided to bring up the subject of my working even though I knew her response would be a definite No.

"Mother," I said, "while staying with Yung-Suk's family, I realized that I had led a too sheltered life."

She looked up with a smile.

"Yes," Mother said, "Maybe I was selfish. Also, I worried a lot the last few months wondering how my innocent boy was handling the hardship alone."

"Because Brother Hi-Seung toughened me up," I said, "I was able to survive without you even though I missed you."

"I am glad," Mother said.

"I even worked for a while in Busan," I said.

Mother's eyes turned round.

"Did you say, 'work'?"

"Yes," I said.

"What kind of work?"

"Cleaning fish."

"Cleaning fish?"

Her spoon shook and the soup spilled on the table.

"Yes," I said. "I learned so much about working and dealing with people."

Mother did not respond, seemingly deep in thought. She looked down at the soup bowl, dipped her spoon in the soup and picked it up. A sliver of the seaweed dangled down from the spoon. She continued to eat quietly without looking at me, first rice, then soup, *kimchee*, abalone, and back again to rice. *What is she thinking? Is she going to tell me not to think of working again but instead, study English?* I decided not to bring up again the subject of my working at this time. It was the first full day with Mother. A time to enjoy.

25. I find a job

For several weeks, I spent the mornings studying English, and the afternoons playing. Like the island boys, I swam in the ocean. I learned to float on my back for minutes, looking up the sky. I found it much easier to swim on my back here than in the Han River by Seoul because the seawater was heavier. I dived deep down in the ocean even touching the floor, looking for abalone or sea urchins, but I couldn't hold my breath long enough on the sea bed to catch any. I jogged up the hill toward Mount Hala until my breath ran out. Then I sat on the top of a big rock, surveying the island and gazing at the horizon surrounding the island in an arc. I struggled between my dream of going to America and my desire to look after Mother. *What should I do? Go to America to be the Edison of Korea and come back home and make Mother proud? Or stay with Mother and look after her?*

While I was studying English at Mother's insistence and was busy getting acquainted with the island life, Mother went to the dock early each morning to meet the fishermen arriving on a boat with their fresh catch of mackerel. She bought one or two fish each day. She cleaned, salted, and broiled them on charcoal. She cooked rice mixed with barley because rice was scarce. After breakfast Mother went to a dress shop to make, sew or alter dresses. Then she returned in the late afternoon. When her pay was good, the rice bowl was filled to the brim with less barley, and there were more side dishes. When her pay was meager, the rice had more barley, and there were fewer side dishes.

One day at lunch time, Mother brought the bowl of rice and about a quarter of a broiled mackerel.

"Here's your lunch, Hi-Dong," Mother said.

"Aren't you going to eat?" I asked.

"I'll eat later," she said. "I have to meet someone at the dress shop. Be sure to cover up your empty bowl with a napkin before you go out. Otherwise, flies will swarm all over the dish."

Maybe, she is going to have some work and we can have a full dinner, I thought.

"OK, Mother," I said and started eating.

But something bothered me. Since coming to the island, Mother and I, sitting across from one another at the table, always ate together. Mother talking the most of the time and I listening. But today I felt strange sitting in the dark hallway eating all by myself for the first time. Also the tone of her voice was strange. Nervous. Her eyes flitted about the room like flies. As I put the last spoonful of rice in my mouth, I realized *that something*. It hit me like lightning. Mother gave me all the food we had left.

I recalled an incident a week earlier when Mother had brought a bowl of rice and a small piece of broiled mackerel with the head on a plate. Having been hungry all day, I gulped down the rice and mackerel leaving the head alone while she talked and watched me eat. When I finished the meal, she took the plate into the kitchen, closing the door. While waiting for her to return, I looked through a crack in the door and saw Mother. She knelt and picked up the left-over mackerel head and chewed the bones with her teeth. I saw her scraping the bottom of the rice pot for a spoonful of what was left over. My eyes froze at the sight. My head did not move. I felt a big lump in my chest. I did not know what to do. Rush into the kitchen? Or pretend that I didn't see her? After seconds of debating, I quietly left the room for the seashore. I had come back home late that night feeling guilty and uneasy. I had told her that I would look for a job, but her response was a definite *No. Study English instead.*

Thinking of that incident, remorse swept over me. I checked the clay pot where the rice was kept. It was empty. I went out to the kitchen where she stored the fish. It was empty. I rushed out to find her. She was not at the dress shop. She was not at Cousin's house down the street. I ran to the pier where we had often gone to sit on a rock or to gather clams. There I saw her, sitting on the rock. All alone.

It was a cloudy day. The sea was violent, with waves crashing against the rocks. She looked over the horizon as if she yearned for eternity.

I imagined her saying, *Please God, take me away. I have had enough. I have reached the end of my rope. All my life I have struggled to support my children while Your servant—my husband—labored and suffered to preach Your word. All those years, I managed to feed, to clothe, and to educate my children. Now my rice bowl is empty. I do not have enough money to feed my growing boy, and I do not have the strength to go on. I am very tired, and am emotionally and physically drained. I am reaching the age of sixty. My bones are weary. My flesh aches. I do not wish to continue to live. Any longer!*

When I thought of those words, a chill swept down my spine. I stood and watched her looking far away over the horizon, where the dark sky met the churning sea. I felt guilty being an additional burden on her life. I wanted to run away. At least she could feed herself without me. On the other hand, running away would cause her greater heartache, even though it would solve her material problem. She had had enough heartache through her years, losing three children before they could talk and walk; seeing Hi-Seung leave for Japan to serve in the military so that his father could be released from the Japanese prison during WWII and returning home to die from his injury; seeing her husband taken away by the North Korean officers during the Korean War; seeing Hi-Bum leave home to avoid his capture by the South when they returned to Seoul during the Korean War. *How will Mother feel if I run away? Her only remaining son? Will she be happy to know that she will not have to worry about another mouth to feed? … No way. She will be in such a shock that she will not survive.* When I realized that she would rather starve with me than eat alone without me, I gained enough courage to walk toward her. I stood quietly beside her. She turned her gaze toward me. My eyes met hers. We talked without words. Her eyes spoke of the pain of existence. My eyes received her pain with helplessness. She reached out to hold my hand. Her hand in mine spoke of her love for me, and I received her love with guilt and gratitude. Tears welled up in our eyes. Those tears fell on the rocks to be washed away by the endless sea.

My heart ached with the sight of Mother sitting on the rock. I did not want her to go through each day to feed me. I did not want to see Mother going hungry. I did not want to see her sitting on the rock looking over the horizon ever again. She had suffered enough. It was my turn to look after my dear mother.

I am fifteen years old. My Brother Hi-Seung volunteered to join the Japanese army at the age of fifteen. He volunteered to save Father from prison. Now I will help Mother. I can clean fish. I can be a delivery boy. I can pick oranges. I can be a waiter or a dishwasher. I can even haul garbage. Any job will do.

In the evening after supper we strolled to the pier and sat on the rock, that had become our own.

"Mother," I said. "Tomorrow, I'm going to look for a job."

"I've been telling you to study English," Mother said.

"But Mother ..." I stopped short of telling her that I was going to be the breadwinner for the family because she wouldn't allow it.

"Mother, what?"

"I'm too hungry to study," I said.

Mother clasped her hands and looked at me. Then she reached out to hold my hand.

"I'm sorry," Mother sighed. "I don't make enough money to feed your growing body."

"I'll look for a job at a restaurant," I said, "so that I don't go hungry."

"But ..." Mother tried to find a response.

"I can always study English at night," I said.

Mother did not resist.

The following day I started my search for a job. I walked by a restaurant that I had passed many times before. *Two Sisters*, written on a wooden block hung crooked on the door. The sign was brushed on plain wood with black paint. It was not like the restaurants in Seoul which had clean entrances with attractive signs. It was more like a small army barracks. So I did not bother to go in and ask for a job. I headed toward the main street with shops lining the street leading to the shore. I asked shop owners for a job. Any job was OK. But none was available. Every job was taken by older people including many refugees with families to feed. Near the shore there were shops selling fish. *I can bring fish from fishing boats. I am an expert in cleaning fish. I can deliver fish to restaurants.* I stopped at one fish store where a wrinkled old man sat on a wooden chair looking out the street. He had on a straw braided hat with a wide rim and was smoking a foot long pipe made of bamboo.

"Sir," I greeted him. "Do you have work that I can do? I worked for a fish store in Busan. I can do anything."

He looked at me. He knew I was not an islander.

"Young man," the old man said in a strong island accent. "You boys from Seoul are too smart and lazy. I hired a boy from Seoul a month ago. I had to let him go."

"I'm not lazy," I said. "Please hire me just for one day, and if you are not satisfied, you can let me go."

The old man puffed on his pipe and smiled.

He said, "I'd like to, but there are so many refugees selling fish and I don't make much money."

"I'm sorry," I said realizing that the refugees were impinging on his livelihood. "Please have a good day."

I went to the next one. No work. The next one. No work. One more shop left on the street. I stopped in at the last shop. A middle-aged lady was chasing flies away on fish with a towel. "You pests," she said. "Stay away from them."

"Hello," I said.

She glanced at me while chasing the flies.

"Yes?" she turned to look at me.

Her voice was gentle and her accent less pronounced. She reminded me of Mrs. Kim, who I had worked for in Busan.

"Do you have a job that I can do for you?" I said. "I'll do anything you tell me."

She stopped talking to the flies and walked over. Like the old man with the pipe, she stared at me.

"Do you live alone?" she asked.

"I am living with my mother," I said.

The picture of Mother sitting on the rock looking over the horizon grabbed my heart. Tears started to swell my eyes. I bit my tongue.

"I want to hire you," she said. "But these days I don't sell enough fish to pay you."

"It's OK not to pay me," I said. "If you can just give me a fish a day, I'll work for you."

She looked at me as if she had been seeing a wounded boy grimacing from pain. She walked closer. She asked my name. She asked about my family. I answered her questions frequently interrupted by her asking for details. Then she saw flies flying over the fish on racks. Some landed on the fish pecking with their small beaks.

"The flies are real pests," she said using a towel to shoo them off the fish.

"Yes," I agreed.

I shooed them away with my hand thinking they are hungry, too.

"Wait for a minute," she said.

She went to the back of the store. *Perhaps she will get an apron for me. Surely she will give me a job.* I felt a tingling start in my toes and travel up to my brain. I'd done it.

She returned with a small bag. *A delivery?*

"I wish that I had a job for you," she said. "But now is not a good time for me to hire you."

Then why did she question me so long? What question did I answer wrong? Now what will I do?

"Take this," she said handing the bag to me.

I looked inside. It was rice, enough for a few days. *What does she think I am? A beggar? A son of a lower-class toilet cleaner? Lady, I am a son of an upper-class Korean family.* My shoulders tightened. I felt nauseated like chewing on an uncooked fish skin with scales. I felt like thrusting the bag at her. Then I realized that Mother always gave food to those who were in need, and they did not throw it back at Mother. Instead, they received the gift with gratitude. I realized that I was on the receiving end, and the lady was like Mother. Giving. Also I pictured Mother sitting on the rock. Hungry. Sad. *Is my pride more important than Mother?*

"Thank you very much," I said pulling the bag close to my body. "Thank you very much."

I've been lucky. Is that all there is to it? Just luck? Why do some people have luck while others do not? Many people helped me. Yung-Suk's family. The fish store lady in Busan. The relative who gave us a place to stay. Now this lady who gave me the rice. When I get older, I will be like them too.

I didn't find work. But at least I tried. Also I had rice for Mother and me to last a few days. I would try to find a job tomorrow and the next day until I found one. I walked back toward home with a bag of rice in my hand, determined to find a job. As I got close to home, again I saw the Two Sisters sign. It was between meal times, and there weren't customers shuffling in and out. *How can a person eat there with that stupid sign? With the stupid name. With handwriting like a child's. The inside must be dirty and the food lousy. I will not work here even if I am offered a job.* Quickly I walked past the restaurant. Then I remembered Mother's words, *Pride leads one to his downfall. Do not look down on people. Do not discriminate. The poor, the rich, the educated, the illiterate, the believers, the nonbelievers ... All are brothers. All are God's children.* My head accepted her words, but my heart didn't. I found my pace slowing. I found my head turning back to the sign, Two Sisters.

Am I going to ignore Mother's advice and continue being proud and discriminate against people? Am I going home after failing in my first attempt to find a job? Am I serious about being a breadwinner? Have I forgotten Hi-Seung's words, "I can do anything that I set my mind to"? Even overcoming my pride?

I turned around and walked into the restaurant, feeling uneasy. I peeked inside. To my surprise, the inside was very clean and pleasant. The floor was laid with flat volcanic rocks. Wooden tables and chairs were neatly arranged on the floor. There were no cheap wall decorations.

A tall lady with chubby arms was cleaning the tables with a kitchen towel while a short lady with chubby arms swept the floor with a broom. They both looked the same except one was taller than the other. They seemed younger than Mother, but not too much younger. Their eyes were thin and narrow. Their chins were reddish and chubby like their arms. Their heads were covered with towels.

"Young man," Sister Tall said glancing at me while wiping the table. "What can I serve you?"

I stood at the door avoiding her glance.

"Oh ... Oh," I hesitated.

Sister Tall stopped wiping and looked straight at me. *Should I walk out like a boneless bean curd? Or should I act like Tarzan?*

"Do ... do you have a job?" I asked looking straight at her. "I can do anything you tell me."

Sister Small stopped sweeping. They looked at each other. Then a smile came over Sister Tall's face.

"Do you want to clean the table and sweep the floor like we are doing now?" Sister Tall asked. "Can you wash dishes and take care of the garbage?"

"No problem," I said.

"It's strange," Sister Tall chuckled. "This morning we were talking about having a young boy like you to help us. And here you are."

"Most people think we're too low class of a place to work for," Sister Small said smiling.

"Can you work every day?" Sister Tall asked.

"Yes," I said.

"Can you get up early in the morning?"

"Anytime you want me," I said

"How much do you want?"

What should I say? Ask for the going wage? What is the going wage? Will it be enough to buy food and new clothes for Mother and me? What if? If it's not enough even to buy food?

"Food for my mother and myself will be fine," I said.

The ladies looked at each other. *Will they go to the back and get me a bag of rice? Or will they give me the job?*

"What's your name?" Sister Tall asked.

"Chai Hi-Dong," I said.

"Call me Aunt Young-Ja and she is Aunt Young-Hae," Sister Tall said pointing to Sister Small. "We start preparing lunch early. Be here at eight tomorrow."

"Yes," I said. "Thank you very much."

Walking back home I felt happy and proud as if I had just bought Mother and me a mansion on the hill. I felt like a man who was in charge of his life. I felt like a man who looked after his aging mother. Also I remembered Mr. Lee, my high school gym teacher, saying, *Even monkeys fall from trees. If you want to succeed in life, don't be afraid to fail, fail and fail.* Today I heard *No* too many times to get one *Yes.* One *Yes* was all I needed.

When I entered the house, the aroma of a freshly broiled fish made my stomach groan. Mother must be cooking in the kitchen.

"Mother, are you broiling a fish?" I said walking toward the kitchen.

"Yes, I'm broiling a mackerel," she said. "The fisherman said that it was just caught an hour ago."

"Good," I said.

Mother sat in front of the charcoal stove flipping the mackerel with a pair of long bamboo chopsticks.

"How was your day?" Mother said.

"Fine," I said putting the bag beside her.

"What's in it?"

"Please look," I said grinning.

Mother opened the bag and looked. Her face looked like a person gazing on a thousand gold coins. Then she turned and looked at me like the time when I, a child, had stolen a piece of candy from a street vendor and proudly showed it to her.

"Where did you get it?" Mother said. "Did you st...eal?"

Today has been a happy day. I found a job. Mother will be happy too when I tell her. But let me scare her a little and have a big laugh.

"Yes," I said nonchalantly, "from a rice vendor."

Her body froze like a statue. Her hand holding the bag didn't move. Her face was motionless. *What is she thinking? Is she angry at me, who was taught that stealing was one of the greatest sins, next to murder? Is she sad because she has not provided enough food, thus causing me to steal from hunger?*

After seconds of silence, she lifted the bag and put it next to me.

"Take it back," Mother said, turning her head away from me.

"Mother," I said, my voice cheerful. "Do you really think that I stole?"

"I don't know," she replied, her voice hollow.

"A gracious lady like you at a store gave me the bag to take home," I said.

Only then her body softened and her voice returned to its usual sound, and I told her what really happened.

"What a wonderful lady," Mother said. "I should go and give my thanks to her tomorrow."

"Also," I said, "do you know what happened today?"

"What?"

"I got a job," I said feeling proud.

"My precious *mangnei*," Mother said, "you got a job so that I don't have to work."

How does she know that I got a job so that she doesn't have to work? I have not told anyone yet. I only told her I would look for a job because I was hungry.

"Well ...," I said, not wanting to admit that she was right.

"Where?" Mother asked.

"Two Sisters," I said.

"What?" Mother's voice hushed. "That dirty-looking place with a crooked sign?"

"Yes," I said. "The owners are two sisters. Very nice people. I'll start working tomorrow morning."

"Well," Mother said, "you are from a *Yangban*—upper-class—family. It's a disgrace to work at a place like that."

"Mother," I said, "you still hold onto the old ways. There is no more *Yangban*, no *Ssangnom*—lower class—these days. Everyone is equal as in America. Also you told me not to discriminate against anyone. You told me that God loves everyone."

Mother reached over and held my hands in hers. I saw tears welling up in her eyes. Then she closed her eyes.

"Thank You, my heavenly Father," she said, "for blessing me with such a thoughtful son ... Bless him and look after him so that he can be a peace-maker and a force for good in the world."

After her prayer, Mother listened to what I would be doing at Two Sisters, and when I would start working in the morning.

"Anyway," Mother said, "with you working, I'll have time to do something else."

"What?"

"You'll find out later," Mother smiled.

What is she going to do? Sewing? If sewing, she would not smile since it's nothing special for her. Visit Uncle and people from Seoul? If so, why does she say, "You'll find out later"? Or maybe, find a person who will teach me English? I am anxious to know what she's up to. But for now, don't bother Mother to find out. It has been a good day for me. I got a bag of rice for Mother. I got a job all by myself. For now, let me relax and wait.

26. I am the breadwinner

I got up at six o'clock in the morning, washed and ate breakfast. I studied English for an hour. Then I walked to Two Sisters, ten minutes away. As I opened the door, Sister Tall was placing jars of salt, black pepper, and hot red pepper on each table. I heard Sister Small chopping something on a wooden board. At eight I started the wood fire under three big iron pots while the two sisters prepared rice and two types of soup— their specialties. *Sul-long-tang*, a mixture of chopped ox tail, intestines and bones. This soup needed to be boiled slowly under medium heat for hours to get the meat and intestines soft and to get nutrients from the bones. The other was fish soup with fish brought by a fisherman that morning. I scaled the fish and removed the innards. Sister Small cut them crosswise and dumped them in scalding water—including the heads and the eyes because some people thought that eating the heads would make them smart and eating the eyes would keep their eyes sharp. Then she sprinkled a generous portion of hot pepper and salt. While the soup was prepared, I walked down to a store to get vegetables to be prepared as side dishes. Next, I made several trips to the nearby well to fill up a big clay drum with water for the day's use.

At eleven o'clock an old man strolled in.

"Welcome, Uncle—a traditional way of addressing an older man," greeted Sister Tall to the old man with many wrinkles and a long gray beard. "How's your day been?"

"Ah, so, so", said the man. "Last night I dreamed of my father waving at me across a river. You know he passed away ten years ago. My day must not be far away."

"Don't say that Uncle," Sister Tall said. "A dream is just a dream. I see my mother almost everyday. She passed away a year ago. And I'm still cooking and serving."

"Hope you are right," the man whispered.

"What can I serve you this morning?" she asked.

"My usual," he said.

"I need to pep you up," she said. "I'll put a lot of hot pepper in your *sul-long-tang.*"

"Good," he said, "I need it to go through another day."

Soon after the man had walked in, other customers started filing in for their lunch. Sister Tall knew them all. They were merchants and workers. The merchants wore traditional costumes while the workers wore unwashed laborers' outfits. They walked in as if they were coming home for their meal.

"What would you like?" Sister Tall asked a man whose face looked like a monkey.

"Oh, I'm here to see the beautiful lady with the chubby arms," he said grinning.

"You are in the right place," she said bringing her reddish arm toward his face. "You like it?"

"Oh, stop it," the man said pushing her arm away. "You know what I like."

"I'll get you a special treat," she said walking in the kitchen.

Within a minute she brought a steaming bowl of *sul-long-tang.*

"A special treat," she said, setting the bowl in front of him. "Enjoy."

The man scooped up a spoonful of hot soup in his mouth and grimaced.

"Man, it's very hot," he said. "You put in a lot of hot pepper on purpose."

Ha! Ha! Sister Tall let out her laugh like a man.

"That'll teach you," she said. "I'll get you another bowl. This time, a regular one."

The place was like a family dining room where people shared whatever was on their minds. Sometimes arguments followed. When conversations got tense, Sister Tall stepped in and calmed them down. The customers did not need to order because Sister Tall knew what each person wanted. She brought soup with more intestines for the first customer. Lots of hot pepper for the second. More ox tails for the third. And so on. The second serving was free. Some even delayed payment for the meal, and she did not complain.

During the first week it was a little hard to get accustomed to the sisters' strong accents and learn to fit into their routine. I had to learn how and when to wash dishes and stack them up. When and where to go to get the produce. What to do with the garbage. The second week on, I had no problem understanding their accent. I felt comfortable with the work routine. Cleaning the dining area and kitchen was not a problem. Washing a couple hundred dishes and cooking pans day after day was boring but doable. The most demanding job was carrying two big buckets filled with water from the well to the restaurant several times a day. The well was three blocks away, and I had to stop along the way and give my arms a rest. But as the days passed, my arms grew stronger and could handle the task without much difficulty. The most distasteful part of my job was disposing of the garbage. The dump was located in one corner of the field behind the restaurant. Every day I made a hole big enough to dump the garbage and covered it up with soil. But with frequent rain and warm and humid weather, some garbage oozed out of the ground. The smell of the decomposing garbage in the ground filled the air. Maggots crawled around, and swarms of flies feasted on the garbage. Every evening while walking to the dump, I kept telling myself, *I can handle anything. The garbage smell. Crawling maggots. Decayed flesh and bones. No problem.* But my nose and my eyes felt otherwise, and to the last day of my work, I hated taking the garbage to the dump.

After working for Two Sisters for two months, everything had become routine. My hands and feet moved like a robot. When I saw dirty dishes piled up in the corner of the restaurant, my feet moved to the dishes, my hands picked the pile up, brought them to the sink, washed them, and put them on racks to dry. When I saw the garbage can filled to the brim, my hands picked up the can took it out to the dump and rushed back to the kitchen to run away from the maggots and the fowl odor. When the water tank was empty, my feet moved toward the well with two big pails, returned with sagging shoulders, and filled up the tank. When the sisters needed produce, my feet took me to the stores and returned with the needed items. All without thinking. Nothing was new. Boredom started to set in.

Then one Saturday, I was memorizing English words like *automobile, forest, restaurant, freedom, and pioneer.* I was bored and tired, and wished that I was out on the pier, swimming. Mother came home from the dress shop with a broad smile. Her voice sounded like the time when she had come home with the news that her niece had delivered a beautiful daughter.

"Mother," I said looking at her. "Anything happened?"

"Yes ... Yes," she said.

"What?"

"Do you remember the name, Chaplain Bob Heinz that Father mentioned when you were a child?"

"No," I said.

"He was the chaplain in the U.S. army in Seoul right after World War II," Mother said. "Father was very close to him, and worked as his interpreter."

"So?"

"Miss Ahn, a lady, visited me this morning," Mother said. "She said that she was a translator for an American missionary who came here a month ago to start an orphanage for children who lost their parents in the war. She mentioned that the name of the missionary was Bob Heinz, who was in Korea as a chaplain after World War II. So I asked her more details about him. He turned out to be the same person whom your father worked with."

"That's good," I said.

"He came with his family," Mother said. "He has a son your age."

What is Mother up to now? Be a friend to this boy? A boy with blond hair, a long nose, and blue eyes? Go and swim together? Climb the mountain together? Everybody on the street will stop and look at us. How embarrassing!

"The chaplain is looking for a person to teach Korean to his son," Mother said.

"So?" I said.

Did Mother volunteer that I would teach the boy Korean? How can I? I can read some English, but I have never spoken to an American.

"When I told Miss Ahn that Father was a good friend of Chaplain,"

Mother said, "the lady was all excited. She said that she would tell Chaplain about us right away and that you would be an ideal person to teach the boy Korean."

"So, you want me to teach the boy Korean?"

"Oh, yes," Mother said.

From the tone of Mother's voice, she was looking ahead. *Teach the boy Korean. In turn, I'll learn to speak English. We'll become friends. Then Mother will ask Chaplain to help me go to America. Boy, Mother's sneaky! But this kind of sneakiness is all right since it will help both me and the boy.*

"How can I teach him Korean," I said, "when I don't even know how to speak English?"

"Your Japanese teacher didn't know how to speak Korean. But she taught you Japanese," Mother said. "You are a creative boy. You can figure out how to help him speak Korean."

I thought what Mother said about learning in Japanese from a Japanese teacher. *Sure, why not?* I thought. *The Japanese teachers did it, and I can do it also. I know simple sentences like "Good morning, thank you. This is a book, He is a Yankee. She is beautiful." To teach him the word 'smile' in Korean, I will point at my smiling face. To teach him the word 'boy', I will point at him and say, "boy," and point at me and say, "boy." Then I will show a picture of a girl to teach him the word 'girl'. To teach him colors, I'll touch his hair and say, "yellow", and touch my hair and say, "black". To teach him lengths, I'll point at his nose and say, "long," and point at my nose and say, "short." Teaching English will be no problem, I thought. And it will be fun.*

Continuing to wash dishes and take garbage away at Two Sisters will turn me into a human robot. But trying to figure out the best way to teach Chaplain's son will keep my mind alive and will free me from boredom. Also I will learn to speak English from him. Eventually Mother will find a way to send me to America. In America, I will become an inventor, the Edison of Korea.

But what about Mother? Mother will be all alone in her old age, without anyone looking after her. Which way should I choose? Look after Mother? Or be the Edison of Korea?

After some brooding, I said to Mother. "No, I can study English by myself."

"Hi-Dong," Mother said, "he needs your help. Also you will learn proper English from him so that you can speak like he does when you go to America."

"Mother, I'm not going to America," I said with my voice firm. "I'm staying with you."

Mother looked at me with her palms touching as if she was going to pray.

"Hi-Dong," Mother said, "you are the only son I have left, and you are fifteen years old."

What's so special about being fifteen years old? I looked at Mother, wondering why she had spoken so. Then I saw her eyes becoming blank as if she was in a trance. Her hands moved to her chest. Her lips trembled. Suddenly, I realized why she had been planning to send me to America. In another year, I would be sixteen years old. Old enough to carry a rifle and shoot. And if the war continued and turned against us, I would be conscripted. I could be sent to the front line and get killed.

I wanted to hold her in my arms, let her feel my love for her, and assure her that I wouldn't die. But I couldn't promise that. If the war raged on for years, the government wouldn't spare me from fighting the enemy because I was the only son left in the family. If I were on the front line facing an enemy's rifle, the bullets would not say among themselves, *He is the only son in his family. Let's leave him alone,* passing around me to spare me from death.

Leave Mother alone in Korea and go to America where I can be safe and where I can maximize my potential? Or stay home with Mother and look after her even though I may be called to fight and get killed? My head said, *Take Mother's advice and go to America. Be the best that I can be, and return home and make Mother proud.* But my heart said, *Stay home and look after Mother regardless of what may happen to me.* I could not decide because I did not know which way was the right one.

27. I teach Korean to an American boy

A few days later, Miss Ahn took Mother and me to Chaplain Heinz's house about a mile away from our place. The western-style house was built on a hill overlooking the ocean. The sky was cloudy as usual, and a strong wind blew inland from the turbulent ocean. Behind the house was land, the size of two basketball courts, where workers were building a long row of one-story buildings to house orphans.

"Oh welcome Mrs. Chai," Chaplain said in Korean with open arms. "I never dreamed of meeting you here."

Chaplain's Korean had a strong American accent but was understandable. *How come doesn't he teach Korean to his own son?* I wondered.

"The world is really small," Mother said bowing politely, "seeing you here on this remote island."

"Yes, it is," Chaplain said turning to a lady and a boy beside him. "Let me introduce you to my family. This is Mrs. Heinz."

Mrs. Heinz welcomed us with her hand held out for a handshake with Mother. Mother ignored her hand and bowed politely because Korean women did not shake hands.

"And this is my boy, David," Chaplain said. "Bow to Mrs. Chai."

"Oh Father," he grunted.

David was a tall, chubby boy with mean brown eyes and curly red hair. He didn't look like the American boy that I had imagined: a boy with blond hair and blue eyes.

"Bow," Chaplain said, his welcoming voice turning to a commanding tone.

"It's alright not to bow," Mother said smiling to David. "I hear people don't bow in America."

He quickly bent his head down and straightened up.

"He must be your son." Chaplain said looking at me.

"Yes," Mother said. "He is Hi-Dong. He feels honored to help your son to speak Korean."

Mother, you shouldn't tell a lie. I never told you that I felt honored to teach Korean to David.

"David, shake your teacher's hand," Chaplain said looking at me with a smile.

David stuck his hand out toward me with mocking eyes. I accepted his hand in a handshake. *What am I getting into? Teaching Korean to that boy with mean eyes and a drooping chin? Will he listen to me? Will we get into a fight?*

"Please come in," Mrs. Heinz said. "You and Rev. Heinz must have a lot to talk about."

"Miss Ahn," Mrs. Heinz said to the interpreter, "please take Hi-Dong and David to the backyard and get them acquainted."

We followed Miss Ahn to the backyard. I sat next to her on a bench by a picnic table. David stood ignoring us. He gazed at majestic Mount Hala looming before him.

"Hi-Dong," Miss Ahn said in Korean. "I already taught David the Korean alphabet. Your job is to teach him conversational Korean. Teach him by talking to him as if he were your friend."

"Why don't you continue to teach him?" I asked.

"Well …," Miss Ahn said glancing at David. "He needs a friend, and …"

And what? How come she stopped speaking in the middle of the sentence? Trouble. Trouble.

"Yes?" I looked at Miss Ahn.

"You have to let him know that you are his teacher," she said. "If not …"

She stopped again in the middle of the sentence. *"If not," what? Will he bully me like Jong-Jin at Mee Dong School?*

"If not, what?" I said.

"If not, he'll run all over you," she said. "If he does, tell him that you will tell his father because he's terribly afraid of his father."

I remembered Hi-Seung begging for mercy when Father whipped him.

220

I pictured Chaplain whipping David who begged for mercy. I looked at David. He didn't seem to be curious about our conversation. He just gazed at Mt. Hala.

"Have you ever told his father when he didn't behave?" I asked.

"Yes, in the beginning, because he wouldn't listen," she said. "So I told his father. After that he settled down."

I wished that Mother had known more about David before volunteering me to be his teacher. *What should I do now? Tell Miss Ahn that I will not teach David? Tell her that she should find an older man than I? But I don't want to pull out like a mushy bean curd. This is a good opportunity to become the fearless Tarzan of the human jungle. He may be much bigger than I, but if he ever attacks me, I will not tell his father like a little kid. Instead, I will knock him down with my karate chop that Hi-Seung taught me.*

A few days later after working at Two Sisters, I went to David's house. It was a hot, humid day, and I wiped the sweat off my face while knocking at the front door. David came out.

"Hello," I said, holding my hand out for a handshake. "How are you?"

He looked down at me with his mocking eyes and drooping chin. Then he turned his head sideways looking disgusted.

"You smell like a pig," he drawled waving his hand.

With my limited English, I understood what he said. My shoulders tightened. My mind raced for a quick response. I looked up straight at him. *How shall I respond? Tell him that he looks like an ugly drooling pig? Tell him that the chaplain's son should be a role model like my elders reminded me as a child? Shall I kick him on his shin and make him cringe? No. Don't act like he. Be a big person, and tell him that I just came from work.* Before I could respond, he turned around and stomped out to the back yard. I followed behind him.

As we reached the picnic table, I said, "I am sorry that I smell like a pig. I just came from work."

"What work?" he asked looking down at me.

I looked up at the tall boy with a forced smile.

"I dish washed," I said.

"What?" he scoffed. "Washed dishes?"

"Yes," I said.

"Go home," he said. "I don't want to learn Korean from a dishwasher."

"But I can teach," I said, my voice tight.

"I don't want to learn from a guy who speaks pig English," he snickered. "Not from a guy who can only say, *I dish washed.*"

My hands turned into fists, tight like rocks ready to smash him down on the ground. But I didn't want to go home and tell Mother the unpleasant news. Instead, I wanted to go home with the good news that I taught David simple sentences.

"Sit down," I said pointing at the table. "I here teach you Korean. No fight."

"What did you say you little pig?" he glared at me. "Did you tell me to sit down?"

"Yes," I eyeballed him. "Sit down."

He lunged to grab me with his long arms. I quickly turned to his side and jabbed his rib cage with a light blow because I did not want to break his ribs. He turned and grabbed hold of my arms. I lifted my foot and hammered onto his toes. He grunted kneeling down in pain.

"If I want, I can break your ribs with one blow," I said. "Instead, I tell your father about you."

I turned around pretending to walk into the house.

"OK, OK," he said still kneeling in pain. "You teach me Korean."

I walked back to David with my right hand out toward him.

"We shake hand," I said eyeballing him.

"OK, OK," he said holding my hand in a handshake.

"I go away today," I said. "I come tomorrow to teach you Korean."

After our first encounter, David's mocking eyes turned cautious and his grunting voice soft. He no longer told me that I smelled like a pig. He no longer snickered at my English. Three times a week, I went to Chaplain's house to help David to be able to engage in ordinary conversation with Koreans. In time my first impression of him changed because he had a sharp mind and good memory. Within several months, he was able to communicate with me in Korean. And also in the process, I learned enough conversational English to be able to talk with Chaplain and his wife.

One day Chaplain wanted to come to our place and have a visit with Mother. Chaplain did not give me the reason why. *Is he going to tell Mother how I have performed as David's teacher? Is he going to pay Mother for my service? Certainly she would refuse.* It was a disgrace to receive payment for service to a friend, especially Chaplain who had come all the way to Cheju to set up an orphanage to help homeless Korean children.

I also didn't want Chaplain to come to our place and see where we lived because he would be shocked. I told him that Mother would go to their place and visit instead, and he agreed.

"Mother," I called from our bedroom, the dark curtain-draped hallway. "Where are you?"

"I'm in the courtyard," she replied.

"What are you doing?" I said walking out of the bedroom to the living room facing the courtyard.

"I'm washing your only pants beside what you have on," she said. "Your pants smell terrible. I don't want David to ever say that you smell like a pig again."

"He wouldn't say that again," I said.

"How do you know?"

"Because he's afraid of me," I replied.

Mother held the wet pants in the air and looked at me. The water dripped down to the pail like huge rain drops.

"Is a big boy like him afraid of you?" Mother chuckled.

Is Mother still thinking I am a tender bean curd? Should I tell her that Hi-Seung taught me to defend myself? Tell her that I am not afraid of anyone? Tell her that I beat him up? No. If I tell her, she will feel so disgraced by my behavior that she will not be able to go and visit with Chaplain.

"Mrs. Ahn told me that David was terribly afraid of his father," I said. "She also told me to tell David right in the beginning that I would report to Father if he didn't behave."

"So you told him?" Mother asked.

"Something like that," I answered because I didn't want to lie.

"You have been teaching David for several months now," Mother said. "Did Chaplain say anything about your teaching?"

Whenever I went to David's house, Chaplain and Mrs. Heinz welcomed me with a big smile. They asked me about Mother. They asked me whether David had been behaving. But they had never told me how I was doing as David's teacher.

"No," I replied. "By the way, Chaplain wants to come to our place and see you."

Mother let go of my pants. They dropped into the pail making a big splash.

"Did you have a fight with David?" Mother said with round eyes.

"No," I said.

Mother looked at me as if she was a policeman talking to a suspect.

"Did he tell you why he wanted to see me?"

"No," I replied.

Mother wiped her hands with her apron without speaking. *What is she thinking?*

"When?" Mother asked.

"When you are available," I said. "But I told him that your work schedule changed from day to day, and that it would be better for you to go to his place."

"What did he say to that?" Mother said.

"He said that it would be fine," I replied.

"Good boy," Mother let out a sigh. "I don't want him to find out where we live. If he finds out we live in a hallway, he will be shocked. I am sure he remembers our two-story house in Seoul."

A few days later, Mother returned home after a visit with Chaplain. From the living room floor I watched her entering the front gate. Her posture was straight. Her gait was light like that of a young girl. She was all smiles. Chaplain must have told her that I had been doing a good job teaching David. Otherwise, she would have come home looking somber. If she had a prayer closet, she would have gone in there without talking to me.

"Mother, what happened?" I said. "You look very happy."

"I'm very, very happy," she said.

"Did he say that I have been doing a good job?" I asked.

"Yes," she said. "And more."

"Did he pay you for my work?"

"Oh, no," she said. "It's much more than the pay."

Much more than the pay. What can it be? I'm sure it's not money since Mother will not accept it. I'm sure that he did not ask her to move to a better place since he did not come and see where we lived. I was curious.

"What?"

"My prayer has been answered," Mother said.

"Please tell me." I was anxious.

"He's going to help you to go to America."

To America? My tongue froze. My heart felt numb. *Should I jump with joy? Or should I beg Mother not to send me away?* I had been dreaming of going to America for a long time, but I did not want to leave Mother alone. Also I dreaded leaving Mother because she had been my life. But I didn't want to insist on my not going because I did not want to dampen her joy.

"O, that's good," I said.

"Chaplain said that he has a friend in New York, who is a principal in a private school," Mother said. "The principal wants to have a boy from Korea so that his students can learn firsthand about Korea and the Korean War."

"So?"

"Even before I could mention your name," Mother said, "Chaplain said that you would be the right person."

"So you agreed?"

"Of course," Mother exclaimed beaming. "Isn't God wonderful?"

If God is so wonderful, why did He let Hi-Seung die? Why did He let Father be taken away by the communists? Why did He let my best friend Kwidong be taken away by a dog warden? Why did He let Hi-Bum become communist, giving us tons of trouble? My fifteen year old brain could not understand Mother being so faithful to the God who did not keep her from suffering. *Maybe Mother has been brainwashed by the church as Hi-Bum would say. Maybe being brainwashed to believe in such a god is a good thing. Maybe that's how Mother survived through all those heartaches.* I had a lot of questions but no clear answers.

Now if I left for America, she would be all alone.

What's the difference between her living near a son in a grave and a son in a far away land whom she will not see for years? Also what will I do alone in America? A far away country where only a few Koreans have gone to study. I will have to stay in a dormitory alone during vacations. I will spend Christmas alone. I will celebrate my birthday alone. I will feel so lonely and homesick. More than anything else, I will be always worried that Mother may die and that I will never get to see her gentle and loving face again.

"When will I be leaving home?"

"As soon as Chaplain makes all the necessary arrangements," Mother replied.

I felt loneliness creeping into my heart. I felt the fear of living in a strange country all alone. Sensing my mood, Mother came over and held my hand.

"I know how you feel," Mother said gently rubbing my hand. "But sooner or later, we all have to leave our parents to start our own lives."

I was silent, lost for words.

"God gave you a good mind," Mother said. "I want you go to America, learn as much as you can, and be the best you can be."

How can I leave Mother alone on this island? She will be spending days, months or years in that dark hallway alone. But her mind is made up, and it's of no use arguing with her. She wants me to be the best that I can be, and I will give my most to fulfill her wish. But what should I be? The Edison of Korea which has been my dream since childhood? Or be a minister following in Father's footsteps to honor him? Or be a person who will promote peace in the world like Mother has done throughout her life? Anyway, my first job is to master English in writing and in speaking.

The next day I went to David's house to teach. He welcomed and congratulated me on my going to America.

"From today you are going to be my student," David said. "Father told me to teach you conversational English."

"Conbersational English?" I said.

"Not *b*," he said, "but *v*."

The Korean language does not have the sounds for *v, f, z* and *th*. David had often laughed when I used words involving those sounds. When I said, 'This is a book', David thought that I said, "Dis is a book." *Zoo* sounded like *Joo*. *Food* like *hood*. *Vase* like *base*.

"OK. You are my teacher," I said. "Teach me how to pronounce English words correctly, especially those with *v*, *f*, *z* and *th*."

"I'll do my best," David said. "Father says that it will probably take three or four months to get your visa. By then, I want you to be able to speak English like my Korean."

For the next several months, I reviewed the English grammar that I had studied in high school. I had to constantly remind myself of the difference in sentence structure between the two languages. In Korean, a sentence sequence is *subject*, *object* and *verb* instead of *subject*, *verb* and *object* as in English. *I apple ate* instead of *I ate an apple*. The words *a*, *an* and *the* did not exist in Korean language. *The apple* in English was *that apple* in Korean. Learning the proper use of *a* and *an* was not difficult, but the hardest one was the proper use of *the*. According to my grammar book, *the* was used to point to a specific item. A very simple concept. But in practice I found it very confusing. *People; the people. Conversation; a conversation; the conversation. The Pacific Ocean. Empire State Building. The Korean War; World War II.* Which one should I use especially in conversation when I would have no time to think?

Several times a week David and I got together. The conversation was strictly in English. No Korean was allowed. David asked questions and made comments. My job was to answer his questions or respond to his comments until I had them right.

"How was your day, Hi-Dong?" David asked.

"Very good," I said.

"You say, *Very good*, to a friend," he said. "But say, *Very good, thank you*, to an older person. What did you eat this morning?"

"I eated rice and drinked soup," I said.

"The past tense of *eat* is *ate* and *drink* is *drank*," David chuckled. "The correct way is *I had rice and soup this morning*."

"For the past tense," I said, "why not use *-ed* at the end of a verb like *eated, sleeped, goed*? It would be so easy this way."

"That's the way my ancestors made it," David said.

"I guess your ancestors had plenty time on their hands and were bored," I said. "And they decided to make English complicated for the future generations to sweat and suffer."

"I am not sweating and suffering," he said. "Anyway, let's get back to work."

"OK," I agreed.

"What did you do today?" he said.

"I worked for the Two Sisters restaurant."

"I worked *at*, not *for*, Two Sisters restaurant," David said. "There is no *the* in front of Two."

"Why not?"

"You don't use *the* before the names of restaurants, stores, and churches," David said. "Like Two Sisters Restaurant, Cheju Market, Jerusalem Church."

"Don't you use *the* for the names of mountains and oceans?" I asked. "Like Pacific Ocean and Mount Everest."

"Well," David scratched his head. "Pacific Ocean is *the* Pacific Ocean, and Mount Everest is just Mount Everest, not *the* Mount Everest."

Unlike Korean, English was so confusing. Korean has twenty-four letters: ten vowels and fourteen consonants. Each letter has the same sound regardless of where it was placed in a word. Past and present tenses were clearly defined. Not *eat, ate; sleep, slept; dig, dug; run, ran.* Korean tenses were more like *eat, eated; sleep, sleeped; dig, digged; run, runned.* Also each word had only one meaning, not multiple meanings as in *fine—fine (ticket) for parking; fine grain; fine person.*

I was getting nervous as the departure date drew closer. *Will I be able to master enough nuances in words to converse without looking like a fool before leaving for America? Will I be able to write compositions and answer questions clearly at school?* All I could do was to try my best while at home. Study English grammar. Converse with David. I remembered my high school teacher's words, *Even monkeys fall from trees. Don't be afraid to fail if you want to succeed.*

While learning English, I continued to work for Two Sisters. Even though it was tiring and boring, I enjoyed working there, meeting people who were uninhibited, learning their crude language and jokes, and learning how to run a successful business. Also I learned how to organize and carry out my work with a minimum use of time and energy. Above all, I felt proud. I took food to Mother, and she no longer had to go hungry. I saw more flesh on her hands, and her once-sunken cheeks disappeared. Every evening, the aunts gave me enough food to feed a big family, and Mother did what she had done all her life. Share what she had.

And time marched on. Without thinking. Without feeling. Like the grandfather clock—tick-tocking–reverberating in the hallway of my vacant home in Seoul.

28. Farewell—February 3, 1953

Six months had gone by since David's father told Mother about my going to America. Two months ago, Mother and I moved to Busan to join Little Aunt, whose family moved down from Seoul a year ago. Also I got to visit—often—Mrs. Park, Yung-Suk and Yung-Ja who had treated me like their own when I waited for Mother to arrive. Whenever we could, Yung-Suk and I got together to play chess and to walk around the town looking for things to do. Mother also visited Mrs. Park just to spend time together and also to share her unending concern for their husbands kidnapped by the communists. And time marched on.

Today, February 3, 1953, I stood on the deck of the Sea Serpent heading for America. The Sea Serpent would sail to the Pacific Ocean. Two and half weeks later, I would debark and step onto the soil of San Francisco. And a new chapter of my life would begin.

For the last sixteen years my life was confined to the area around Seoul. To the north I traveled to Kae-Sung, forty miles away. To the west, In-Chon, twenty miles away. To the south, Busan, two hundred miles away. Then Cheju Island. *But today I will be heading for a country ten thousand miles away. I am going to America. The country that I have dreamed of since my childhood.*

I am excited. In America I will be able to get the best education. Get a Ph.D. I will invent something that people all over the world will use, like my hero Thomas Edison's light bulb. Then I will come back home. When the people welcome me with shouts and adoration, I will stand behind Mother and tell them, "It is the person in front of me who deserves all the praise. It is my father who is looking down from heaven who deserves all the glory."

Also I am sad. Since birth, Mother has been my life. When she laughed, I laughed. When she cried, I cried. When I was alone without her, living was no fun. When I was with her, I felt that I could climb any mountain and swim across any river. Soon I will be all alone. Who will I run to when I have a bruise? Who will I talk to when I am upset? Who will I show my report card filled with straight As?

I was afraid of leaving Mother in the country where the war raged on. *What will happen to Mother after I'm gone? Will she go hungry? No, Little Aunt will take care of her. She's not going to leave Mother alone. She will probably force Mother to live with her when I'm gone. But what about the police? Will the police torment Mother because of my communist brother Hi-Bum? Will they take her to a police station and question her about Hi-Bum like they did to me and Mother in Seoul more than two years ago? Please God, don't let that happen again. Please keep her safe till my return.*

Last night Mother put a ring on my finger. A gold ring. She put it on my ring finger, and said, *When you look at this ring, remember that I am praying for you day and night. When you touch this ring, feel that my love is with you. I will pray for you always, and I will send my love your way.*

Thank you, Mother. I will carry this ring wherever I may be. When I am happy, I will look at the ring, picturing you sharing my happiness. When I am sad, I will look at the ring picturing you holding my hand and consoling me. When I feel lonely, I will look at the ring picturing you praying for me. Above all, when I feel the ring with my finger, I will feel your gentle hand holding mine. I will also pray like you have been praying. Praying for your well-being. Praying that I would succeed in my endeavor. Praying that I would be a force for peace and harmony in this world—just like you.

When we arrived at the dock, the sailors were getting ready for the long journey ahead. Some men pulled up the anchors that made a creaking sound. The engine groaned warming up to turn the propellers. The captain walked along the rail and looked down from the deck. Soon I would have to walk up that ramp. My insides churned. I did not want to walk up the ramp. I did not want to say *goodbye*. I wanted to stay with Mother. But I was not going to turn back. Hi-Seung told me to be brave. I was sixteen years old. I was not a mama's boy anymore. A bright future waited for me.

"Mother," I said bowing. "Please take good care of yourself until I come back."

She held my hand in hers. Her hands felt cold. I could feel the bones through her flesh. I could feel the wrinkles on her hands. She gazed at me. I avoided her gaze because I did not want to break down.

"You write me as soon as you land in America," Mother said.

"Yes, I will."

"Get on board," I heard a sailor yell.

Mother held my hand and did not let go.

"The boat will be moving soon," the sailor yelled.

Mother squeezed my hand and then let go. I picked up my bags and walked up the ramp.

Once on the boat, I put the bags on board and looked down at the deck. I saw sailors lifting the ramp leading to the dock. I realized that, soon, I could no longer touch and smell the soil of my beloved country, that nourished me with the fruits of its land, exposed me to the pain and humiliation of being a citizen of the conquered, and showed me the futility and suffering that came with the wars. No longer could I climb mountains, swim in rivers and just play with friends, carefree. No longer could I walk beside Mother, suffer, cry, talk and experience the warmth of her love. My heart ached with pain that I could not describe in words.

As I looked down at Mother, I felt that this was the last time that I would see her face. I wanted to look at her very carefully, so that I could etch her face in my heart, and carry it with me for the rest of my life. Before coming on board, I wished I could have embraced her, and told her how much I loved her. Now the ramp was up, and it was too late. I just shook her hand politely, saying, *Please take care of yourself.* I was too timid. I was too much bound by tradition.

I heard the creaking sound as the sailors were pulling up the anchors. I saw the captain at the helm, and workers at their assigned stations. I heard the engine starting and the propeller turning. The ship was about to depart.

Mother, the ship is moving. It is inching away from you. I am becoming very frightened. I am only sixteen years old, and I don't feel ready to weather the storms alone in a faraway country. I need you. You know how innocent I am. You know how trusting I am. I will be totally lost in America, where I will mingle with people who look very different from me. I am scared. Very scared!

Last night Mother held my hand and told me to trust in God always. She told me to rush to Him with any problem, no matter how great or small. She said that God would give me strength to rise above any worldly problems. I knew that was how she had overcome her suffering, and I would try to do the same.

The boat was moving further and further away from the dock. The murky water looked ugly. The clouds above seemed very dark. The sound of the fog horn was deepening my sorrow. I could still see Mother's face. Out of all those people standing on the dock and waving handkerchiefs in the air, her face was the only one that I saw: the face etched with suffering, yet ever gentle, with great wisdom, and the face firm with faith in God.

The boat was now too far away to see her face. I could still see her standing. I could see her white handkerchief fluttering in the air.

Mother, can you see my face? Can you see the tears falling down my cheeks? Can you hear me yelling at you, "Farewell, Mother?"

Farewell!

     Farewell!

          Farewell!"

Mother, I love you!

     If not in this world,

          I will see you in the world to come!

Other family members

In the book my family consists of Father, Mother, Brother Hi-Bum, Brother Hi-Seung and me since we were the ones who experienced the brunt of the wars. The rest of my siblings escaped the hardship. Hi-Sook, my oldest sister, was twenty-two years older than I was. Soon after my birth, she was married and lived away from home; after WWII her family moved to New York where her husband received a position on the Voice of America. Hi-Chang, an elder brother next to Hi-Bum, was fifteen years older. During WWII he served in the Japanese air force. After the war, he returned home without an injury, attended college for an engineering degree, and left for the United States for graduate work before the Korean War broke out. Hi-Hyun and Hi-Myung, my twin sisters who were five year older, were in their pre-teens during WWII, too young to serve in the Japanese war effort. During the Korean War, Mother sheltered them at her elder sister's home where Mother thought that they would be safer living with a widow who was over sixty years old.

Acknowledgements

My appreciation goes to:

My sister, Hi-Hyun; my family friend, Byung-Mok; and many friends who read my earlier versions of the story and encouraged me to go on.

Phyllis, my wife, who corrected my English from the start to the end.

David Rim, my nephew, whose photograph of my mother praying is in the book.

Jennifer Pillari at 52Novels.com, who read and critiqued the story.

Dan Emmerson at 51Novels.com, who designed the cover.

Erica Orloff at editingforauthors.com, who edited and formatted the story.

About the Author

A native of Seoul, Korea, Hi-Dong Chai was educated in the United States. He received a Ph.D. in electrical engineering. As an engineer he worked nineteen years with IBM and fifteen years as a professor of electrical engineering at San Jose State University. He was recognized as a leading authority of magnetic actuator design. He published extensively in the field of magnetic aspects of electromechanical devices including a book, *Electromechanical Motion Devices*, Prentice Hall. He is a holder/co-holder of over forty inventions that were either published in the IBM Invention Disclosure Bulletin or filed for U.S. patents.

With all his professional accomplishments, he did not forget his life's journey through Korea as the last son of a Christian minister. He did not forget his father in prison under Japan's rule. He did not forget his fifteen-year-old brother volunteering to join the Japanese military in the hope of having his father released from the prison, and coming home after WWII and dying from his injury. He did not forget his father taken away by the communists during the Korean War, never to return. He did not forget his mother whose life had been shattered by the wars, but who led her last son with love and wisdom.

After retiring in 2002, he decided to spend his remaining years sharing his life stories with the world. *My Truest Hope* was published in the 2012 August issue of Guideposts magazine. *My Truest Hope* won the award for Writerstalk Challenge for Memoir by South Bay Branch of California Writers Club in February, 2013. Also *Blossoms and Bayonets* co-authored with Jana McBurney-Lin was e-published in October, 2012, and the print version in 2013. *Cindy and a Korean Boy*, a short endearing love story that tells of Cindy's caring for the lonely Korean boy and the fragility of life, was e-published in January 2013. In coming years he will work on *Journey Through America*, an autobiography describing his life in America since 1953.

More of his work can be found on his website, www.hidongchai. com, where he shares his singing, his thoughts, his feelings, and his life experiences.

CPSIA information can be obtained at www.ICGtesting.com
Printed in the USA
BVOW03s0916160114

341991BV00002B/9/P